I0212539

For years I have taught the Doctrinal Preaching seminar for PhD students at The Southern Baptist Theological Seminary, and each year I lament the lack of a thorough treatment of the subject, let alone one that is actually practical and helpful. Imagine my delight that one of our graduates has finally written the book I have looked for so long! Filled with scriptural insight as well as homiletical instruction, Joel Breidenbaugh's *Preaching for Bodybuilding* finally provides preachers with a methodology and an inspiration for combining engaging exposition with the spiritual nutrition of doctrinal instruction. Proving wrong those critics who assert that contemporary church audiences won't sit still for doctrinal preaching, Dr. Breidenbaugh insists that not only will they sit still for it, they will *love* it and *grow*! Honoring to Christ and faithful to the Word, *Preaching for Bodybuilding* is a gift to pastors and parishioners alike.

> Hershael York
> Victor and Louise Lester Professor of Christian Preaching
> Southern Baptist Theological Seminary
> Louisville, Kentucky
> Senior Pastor
> Buck Run Baptist Church
> Frankfort, Kentucky

Vibrant biblical preaching will wed the twin disciplines of exposition and theology. *Preaching for Bodybuilding* shows us how to do just that and to do it well. Healthy churches require such a diet and faithful heralds of the Word of God will provide such nourishment. This book is a much needed remedy for the anemic pulpits that tragically dot the landscape of so much preaching today.

> Daniel Akin
> President
> Southeastern Baptist Theological Seminary
> Wake Forest, North Carolina

This readable, practical book challenges the superficiality and limited scope of much modern preaching. Breidenbaugh examines many sermons in the Bible itself in order to argue that truly biblical preaching must teach not only the specific details of a passage but also its contribution to the entire doctrinal structure of the Bible and its practical application to life. This book will be a significant help to every preacher!

> Wayne Grudem
> Research Professor of Theology and Biblical Studies
> Phoenix Seminary
> Phoenix, Arizona

Christian books are a unique genre. Many times, they are practically-driven but biblically empty, or they are deep and thoughtful theological works that cannot be applied to life in any meaningful way. Dr. Joel Breidenbaugh has accomplished an astonishing feat—he has written a biblically driven book that can be used every single day. This book on preaching is not just for Senior Pastors—Bible teachers, class leaders and any Christian who speaks publically can benefit from this book. Read it with a pen in hand; you will be writing and marking on every page. More importantly, it will make you a better communicator for Jesus Christ.

Ergun Caner
Retired Professor
Center for Global Apologetics
Weatherford, Texas

Preaching for Bodybuilding

Integrating Doctrine and Expository Preaching for the 21st Century

Joel Breidenbaugh

Copyright © 2010, 2016 Joel Breidenbaugh

All rights reserved.

ISBN: 0-9907816-7-4
ISBN-13: 978-0-9907816-7-7

DEDICATION

To Annthea, my wife and greatest supporter of my preaching ministry.

CONTENTS

PREACHING FOR BODYBUILDING

ACKNOWLEDGMENTS

This book is by no means a solo effort. Many people aided me in this project with words of instruction, encouragement, and prayer. I would like to thank several of these people by name.

First, I am grateful for the supervisory committee under which I began this project several years ago—Drs. Hershael York, Tom Nettles, and John Polhill. Each scholar has contributed to forming me into a lifelong student. They also encouraged me to publish this work.

Moreover, I would like to thank the following churches: Bethel Baptist Church in Henderson, Kentucky; CornerStone Baptist Church in Panama City Beach, Florida; First Baptist Sweetwater in Longwood, Florida; and Gospel Centered Church in Apopka, Florida. These churches have allowed me to stand in their pulpits and declare God's precious Word. Whether the people of these churches knew it or not, these pulpits have given me something of a laboratory in carrying out doctrinal exposition.

Furthermore, I have grown to appreciate my family and in-laws more and more as each year has passed. Surely, whatever may be commendable in me is a direct result of the discipleship from my parents, grandparents, and parents-in-law. My time spent in ministry, rather preaching, praying, counseling, visiting, researching, writing, traveling or more often cut our gatherings short and many times kept us from getting together at all. Yet through these years, I have received innumerable blessings from them—spiritually, financially, and emotionally, to name a few.

The family member I am most thankful for is my wife, Annthea. We married in 1996 and my life has been far more wonderful with her by my side. She pours her life into our kids—Hannah, John Mark, Alethea, Lukas and Joanna—and I am convinced that they could have no finer teacher. I can think of no greater life than the life I have in Christ and the life I get to share with Annthea and our children. I cannot wait to see what else God will do through our years together.

Finally, words cannot express my love and gratitude for our Lord and Savior Jesus Christ. Who would have imagined that God would be gracious enough to transform a prideful boy from the farmland of Indiana into a preacher of the gospel of God's grace in Christ? Though far from perfect, this work is an offering to Jesus Christ because of who He is and what He has done.

Joel Breidenbaugh

PREFACE

Two of the most influential preachers on my preaching ministry in recent years have been John Piper and John MacArthur. Each of these men has impacted me through both his sermons and his writings. Two characteristics they share stand out to me—they preach expository messages and these messages are rich in doctrine. It is accurate to say that expository preaching is the most biblical form of preaching, for its concern lies with the text's meaning within the immediate and larger contexts. At the same time, the best expository preaching I have heard is full of theology. It is with regret, however, that what I have read about expository preaching gives little attention to doctrine.

My initial interest with doctrinal expository preaching came at the task of producing a twenty week preaching calendar over a doctrinal-expository series in Hershael W. York's Doctrinal Preaching seminar. I was able to divide the Epistle to the Hebrews into twenty sermons and I put this model into practice in my own church. I gained additional interest in the topic after I wrote a paper on "Preaching Christology" for the same seminar. Furthermore, after reading the leading texts on expository preaching for comprehensive exams and after analyzing the books for the Doctrinal Preaching seminar, I realized the need to address this issue. To be fair to those who advocate expository preaching, they would probably want biblical doctrine to shine brightly in their messages. The reality is, nevertheless, that proponents of expository preaching have not explicitly argued for strong doctrinal content nor have they explained how preachers can incorporate theology and exposition.

Moreover, one of the contentions made in York's seminar was that doctrinal preaching's greatest downfall occurred during the 1970s and 1980s as Walter Kaiser, Jr. and others led preachers away from systematic theology toward biblical theology. While there may be some truth to this claim, I will argue that it is possible to recover strong doctrinal preaching through incorporating both biblical and systematic theologies.

A second reason for exploring this issue lies with the increasing downplay of doctrine among evangelicals today. Recent studies reveal that many evangelicals are biblically illiterate and theologically ignorant. It seems to me that the discipline of homiletics needs to re-address doctrinal preaching, especially within the framework of expository preaching.

Furthermore, anyone studying evangelicalism cannot escape the fact that the majority of evangelicals have gotten weaker theologically over the last century. This doctrinal "flabbiness" has contributed to the numerous adherents to evangelical life who give little more than sociological, or cultural, reasons for being a Christian.

Therefore, with these interests and concerns, I have undertaken this task of proposing and analyzing a way in which preaching can integrate theology and exposition.

Finally, I should add a brief word about the masculine language I tend to use in reference to preachers. While I do believe God calls women into ministry, and some of those women preach (really well), I find it difficult grammatically to reference anyone (male or female) as a preacher and then use the wrong possessive pronoun (their) to avoid ambiguity. Thus, I might say something like "God does not just choose to use a preacher, but He wants to use every facet of his life—heart, soul, mind and strength—in declaring and living out His Word." Rather than switch from his to her (or use the awkward "his or her"), I have sought consistency in this work. Ladies, please forgive me.

CHAPTER 1
INTRODUCTION: WHAT IS BODYBUILDING?

The issue of blending doctrinal and expository preaching has received minimal treatment in textbooks and articles on preaching. Since the appearance of Haddon Robinson's *Biblical Preaching* in 1980[1] homileticians have published a vast amount of material about expository preaching—so much that it is proper to speak of a recovery of *expository* preaching. Within the same period, however, one has difficulty in locating substantial writings which handle the subject of *doctrinal* preaching. R. Albert Mohler, Jr. observes that this lack of emphasis on preaching doctrine has encouraged many preachers to become slack in this area, resulting in their own doctrinal ignorance. Theological ignorance among those occupying the pulpit inevitably has been passed on to people in the pews.[2]

Due to this dearth of doctrinal certainty, it is little wonder that the current trend in preaching often minimizes any theological elements in favor of preaching to the people's felt needs. Harry Emerson Fosdick's (1878—1969) impact on the last fifty years of preaching has led many preachers to define their roles primarily as counselors. Even some theologically conservative preachers have accepted his criticism of expository preaching and his counter-proposal. Fosdick claims that many preachers

indulge habitually in what they call expository sermons. They take a

---

[1] Haddon W. Robinson, *Biblical Preaching: The Development and Delivery of Expository Messages* (Grand Rapids: Baker Books, 1980).

[2] R. Albert Mohler, Jr. "The Primacy of Preaching," in *Feed My Sheep: A Passionate Plea for Preaching*, ed. Don Kistler (Morgan, PA: Soli Deo Gloria, 2002), 23. See also Tom Ascol, "Systematic Theology and Preaching," *The Founders Journal*, no. 4 (1991); founders.org/FJ04/editoria_fr.html.

passage from Scripture and, proceeding on the assumption that the people attending church that morning are deeply concerned about what the passage means, they spend their half hour or more on historical exposition of the verse or chapter, ending with some appended practical application to the auditors. Could any procedure be more surely predestined to dullness and futility? Who seriously supposes that, as a matter of fact, one in a hundred of the congregation cares, to start with, what Moses, Isaiah, Paul or John meant in those special verses, or came to church deeply concerned about it? Nobody else who talks to the public so assumes that the vital interests of the people are located in the meaning of words spoken two thousand years ago. The advertisers of any goods, from a five-foot shelf of classic books to the latest life insurance policy, plunge as directly as possible after the contemporary wants, felt needs, actual interests and concerns.[3]

Fosdick clearly denounces *bad* expository preaching, for expository preaching by its own nature engages the audience with the biblical text.[4]

Against Fosdick's criticism, the recent rise of expository preaching rightly emphasizes preaching the Word of God as it is—doctrines and all—but the emphasis lies with the text's meaning and significance, or exposition and application. Furthermore, expository preaching textbooks rightly note the need to convey the central idea of the *Scripture* so that the central idea of the *sermon* addresses the audience. Throughout this discussion on expository preaching, however, homileticians say little or nothing about preaching doctrinally within such an expository framework. Because the Bible, as the Word of God, is a theological book, it is possible and even necessary to convey the central idea of a biblical passage from a *doctrinal* standpoint. The last several years have produced a few publications showing that theology and preaching in general are once again receiving treatment as overlapping disciplines.[5] Further, expository preaching that addresses the contemporary

---

[3] Harry Emerson Fosdick, "What Is the Matter with Preaching?" *Pulpit Digest* 63 (reprint, September-October 1983): 9.

[4] Hershael W. York and Bert Decker argue for "engaging exposition" in *Preaching with Bold Assurance: A Solid and Enduring Approach to Engaging Exposition* (Nashville: Broadman & Holman, 2003). See also York, *2001 Power in the Pulpit Conference: Speaking with Bold Assurance* (Louisville: The Southern Baptist Theological Seminary, cassette). See chapter 14 below on doctrinal exposition and the audience.

[5] See, for example, Millard J. Erickson and James L. Heflin, *Old Wine in New Wineskins: Doctrinal Preaching in a Changing World* (Grand Rapids: Baker

world continues to be a growing interest. A need remains, nevertheless, for integrating the two disciplines of *theology* and *exposition*. Even though some expository preachers rely heavily on doctrine and some doctrinal preachers deliver sermons in an expository fashion, it is still necessary to blend doctrinal and expository preaching. This integration is what I call *Preaching for Bodybuilding*.

Aim of This Book—Preaching for Bodybuilding

This work will describe and analyze the integration of expository preaching and doctrinal preaching in addressing a postmodern world (defined below). An assumption of this work is that expository preaching best fits the biblical model.[6] Furthermore, both biblical theology and systematic theology are faithful approaches to understanding biblical doctrine.[7] How one is taught (expositional preaching) and what one is taught (the Bible's theology) should be every preacher's concern for his church.[8] Thus, blending expository preaching and systematic-biblical theology provides what I label "doctrinal expository preaching." Additionally, since expository preaching necessarily includes application, it is imperative to convey how doctrinal exposition can, and should, address the contemporary world.

Thus this proposal of doctrinal expository preaching for a postmodern

---

Books, 1997); Robert G. Hughes and Robert Kysar, *Preaching Doctrine: For the Twenty-First Century* (Minneapolis: Fortress Press, 1997); Ronald J. Allen, *Preaching Is Believing: The Sermon as Theological Reflection* (Louisville: Westminster John Knox Press, 2002); Robert Smith Jr., *Doctrine That Dances: Bringing Doctrinal Preaching and Teaching to Life* (Nashville: B&H Academic, 2008).

[6] See chapter 5 for a definition of expository preaching as a foundation to understanding doctrinal expository preaching.

[7] This is not to say that one necessarily concerns itself with the text of Scripture more than the other. Biblical theology focuses on a particular author's writings, seeking to understand what is meant by certain words, phrases, and concepts. Systematic theology, on the other hand, aids one in seeing what the entire canon teaches about a particular doctrine, emphasizing the unity of the Scriptures. I contend, therefore, that both biblical theology and systematic theology are faithful both theologically and textually. For more on this notion, see Ascol, "Systematic Theology and Preaching," as well as chapter 10 below.

[8] Mark E. Dever, *Nine Marks of a Healthy Church* (Wheaton: Crossway Books, 2000), 45-46.

world will show the need for emphasizing doctrinal truth within expository sermons. Because of the influence of postmodernism on today's church, preachers now more than ever need to declare the whole counsel of God. This kind of preaching demands both a doctrinal soundness and an expository style in setting forth the truth in its proper context. Although books and articles on expository preaching are abundant, doctrinal preaching receives little space in comparison. Furthermore, except for a chapter or section in a few isolated places, a tremendous void in resources supporting doctrinal expository preaching remains. The lack of theological and biblical clarity and conviction in most of the modern pulpits—as well as the pews—makes this study both necessary and relevant.

Preaching for Bodybuilding argues that the most faithful preaching begins by developing the preacher, who then proclaims God's message to the listeners, helping them build their spiritual bodies into the image of Christ.

An Exercise Plan—the Layout of Preaching for Bodybuilding

To begin this discipline, I will lay out a plan, much like a trainer would do for a serious bodybuilder. This exercise plan builds the necessary foundation, develops it, and then critiques the process along the way to adapt it to the individual preacher. Ultimately, I will propose and analyze the incorporation of the all-too-often separated disciplines of doctrinal preaching and expository preaching with an eye on the contemporary, postmodern world. This plan will demonstrate doctrinal expository preaching distinctively, biblically, systematically, and practically.

First, I will establish the relevancy and necessity for this study. This section will include the rise of expository preaching and the decline of doctrinal preaching. Additionally, an analysis of the transformation of the audience over the last few decades with special concern for the roles of postmodernism and evangelicalism will help set the context for the rest of this work.

Second, in light of the volume of work on expository preaching, this study will look at significant components of some of the leading definitions. I am not trying to "reinvent the wheel" when it comes to exposition, but I do want to make a case for its neglect of theological substance. Moreover, a discussion of doctrinal preaching will help serve as a foundation for understanding doctrinal expository preaching.

Third, an investigation of the Scriptures' terminology and preaching models should validate the biblical basis for doctrinal expository preaching. Fourth, a proposal on the roles of biblical and systematic theology in doctrinal exposition will aid in theological interpretation, refining this discipline and tailoring it to fit the preacher's gifts and comfort with various approaches. To help avoid forcing particular doctrines onto certain passages of Scripture, I remind the reader that hermeneutics has a voice in determining theological interpretation. The product of this theological exegesis will serve the discipline of forming the sermon. This section closes by offering two models for implementing doctrine and exposition.

Finally, cultural concerns of truth, entertainment, language, image, and story highlight this study's relevancy and practicality in a postmodern world. This work then concludes with several practical elements of doctrinal exposition, showing why it is preaching that builds spiritual bodies.

Part 1: Historical Issues for Doctrinal Exposition

CHAPTER 2
THE RECOVERY OF EXPOSITORY PREACHING:
WATCHING AND LEARNING FROM OTHERS
WHO HAVE PREACHED FOR BODYBUILDING

Before you jump into a serious workout routine, it is helpful to sit down and watch how others workout. You can gain insights into how you may want to approach the discipline. Studying what others have said and done will help you begin to develop the basis for serious bodybuilding—both for yourself and your audience—those you train.

Men of God have practiced expository preaching since the biblical era. Expositors of God's Word include Moses (Deut 1:5), Ezra (Neh 8:5-8), Jesus (Luke 24:27), and Paul (Acts 13:15ff). Although explanation was clearly at the heart of their preaching, exhortation and application were also essential components, telling the audience what to do with the messages.

Furthermore, the early church modeled the kind of preaching that explained the biblical text and applied it to the contemporary listeners. Men such as John Chrysostom (347—407) and Augustine of Hippo (354—430) stand out as noteworthy expositors. Known as the Golden Mouth, Chrysosom's preaching was tied closely to the Scriptures, so close that he delivered three homilies on the very first verse of John's Gospel![1] As far as Augustine goes, one usually remembers him as a theologian. His rich explanation of the Scriptures, however, made an impact on both his

---

[1]John Chrysostom, *Homilies of St. John Chrysostom Archbishop of Constantinople on the Gospel of St. John* 30-64, in The Nicene and Post-Nicene Fathers First Series, vol. 14, ed. Philipp Schaff, in The Master Christian Library [CD-ROM] (Albany, OR: AGES Software, 1997). Significant writings exist from both Chrysostom and Augustine as are found in the first fourteen volumes of *The Nicene and Post-Nicene Fathers*.

generation and the Reformers of the sixteenth century. His clear explanation of the Bible's message placed him as the leading defender against the heresies of his day.

During the Middle Ages, solid biblical preaching began to fade from the scene as the sacraments grew to replace the role of the Scriptures in worship. The Reformation not only returned the priority of the Word in worship, but it also recovered expository preaching. Looking at how the Reformation had an impact on preaching, nineteenth-century homiletician John Broadus cites four characteristics. The first two occur here, and the last two are below. Reformation preaching was, first of all, "a *revival of preaching*."[2] Such an outburst of faithful proclamation had not occurred since the biblical era. Second, "it was a revival of *Biblical* preaching," the greater part of which "was *expository*."[3] The Reformers' exposition had not had an equal since the days of Chrysostom, for it featured a return to the study of the original languages in order to explain carefully to the people the Scriptures' teachings—passage by passage and book by book. Careful and consistent exposition, sound exegesis, and orderliness abound in Reformation preaching.[4] Broadus concludes this point by saying that "in general, it may be said that the best specimens of expository preaching are to be found in Chrysostom, in the Reformers, especially Luther and Calvin, and in the Scottish pulpit of our own time."[5]

In the Face of Thematic Preaching

Although the Reformation recovered expository preaching, it did so only to a degree. The Reformation's successors did not, for the most part, rival the steady verse-by-verse, passage-by-passage, and book-by-book approach of Luther and Calvin. The English Puritans latched on to the theological teaching of the Reformation, resulting in a doctrinal-thematic style of

---

[2]John A. Broadus, *Lectures on the History of Preaching* (New York: Sheldon & Co., 1876), 113.

[3]Ibid., 114. Cf. John H. Leith, *The Reformed Imperative: What the Church Has to Say That No One Else Can* (Philadelphia: The Westminster Press, 1988), 24-28.

[4]Broadus, *History of Preaching*, 114-16. Broadus' push for expository preaching in his own day is quite significant. Students of preaching should view his argument for exposition as foundational to Robinson's work in the same field (see also chapter 5 below).

[5]Ibid., 116. For Broadus' treatment of expositors in his own day, including Spurgeon, see Broadus, *History of Preaching*, 229-31.

preaching.[6] Thematic preaching, often understood as topical preaching in the twentieth and twenty-first centuries, is preaching which "gives a systematic or integrated treatment of a theme considered worthy of discussion."[7] The kind of thematic preaching which had its roots in biblical truth would eventually give way to a type of thematic preaching which originated from the "hot" issues of contemporary culture.

The Puritan Model of Thematic Preaching
Shortly after the Reformation, the Puritans entered the scene both in England and, later, in America. Doctrinal preaching may very well have reached its climax within this group of ministers. Puritan sermons, often one to two hours in length, were full of theological explanation and argumentation. In addition to Sunday sermons, special weekday or "occasional" sermons addressed the current circumstances. Puritan ministers were well-equipped to address both theology and culture.

A noteworthy feature of Puritan preaching is its "plain style." This style has at least three characteristics in regards to substance and structure. First, beginning with the biblical text, it provides a doctrinal thesis. Second, it offers careful and comprehensive explanation of the theological statement. Finally, the plain style consists of several observations for applying the doctrine to one's life.[8]

---

[6]For writers who classify Puritan preaching as expository preaching, see John MacArthur, Jr. and the Master's Seminary Faculty, *Rediscovering Expository Preaching: Balancing the Science and Art of Biblical Exposition*, ed. Richard L. Mayhue (Dallas: Word, 1992), 51-60; John R. W. Stott, *Between Two Worlds: The Art of Preaching in the Twentieth Century* (Grand Rapids: William B. Eerdmans, 1982), 28-33; J. I. Packer, *A Quest for Godliness: The Puritan Vision of the Christian Life* (Wheaton: Crossway Books, 1990), 284. Although Puritan preaching has elements of expository preaching, I identify it, nevertheless, as doctrinal-thematic (for clarification sake, I provide a working definition of expository preaching in chapter 5). The Puritans did not normally practice the now-famous book-by-book approach to expository preaching. Since the Puritans were so well-versed in the Scriptures, many of their sermons include a barrage of biblical verses to support their doctrinal theses. For other homiletical models which fall outside expository preaching, see Derek Thomas, "Expository Preaching," in *Feed My Sheep*, 74-80.

[7]James W. Cox, "Topical Preaching," in *Concise Encyclopedia of Preaching*, ed. William H. Willimon and Richard Lischer (Louisville: Westminster John Knox Press, 1995), 492.

[8]Harry S. Stout, "Puritan Preaching," in *Concise Encyclopedia of Preaching*, 394-97.

Although a full analysis of Puritan preaching is impossible at this juncture, the impact it made on future preaching is difficult to overstate. The need for sermons to revolve around a theme or idea has its origin in the Puritan model. Thus, it appears that the *structure* of Puritan preaching has had at least a small part in shaping the thematic preaching so prominent throughout much of the last one hundred years. Some preachers of the 1900s focused so much on relevancy that they had less and less to say about doctrine. Thus, the Puritans' doctrinal-thematic approach *grounded in the Scriptures* would eventually give way to something of a topical-thematic preaching *founded on the preacher's idea*. So, while a vast difference exists between the *substance* of Puritan preaching and much of contemporary preaching, there seems to be a connection with the *structure* between the two.

The Modern Method of Thematic Preaching

Puritan preaching helped preachers narrow their sermon's focus to a single theme. Although Puritans always began with the biblical text as the foundation for the sermon's doctrinal theme, preachers since at least the early-twentieth century have moved away from a semi-doctrinal exposition of Scripture to a thematic discussion of popular trends. The impact of Fosdick helps explain this shift in preaching.

Fosdick's roles both as pastor of Riverside Church and as professor of Union Theological Seminary provided two influential speaking platforms. On the one hand, as a professor, he was well-versed in the theological trends of his day. His writings on the Bible, preaching, and religion supplemented his classroom discussions. On the other hand, as a pastor, Fosdick used the Bible to offer words of advice and comfort. He viewed himself as something of a therapist. Many students and preachers valued his opinions as a theologian and trusted his advice as a pastor.

As noted above, Fosdick's distaste for some bad expository preaching led him to criticize the whole lot of expositional preaching. Furthermore, his modernist view of the Scriptures directly influenced his preaching. Contemporary preaching still feels the rippling-effect of Fosdick's view of preaching.

Fosdick's "What Is the Matter with Preaching?" has become one of the most influential articles on preaching in the twentieth-century. He argues against expository and topical preaching because they both start at the wrong end of preaching—the Bible and the preacher, respectively. As an alternative, Fosdick offers what he calls the project method, or problem-solving method. This type of preaching begins with the audience and results from cooperative thinking between the preacher and the congregation, using psychological practices.[9]

One of the biggest ironies about Fosdick's proposal is that many of his followers see him as "the progenitor of what might be called 'topical' preaching. Topical sermons often dealing with 'problem-solving' or 'life-situations' have dominated the pulpits of American churches"[10] since Fosdick's proposal. Even though Fosdick criticizes topical preaching, others observe that he has simply given it a different name.

This topical or thematic preaching continues to dominate mainline evangelicalism. A study of sermons by Fosdick and his followers shows that they offer little biblical explanation, often favoring narrative discourse.[11] What they do advance, however, are ideas of ways people can feel better about themselves or how they can be of service to others. Although preaching themes could treat doctrines such as the Trinity, creation, grace, or sin, contemporary concerns for drug addiction, aging, depression, racism, and vocation have moved to the forefront in many of the mainstream evangelical pulpits of the last half-century.[12]

Where thematic preaching has become skewed is in its place of authority. Although the Puritans' authority was the Bible, many preachers today see themselves as the authority. That is to say, the theme often originates in the preacher's mind before turning to find a supporting text.

In explaining this move towards more of a subjective approach to

---

[9]Harry Emerson Fosdick, "What Is the Matter with Preaching?" *Pulpit Digest* 63 (reprint, September-October 1983): 9-12.

[10]Ronald E. Sleeth, "'What Is the Matter with Preaching?': A Fosdick Retrospective," *Pulpit Digest* 63 (September-October 1983): 17.

[11]See Harry Emerson Fosdick, *On Being Fit to Live With: Sermons on Post-War Christianity* (New York: Harper & Brothers, 1946); John R. Claypool and others, *Protestant Hour Classics: The 12 Most Requested Sermons, 1953-1988* (Nashville: Abingdon Press, 1992); Barbara Lundblad and others, *The Past Speaks to the Future: 50 Years of the Protestant Hour* (Nashville: Abingdon Press, 1995); Thomas G. Long and Cornelius Plantiga, Jr., eds., *A Chorus of Witnesses: Model Sermons for Today's Preacher* (Grand Rapids: Wm. B. Eerdmans, 1994).

[12]For ways these and similar subjects are supposed to help in addressing contemporary listeners, see James W. Cox, ed., *Handbook of Themes for Preaching* (Louisville: Westminster John Knox Press, 1991). One needs only to observe the number of Baptist, Presbyterian, Lutheran, and Methodist contributors in order to realize the popularity of this book among mainstream denominations.

preaching, especially preaching directed at people's needs, Robinson argues that the way preachers have viewed their roles reflect the shift of authority in the American culture. Prior to the 1950s, preachers saw themselves as evangelists. From 1950-1970, they viewed themselves as teacher. The 1980s and 1990s ushered in the preacher as therapist role.[13] The first few years of the twenty-first century has carried the preacher as therapist into the preacher as a "feel good" helper. These role transformations caused changes in sermon content as well as in the authority in preaching. The recovery of expository preaching in the face of these changes underscores the renewed emphasis upon biblical authority.

In Efforts to Be Biblical

When many preachers were viewing themselves as therapists, others were sensing the need to find their authority in the Scriptures. Thus, the primary reason for the recovery of expository preaching since 1980 is the need for preaching to be biblical once again. The route of thematic preaching was giving little more than lip service to Scripture. Of course, much of this direction resulted from a low view of Scripture. As more evangelicals asserted the inerrancy of Scripture, the natural way of preaching Scripture was expositionally. After all, "biblical exposition comes only from those with a high inerrantist view of Scripture."[14] This relationship between Scripture and preaching is even clearer in the role doctrine has played in preaching.

---

[13]Haddon W. Robinson, "When Flint Strikes Steel," *Reformed Worship* 40 (June 1996): 15-16. David F. Wells makes a similar argument in his *No Place for Truth, or Whatever Happened to Evangelical Theology?* (Grand Rapids: Eerdmans, 1993), 101.

[14]R. Kent Hughes, "The Anatomy of Exposition: *Logos, Ethos, and Pathos*," *The Southern Baptist Journal of Theology* 3, no. 2 (1999): 46. Conservative evangelicals' insistence on inerrancy in the late 1970s undoubtedly contributed to the recovery of expository preaching, for if one can trust that the Bible is God's Word, he can preach *it* rather than his *own* ideas.

CHAPTER 3
THE NEED FOR DOCTRINAL PREACHING:
TO GROW STRONGER, YOU MUST WORK OUT!

Far too often someone realizes the need to begin a workout routine only to fail in actually working out! The spiritual decline of preaching has often been attributed to nothing more than a failure to put the time into the preparation of delivering the Word of God.

One finds different kinds of doctrinal preaching throughout church history—both strong and weak. Even in the doctrinally-weak sermons, the church has never completely lost doctrinal preaching. Nevertheless, periods of significant neglect of the sermon's theological content mark the history of the church. This section highlights both the high and low points of the history of doctrinal preaching.

When Doctrinal Preaching Dominated

Doctrine will always remain an integral part of gospel preaching, for the gospel consists of such doctrines as the holiness and love of God, the sinfulness of man, the deity and sinlessness of Christ, the substitutionary atonement, Christ's resurrection from the dead, the regenerating work of the Holy Spirit, and the necessity of repentance and faith for conversion. The truth of the gospel is at stake whenever people dismiss, or redefine in unbiblical terms, any of these key doctrines.

These key doctrines and their formations find their roots in the biblical era and the early church. It should serve as no surprise that today's homileticians remember the most noted expositors of Christian history as some of the best doctrinal preachers. Due to the absence of strong preaching during much of the medieval period, however, there was a need to recover the role of Scripture in worship. Thus, preaching and teaching the Word of God became of paramount importance during the Reformation Period. The Second Helvetic Confession of 1566 states, "The preaching of the Word of God is the Word of God."[1] Because of this return to the Scriptures and its doctrines, many scholars agree that the Reformation Period and the next few centuries saw doctrinal preaching at its highest.

Broadus' comments about doctrinal preaching in his discussion of Reformation preaching are noteworthy. Within his treatment of the Reformers' biblical preaching, he states that "the preacher's one great task was to set forth the doctrinal and moral teachings of the Word of God."[2] As stated above, Reformation preaching was not only "a *revival of preaching*," but it was also a revival of biblical or expository preaching.[3] Furthermore, it "involved a revival of *controversial* preaching"[4] when truth would not be allowed to stand beside error. Finally, Reformation preaching was "a revival of preaching upon the doctrines of grace. . . . freely proclaimed by *all* the Reformers."[5] Truth and doctrine are clearly at the core of these final two characteristics.

Combining both the point made above and this one, it is worth noting that Broadus emphasizes both *expository* preaching and *doctrinal* preaching within his discussion on biblical preaching, as if to say that true biblical preaching is both expository and theological in substance. The Reformation recovered the same practice of preaching that had occurred during the first few centuries of Christendom. Elsewhere, Ascol claims that in Calvin, Luther, and Zwingli, "theology resulted from and was given expression in expository preaching."[6] Although doctrinal preaching would continue for a

---

[1] John H. Leith, *Creeds of the Churches* (Atlanta: John Knox Press, 1982), 131.

[2] John A. Broadus, *Lectures on the History of Preaching* (New York: Sheldon & Co., 1876), 114. Charles J. Duey notes that in the Reformation "biblical preaching became the prime element in Protestant worship. And this preaching was theological preaching, not topical or life-situation preaching or any other form of public address than theological presentation of the Word of God" ("Let's Preach Theology," *The Covenant Quarterly* 21, no. 2 [1963]: 11).

[3] Broadus, *History of Preaching*, 113-14.

[4] Ibid., 116.

[5] Ibid., 117. Even if one does not ascribe to the doctrines of grace, the point here is that Reformation preaching included the proclamation of doctrine.

[6] Tom Ascol, "Systematic Theology and Preaching," *The Founders Journal*, no. 4 (1991); founders.org/FJ04/editorial_fr.html. Elsewhere Ascol asserts that

few centuries following the Reformation, pure exposition took something of a backseat in most pulpits.

During the sixteenth through nineteenth centuries, doctrinal preaching abounded, thanks in large part to the influence of the Puritans. Their high view of the Scriptures provided the foundation for their high view of preaching. They insisted that one have a firm grasp of the theology of the entire Bible before seeking to explain a part of it. J. I. Packer writes,

> The Puritans received the Bible as a self-contained and self-interpreting revelation of God's mind. This revelation, the 'body of divinity' as they called it, is, they held, a unity, to which every part of 'the best of books' makes its own distinct contribution. It follows that the meaning of single texts cannot be properly discerned till they are seen in relation to the rest of the 'body'; and, conversely, that the better one's grasp of the whole, the more significance one will see in each part. To be a good expositor, therefore, one must first be a good theologian. Theology—truth about God and man—is what God has put into the texts of Scripture, and theology is what preachers must draw out of them. To the question, 'Should one preach doctrine?', the Puritan answer would have been, 'Why, what else is there to preach?'[7]

It follows, then, that to a Puritan, preaching is doctrinal by definition.

In further support of this claim, one of the most beneficial works on preaching came from the hand of a Puritan, William Perkins.[8] He believed that the preparation of a sermon must begin with doctrine: "First, fix clearly in your mind and memory the sum and substance of biblical doctrine, with its definitions, divisions and explanations."[9] The Scriptures' theological teaching, thus, shapes the rest of the preparation and proclamation process.

---

during the sixteenth through nineteenth centuries people assumed pastors were also theologians. "The Pastor as Theologian," *The Founders Journal*, no. 43 (2001); founders.org/FJ43/editorial_fr.html.

[7]J. I. Packer, *A Quest for Godliness: The Puritan Vision of the Christian Life* (Wheaton: Crossway Books, 1990), 284-85. Timothy George asserts that the Puritans developed one of the most biblically-based, theologically-responsible patterns of preaching ("Doctrinal Preaching," in *Handbook of Contemporary Preaching: A Wealth of Counsel for Creative and Effective Proclamation*, ed. Michael Duduit [Nashville: Broadman Press, 1992], 96).

[8]William Perkins, *The Art of Prophesying; with the Calling of the Ministry* (Cambridge: J. Legatt, 1592; reprint, Carlisle, PA: The Banner of Truth Trust, 1996).

[9]Ibid., 23.

As for Puritan preaching, many Christians continue to benefit from the theologically-saturated sermons from the well-known preachers of that era, such as John Owen, Richard Baxter, John Bunyan, George Whitefield, Jonathan Edwards, and Charles Spurgeon. Although an in-depth look at the preaching of these men falls outside the scope of this work, the main concern here is to see how and when the disciplines of theology and preaching became disconnected.

When Doctrinal Preaching Diminished

It should be evident that preaching and theology have a direct relationship to the Scriptures. Apart from the authority and trustworthiness of the Bible one ends up with a dramatic shift in doctrine and preaching. Thus, it is not surprising that several writers trace the decline of doctrinal and/or expositional preaching to the decline of biblical authority.

Stated slightly differently, the movement away from doctrinally-substantive preaching finds its origin in the decline of biblical authority. As preachers lost confidence in the Scriptures' truthfulness, they made fewer appeals to its doctrines. The decline of biblical authority and the subsequent lack of doctrine in preaching find their roots in the rising liberalism of the late nineteenth century. Mohler writes,

> The intellectual roots of liberal trend within Protestantism are found in the enlightenment and the rise of modernist thought. By the late nineteenth century, liberal scholars in the academic world, especially in Germany and England, began to question some of the most basic teachings of the Bible. In particular, these skeptics began to deny the truthfulness of the Bible with regard to matters of history, creation, and the permanence of objective truth. . . . The Bible was no longer seen as a perfect treasure of divine truth, but was seen as the faulty testimony of ancient religious peoples.[10]

In order to observe this change in doctrinal preaching, several timeframes stand out.[11] Although these timeframes are not concrete-like

---

[10]R. Albert Mohler, Jr., "A Conflict of Visions: The Theological Roots of the Southern Baptist Controversy," *The Southern Baptist Journal of Theology* 7, no. 1 (2003): 5. For liberalism's impact on twentieth-century mainline Protestantism and the Southern Baptist Convention, see Mohler, "Conflict of Visions," 5-8.

[11]Mark Coppenger observes similar timeframes in tracing the human depravity in Southern Baptist preaching during the nineteenth and twentieth centuries. "The Ascent of Lost Man in Southern Baptist Preaching," *The Founders Journal*, no. 25 (1996); founders.org/FJ25/article 1_fr.html.

parameters, they do help in tracing the decline in biblical authority and preaching. This section, therefore, outlines the roots and steady growth of doctrine-less preaching.

1870—1900—The Root of Decline in Doctrinal Preaching

The 1870s serve as a good indicator as to when this decline in biblical authority began within mainline Protestantism. Even though Schleiermacher's influence from the turn of that century was foundational to the rise of liberalism, its impact on American Protestantism would appear several decades later. Furthermore, the decade of the 1870s was a time when America began to identify itself anew in a post-Civil War era.

Several important figures began addressing the growing problem of liberalism during this decade. Princetonian scholars Charles Hodge (1797—1878) and, a few years later, B. B. Warfield (1851—1921) took a hard stand for biblical inspiration and inerrancy as they fought the criticism and Modernism creeping out of the European universities.[12] Hodge, for instance, opposed the promotion of Darwinian evolution because of its refusal to pay heed to biblical theology. The Bible is the supreme source of truth, and every theologian must subject himself, first of all, to the truths of Scripture. He wrote,

> It may be admitted that the truths which the theologian has to reduce to a science, or, to speak more humbly, which he has to arrange and harmonize, are revealed partly in the external works of God, partly in the constitution of our nature, and partly in the religious experience of believers; yet lest we should err in our inferences from the works of God, we have a clearer revelation of all that nature reveals, in his word; and lest we should misinterpret our own consciousness and the laws of our nature, everything that can be legitimately learned from that source will be will be found recognized and authenticated in the Scriptures.[13]

---

[12]Carson is surely correct in his claim that "the Princetonians had more to say about Scripture than their forebears, precisely because that was one of the most common points of attack from the rising liberalism of the (especially European) university world" (D. A. Carson, "Domesticating the Gospel: A Review of Stanley J. Grenz's *Renewing the Center*," *The Southern Baptist Journal of Theology* 6, no. 4 [2002]: 90).

[13]Charles Hodge, *Systematic Theology* (New York: Charles Scribner's Sons, 1871; reprint, London: James Clarke & Co., 1960), 1:11. Hodge specifically attacks Darwinian evolution in *What Is Darwinism?: And Other Writings on Science and Religion*, ed. Mark A. Noll and David N. Livingstone (1874; reprint, Grand Rapids: Baker Books, 1994). For more on the Princetonian doctrine of

Hodge also claimed that experience must be subject to the Scriptures' authority, for

> the Bible gives us not only the facts concerning God, and Christ, ourselves, and our relation to our Maker and Redeemer, but also records the legitimate effects of these truths on the minds of believers. So that we cannot appeal to our own feelings or inward experience, as a ground or guide, unless we can show that it agrees with the experience of holy men as recorded in the Scriptures.[14]

B. B. Warfield also defended biblical inspiration and doctrine in the face of growing liberalism. Concerning the latter, Warfield warned against creeping heresies:

> "Modern discovery" and "modern thought" are erected into the norm of truth, and we are told that the whole sphere of theological teaching must be conformed to it. This is the principle of that reconstruction of religious thinking which we are now constantly told is going on resistlessly about us, and which is to transform all theology. What is demanded of us is just to adjust our religious views to the latest pronouncements of philosophy or science or criticism. And this is demanded with entire unconsciousness of the fundamental fact of Christianity—that we have a firmer ground of confidence for our religious views than any science or philosophy or criticism can provide for any of their pronouncements. . . .
>
> . . . We are "orthodox" when we account God's declaration in his Word superior in point of authority to them, their interpreter, and their corrector. We are "heretical" when we make them superior in point of authority to God's Word, its interpreter, and its corrector. By this test we may each of us try our inmost thought and see where we stand—on God's side or on the world's.[15]

Moreover, Warfield addressed the significance of theology in preaching by stating

> if there be any validity at all in these remarks, the indispensableness of Systematic Theology to the preacher is obvious. For they make it clear not only that some knowledge of Christian truth is essential to him who essays to teach that truth, but that the type of life

---

Scripture, see John Battle, "Charles Hodge: Inspiration, Textual Criticism, and the Princeton Doctrine of Scripture," *The WRS Journal* 4, no. 2 (1997); wrs.edu/journals/897/text.html.

[14]Hodge, *Systematic Theology*, 1:16.

[15]Benjamin B. Warfield, "Heresy and Concession"; bibleteacher.org/BBW5.htm.

which is produced by his preaching, so far as his preaching is effective, will vary in direct relation to the apprehension he has of Christian truth and the type of proportion of truth he presents in his preaching.[16]

Not only did Princeton's scholars stake their claims on biblical authority, but other evangelical leaders also contributed. In the middle of the 1870s, Broadus wrote, "It becomes every day more important to draw a firm line of demarkation between Physical Science and Theology, and to insist that each party shall work on its own side the line in peace."[17] Broadus believed that the Word of God is the highest authority, and even marginal departures from biblical teachings devastate a faithful biblical theology. Allowing modern science and its quest for truth an equal plane alongside the Bible's teachings would eventually result in a denial of several key Christian doctrines.

Furthermore, James P. Boyce confronted liberalism in a personal way at the young, struggling Southern Baptist Theological Seminary in Louisville. In 1878 Boyce approached Old Testament Professor Crawford H. Toy because of the latter's recent acceptance and advancement of higher criticism in the classroom. As seminary President, Boyce could not, and would not, allow such destructive views to be taught to future ministers no matter how popular Toy was with the students. Although Toy at first agreed to refrain from teaching his personal views, students asked too many questions about his opinions. Unable to remain quiet on his views, Toy eventually offered his resignation in 1879.[18] Even though Boyce was a personal friend of Toy, he stared liberalism in the face and fought against it.

On the other side of the Atlantic, Charles Haddon Spurgeon stood against higher criticism in what is known as the "Down Grade" Controversy among English Baptists. In setting the stage to this controversy, biographer Lewis Drummond writes about nineteenth century

---

[16]Benjamin B. Warfield, "The Indispensableness of Systematic Theology to the Preacher," *The Master's Seminary Journal* 7, no. 2 (1996): 245-46.

[17]Broadus, *History of Preaching*, 231.

[18]John A. Broadus, *A Memoir of James Petigru Boyce* (New York: A. C. Armstrong & Son, 1893), 264; see also Gregory A. Wills, *Southern Baptist Theological Seminary, 1859-2009* (Oxford: Oxford University Press, 2009), 108-149; Thomas J. Nettles, *James Petigru Boyce: A Southern Baptist Statesman* (Phillipsburg, NJ: P&R Publishing, 2009), 317-355. Boyce began noticing the crisis in Baptist doctrine at least as early as 1856 in an address before the Furman University Board of Trustees. James Petigru Boyce, "A Crisis in Baptist Doctrine" *The Founders Journal*, no. 7 (1992); founders.org/FJ07/ article4.html.

European liberalism and how

> the continental philosophical atmosphere, aided by the theory of evolution, spawned pure rationalism, growing scientism, humanism and higher biblical criticism. And this atmosphere began to make strong footholds in the British scene, throwing the Church on the defensive.
>
> Spurgeon reacted strongly against this liberal trend. When he read a book he felt truly heretical, he would tear it into small pieces lest anyone read it and be led astray.[19]

Having been suspicious for some time about the Baptist Union and certain Baptist preachers, Spurgeon finally gathered enough information to critique openly those who had accepted unorthodox teaching. About their preaching Spurgeon wrote,

> The Atonement is scouted, the inspiration of Scripture is derided, the Holy Spirit is degraded into an influence, the punishment of sin is turned into a fiction, and the resurrection into a myth, and yet these enemies of our faith expect us to call them brethren and maintain a confederacy with them.[20]

Although Spurgeon ended up on the minority side of the controversy, evangelicals around the world have benefited from his stance on biblical truth.

This growing liberalism would have an even greater impact on the next century. It would continue to affect the role of the Scriptures. What started in the classrooms of the world's leading universities would creep its way into the institutions of school, state, and church in just a few short years.

1900—1940—Preaching the Truth Takes on New Meaning

The birth of the twentieth century brought with it the continual growth of liberalism in the university world. As teachers advanced modern science and evolutionary principles in the classroom, students became more and more susceptible to higher critical methods.[21] Numerous Christian colleges,

---

[19]Lewis Drummond, *Spurgeon: Prince of Preachers* (Grand Rapids: Kregel, 1992), 663. For a thorough treatment of the Down Grade Controversy, see Drummond, *Spurgeon*, 661-716.

[20]Charles H. Spurgeon, "Another Word Concerning the Down Grade," *The Sword and the Trowel* 23 (August 1887), 397; quoted in Drummond, *Spurgeon*, 820.

[21]Since the writing of Charles Darwin's *Origin of Species* in 1859, the subject of evolution had become increasingly popular among Western thought. By the first two decades of the twentieth century, evolution had gained wide

universities, seminaries, and divinity schools accepted the claims of science, all-the-while rejecting little by little the authority of the Bible as divinely revealed.

Somewhat of a climactic moment came by 1925, when the Church went head-to-head with the State in the famous *State v. John Scopes* (a.k.a. the Scopes' Monkey Trial) over the teaching of Darwinian evolution in the public school system. The roles of Fundamentalist William Jennings Bryan and atheist Clarence Darrow brought most of America up-to-speed on the larger scale of the controversy. While disagreements came from both sides of the evolution issue—due to the larger war between supernaturalism and naturalism—this controversy boiled down to a battle of science versus the Bible in discovering the *truth*. Bryan's inability to match Darrow's wit, along with the media's modernist tendencies, eventually led to a significant setback to the anti-evolutionary forces.[22]

Within the church realm, Modernists represented the adherents of modern science's claims. On the other side of the debate, the Fundamentalists characterized many who continued to take their stand with the full authority of the Scriptures. Although many personalities embodied both sides of the Modernist-Fundamentalist debate, two stood out as leading voices—Harry Emerson Fosdick (1878—1969) and J. Gresham Machen (1881—1937).

Believing evolution to be factual and questioning much of the Bible's integrity, Fosdick preached with a strong emphasis on how one should live in the world. Among his sermons and numerous writings, one is hard-pressed to find solid biblical claims in support of the message he proclaimed.

Fosdick's message "Shall the Fundamentalists Win?" in 1922 was aimed at stirring up like-minded Modernists.[23] This sermon has gone down

---

acceptance throughout America, impacting the institutions of church and school. Moreover, a study of the Lyman Beecher Lectures on Preaching reveals that sound doctrine had a strategic place in the pulpit during the latter half of the nineteenth century. A couple of decades into the next century, however, show a decline in doctrine (see Edgar DeWitt Jones, *The Royalty of the Pulpit* [New York: Harper & Brothers, 1951], 385-94).

[22]For a helpful summary of this trial, see Doug Linder, "State v. John Scopes ('The Monkey Trial')" (2002); accessed 15 April 2003; available from law.umkc.edu/faculty/projects/ftrials/ scopes/evolut.html.

[23]It appears that the sermon was first published under Harry Emerson Fosdick, *The New Knowledge and the Christian Faith* (New York: n.p., 1922). The better-known title stuck shortly thereafter as is found in Harry Emerson

in history as his most famous, however, because it sounded the alarm to many Fundamentalists. In this sermon, Fosdick dismissed four doctrines championed by Fundamentalists—specifically the doctrines of the plenary inspiration of the Scriptures, the virgin birth of Christ, His propitiatory sacrifice, and His literal return to earth.

As to these doctrines, Fosdick began by asserting that, although many gracious people hold to a literal virgin birth, there are a number of other evangelicals "who would say that the virgin birth is not to be accepted as an historic fact."[24] Also, Fosdick misrepresented the doctrine of plenary inspiration, describing it in terms of mechanical dictation. Finally, he discredited a literal, bodily return of Jesus Christ to the earth in favor of God's work of grace through human lives. He stated that there are evangelicals that claim,

> 'Christ is coming!' They say it with all their hearts; but they are not thinking of an external arrival on the clouds. They have assimilated as part of the divine revelation the exhilarating insight which these recent generations have given to us, that development is God's way of working out His will. . . .
>
> And these Christians, when they say that Christ is coming, mean that, slowly it may be, but surely, His will and principles will be worked out by God's grace in human life and institutions.[25]

Fosdick rejected these core doctrines of Christianity because of his modernist view of the miraculous. He wrote that modern man "feels that miracles are a priori improbable. . . . [and] feels that stories of miracles are historically unreliable."[26] Miracle stories, Fosdick asserted, were added in later New Testament writings, those which were second-hand accounts. First-hand accounts, the most reliable, rarely record the miraculous—the epistles never record it and the "we" sections in Acts list very few miracles. Because of his naturalistic views, it is little wonder that Fosdick could preach that "Christians are unpayably indebted to science for the new note of straightforwardness and honesty in dealing with facts."[27]

Fosdick, "Shall the Fundamentalists Win?" *Christian Work* 102 (10 June 1922); historymatters.gmu.edu/d/5070/.

[24]Fosdick, "Shall the Fundamentalists Win?"

[25]Ibid.

[26]Harry Emerson Fosdick, *The Modern Use of the Bible* (New York: The Macmillan Company, 1924), 142-43 (cf. 146-47).

[27]Harry Emerson Fosdick, *Religion's Indebtedness to Science* (New York: n.p., 1927), 16.

Based on these assertions by Fosdick, it appears that he wanted to offer Jesus Christ and His teachings as the solution to the world's problems, all-the-while presenting a view of Christ which is radically different than the New Testament. Whenever the New Testament offers a doctrine which is puzzling to science, Fosdick either totally rejected it or redefined it. The authority, therefore, is not in the biblical text, but in the scientific assertions. This shift in authority impacted a number of scholars and preachers by the middle and late twentieth century.

Countering the denial of Christian fundamentals, Machen wrote to fight off modern science in the realm of Christianity. His clear and careful argument that "Christian doctrine lies at the very roots of faith" makes his *Christianity & Liberalism* one of the strongest defenses ever for Christian orthodoxy.[28] Although Machen addressed key doctrines such as God, Christ, man, salvation, and the Bible, his *claims* on doctrine during this timeframe are of special interest.

Machen stated up front that naturalistic modernism/ liberalism is not only a non-Christian religion, but it falls in a different classification of religions altogether.[29] Upholding Christianity as simply a way of life, modernism rejects the doctrinal framework of the Christian faith. In doing so, however, the modernist's claim against doctrine looks more like a mere objection "to one system of theology in the interests of another."[30]

Showing the validity of a clear doctrinal foundation in Christianity, Machen asserted that the entire Christian message stands on doctrine. The fundamental nature of the gospel means that certain historical events actually happened. From the time of the primitive Church,

> the meaning of the happening was set forth; and when the meaning of the happening was set forth then there was Christian doctrine. "Christ died"—that is history; "Christ died for our sins"—that is doctrine. Without these two elements, joined in an absolutely indissoluble union, there is no Christianity.[31]

Although some critics of the 1920s were blaming the Reformation for the twentieth century emphasis upon key doctrines, Machen noted, "Ultimately the attack is not against the seventeenth century, but against the

---

[28]J. Gresham Machen, *Christianity & Liberalism* (Grand Rapids: Eerdmans, 1923; reprint, Grand Rapids: Eerdmans, 1999), 44.

[29]Ibid., 2, 7.

[30]Ibid., 19.

[31]Ibid., 27 (cf. 28-29 for the extended argument).

Bible and against Jesus Himself."[32] Therefore, Modernists fought against biblical authority and Jesus Christ's deity, and a Christianity grounded in ethical practices replaced the Christian faith consisting of doctrinal assertions.

While one could say more about these early decades of the twentieth century, the Fundamentalist-Modernist controversy of the 1920s stresses the changing role of doctrine in the sermon. With the help of the leading universities and the media, modernism continued to gain ground. Doctrinal conviction and clarity within the Church was beginning to fade.

1940—1980—The Last Hurrah for Doctrinal Preaching?

The decades from 1940-1980 reveal a good deal about the role doctrine played in preaching. Books and journal articles on this subject appear to abound in comparison with both earlier and later decades.[33] As doctrinal preaching was making its last great run, one could sense the troubled times ahead. Thus, one might say concerning the doctrinal preaching of this era, "It was the best of times, it was the worst of times."

In one sense, it was as if preaching had rediscovered theology anew. One scholar observed,

> The statement that contemporary preaching has rediscovered theology needs a double qualification. On the one hand, theological preaching has never been altogether lost in the life of the church, though in various periods it has suffered neglect or abuse. On the other hand, the preaching in a multitude of churches today gives scant evidence of a theological concern or enlightenment. By "preaching's rediscovery of theology" is meant that in the life of the church as a whole, there is a new and deepening realization of the necessity of preaching which is theologically informed.[34]

---

[32]Ibid., 46.

[33]Some of the books on doctrinal preaching and/or sermons during this timeframe include Merrill R. Abbey, *Living Doctrine in a Vital Pulpit* (Nashville: Abingdon, 1964); Edmund P. Clowney, *Preaching and Biblical Theology* (Grand Rapids: Eerdmans, 1961); Douglas W. C. Ford, *A Theological Preacher's Notebook* (London: Hodder and Stoughton, 1962); Robert Mounce, *The Essential Nature of New Testament Preaching* (Grand Rapids: Eerdmans, 1960); James Stewart, *A Faith to Proclaim* (New York: Charles Scribner's Sons, 1953; reprint, Grand Rapids: Baker Book House, 1972); Theodore Wedel, *The Pulpit Rediscovers Theology* (Greenwich, CT: Seabury Press, 1956); Jerry Vines, *Fire in the Pulpit* (Nashville: Broadman Press, 1977).

[34]Thomas E. McCollough, "Preaching's Rediscovery of Theology," *Review*

At the same time doctrinal preaching was making its last great run during the middle of the twentieth century, it was also facing a growing, ever-critical voice. Some complained that theological preaching was boring and should not be practiced. James S. Stewart answered such criticism,

> How foolish then, the clamour for non-doctrinal preaching! And how desperately you will impoverish your ministry if you yield to that demand! The underlying assumption is, of course, that doctrine is dull: a perfectly absurd misapprehension. . . . But to maintain that doctrine, as such, is necessarily a dull affair is simply a confession of ignorance or downright spiritual deficiency. Only a crass blindness could fail to see that such a truth as that presented in the sentence "The Word was made flesh" is overpoweringly dramatic in itself and utterly revolutionary in its consequences. "If this is dull," exclaims Dorothy Sayers, "then what, in Heaven's name, is worthy to be called exciting?"[35]

Stewart obviously considered doctrinal preaching as the only way to preach the full gospel of Jesus Christ. One could not truly classify anything less as preaching.

In light of criticisms of doctrinal preaching as irrelevant, several evangelicals began to note the need to refill the tank of doctrinal preaching. E. C. Rust, speaking to both liberals and conservatives, wrote,

> Indeed, more than ever today there is a need for theological preaching. By this I mean preaching which relates the central doctrines of our faith to the challenging and portentous movements of our time and to the everyday life of our people. For too long our preaching, at all levels, has been remarkable for the absence of the doctrinal note.[36]

Furthermore, some preachers reaffirmed the necessity of theology in preaching, especially a cross-centered theology. The person and work of Jesus Christ remained at the heart of preaching. One could not explain such a subject without dealing with doctrinal matters.

Even though some great strides were made in theological preaching during this era, the biblical theology movement was just beginning to take

---

and Expositor 56, no. 1 (1959): 43.

[35]James S. Stewart, Heralds of God (New York: Charles Scribner's Sons, 1946), 67-68.

[36]E. C. Rust, "Theology and Preaching," Review & Expositor 52, no. 2 (1955): 145. Rust's general assessment is correct, but what he offers by way of liberal and neo-orthodox theology as the answer lacks a solid, biblical foundation from which to build doctrinal preaching.

its toll on preaching doctrine. More evangelicals were championing biblical theology as the foundation to preaching. Little did they suspect the dramatic decline in doctrinal preaching in the coming years.

1980—Present—Is There Any Hope for Doctrinal Preaching?

The last thirty years reveal, now more than ever, the tremendous lack of doctrinal preaching. As noted above, the 1970s helped pave new roads for biblical theology at the expense of systematic theology. This change in theology has cost many conservative evangelicals more than they bargained. Ascol rightly observes,

> The near extinction of doctrinal preaching today strictly correlates to the modern disenchantment with systematic theology—the discipline which seeks to arrange in an orderly and coherent (i.e. "systematic") fashion the revealed truth concerning God in His various relationships. Quite obviously such an attempt is valid only if there is an inherent unity in the Scriptures. If there is no overall unity in the Bible, no coherence in all its parts, then the systematic theologian is on a fool's errand.[37]

Without the Bible's unity, there is no foundation for systematic theology. Without systematic theology, preaching suffers from doctrinal malnourishment. Without solid doctrinal preaching, the Christian message is at stake.

Other than the rejection of biblical authority, another reason for the decline in doctrinal preaching concerns the cultural shift from modernism to postmodernism and the latter's influence on both the academic and ecclesiastical arenas.[38] Recent writers continue to lament the lack of doctrine in preaching: "How hard theology has fallen! Once considered the queen of sciences, today it is not even in the royal court."[39] Another says,

> Contemporary homiletical methods have unintentionally moved preachers away from teaching doctrine in the sermon. . . . [and] have often been interpreted in ways that diminish the role of

---

[37] Ascol, "Systematic Theology and Preaching."

[38] Robert G. Hughes and Robert Kysar accurately blame both the church and the culture for the current demise in theological understanding (*Preaching Doctrine: For the Twenty-First Century* [Minneapolis: Fortress Press, 1997], 2-6).

[39] Matthew Ristuccia, "Bringing Theology to Life," *Leadership* 15, no. 1 (1994): 25. John H. Leith (*From Generation to Generation: The Renewal of the Church According to Its Own Theology and Practice* [Louisville: Westminster/John Knox Press, 1990], 83) also observes the "great need for preaching with theological depth in our particular day."

teaching in general and theological reflection in particular.[40]

All hope is not lost, however, for preachers are at least noticing the need for theological preaching and many preachers have a desire to return to it. Timothy S. Warren writes,

> In the last few years the study of preaching has taken an explicitly theological turn. Both the theological basis for preaching and the theological process in preaching are topics that have precipitated significant writings.[41]

It is with great hope, therefore, that homileticians recover sound doctrinal preaching afresh in this day. With the rise of expository preaching, along with a bit of an interest in theological sermons, there is a tremendous opportunity at (re-)implementing these two disciplines. The field of biblical preaching is ripe for harvest, if only the preachers themselves will get busy about the work. Genuine Christians crave spiritual exercises to build their spiritual bodies. Doctrinal expository preaching can aid these people!

---

[40]Robert Kysar, "New Doctrinal Preaching for a New Century," *Journal for Preachers* 20, no. 3 (1997): 17.

[41]Timothy S. Warren, "The Theological Process in Sermon Preparation," *Bibliotheca Sacra* 156, no. 623 (1999): 336. Some of the more recent publications on doctrinal preaching include Jerry E. Oswalt, *Proclaiming the Whole Counsel of God: Suggestions for Planning and Preparing Doctrinal Sermons* (New York: University Press of America, 1993); Ronald J. Allen, *The Teaching Sermon* (Nashville: Abingdon Press, 1995); idem, *Preaching Is Believing*; Thomas G. Long and Edward Farley, eds., *Preaching as a Theological Task: World, Gospel, Scripture: In Honor of David Buttrick* (Louisville: Westminster John Knox Press, 1996); Hughes and Kysar, *Preaching Doctrine*; Erickson and Heflin, *Old Wine in New Wineskins*; Robert Smith Jr. *Doctrine That Dances: Bringing Doctrinal Preaching and Teaching to Life* (Nashville: B&H Academic, 2008). Chapter 6 deals with some of these writers' contributions to doctrinal preaching.

CHAPTER 4
THE AUDIENCE OF THE TWENTY-FIRST CENTURY: WHO'S WATCHING YOU WORKOUT?

In addition to proposing a way of integrating doctrine and expository preaching, we must not overlook the contemporary audience. The twenty-first century has reaped the technological advances—radio, television, computers, and the Internet—of the twentieth century. The thirty minute sitcom has affected both the length of sermons and the way ministers preach. The ever-increasing visual technology enhanced by computers reminds preachers of the impact of visual, as well as vocal and verbal, communication.[1]

Think of the issues in this chapter in light of our analogy of bodybuilding. If the best biblical preaching—doctrinal exposition—helps build others up in the Christian faith, surely the preacher himself is conscious of those learning from him. If you were undergoing strenuous exercise, would you want your trainer to be flabby and out of shape? Of course not. Just as physical fitness trainers practice what they teach because others are learning from them, so preachers must realize the importance of their audience.

Even though part 5 addresses preaching to a twenty-first century audience in greater detail, a few preliminary words are in order here. The

---

[1]Bert Decker, *You've Got to Be Believed to Be Heard* (New York: St. Martin's Press, 1992), 81-85. See also Bert Decker and Hershael W. York, *Speaking with Bold Assurance* (Nashville: Broadman & Holman, 2000). Neil Postman has picked up on America's visual-orientation in what he calls the "Age of Show Business" in his *Amusing Ourselves to Death: Public Discourse in the Age of Show Business* (New York: Penguin Books, 1985). This age has resulted in a "dumbing-down" of the average American mind.

rise of postmodernism has influenced preaching. Also, the ever-growing struggles within evangelicalism will help determine what doctrines preachers should declare in these uncertain days.

The Rise of the Postmodern Mindset

Perhaps David S. Dockery summarizes the current era best: "A new day has dawned. A new generation has come of age. The new generation is post-Christian, post-Enlightenment, and postmodern."[2] Many believe postmodernism, whatever it is, currently influences mostly the academy and intellectual world.[3] Postmodernism has, nevertheless, begun to impact preaching both in substance (what is preached) and style (how it is stated). The complexities of postmodernism demand attention, if preaching is to address people immersed in a postmodern culture.

It should be clear at the forefront that postmodernism is difficult to define with precision. By definition it refers to the age which follows modernism.[4] The current application of the term reveals it as "an umbrella concept covering styles, movements, shifts, and approaches in the fields of art, history, architecture, literature, political science, economics, and philosophy—not to mention theology."[5] It seems safe to say that every area of life has been touched by postmodernism.

Dockery views the heart of postmodernism's challenge as the rejection

---

[2]David S. Dockery, ed. *The Challenge of Postmodernism: An Evangelical Engagement*, 2nd ed. (Grand Rapids: Baker Academic, 2001), 9.

[3]R. Albert Mohler, Jr., "The Integrity of the Evangelical Tradition and the Challenge of the Postmodern Paradigm," in *Challenge of Postmodernism*, 69-70. See also idem, *Culture Shift: Engaging Current Issues with Timeless Truth* (Sisters, OR: Multnomah Books, 2008).

[4]The dates for modernism vary. Thomas C. Oden ("The Death of Modernity and Postmodern Evangelical Spirituality," in *Challenge of Postmodernism*, 23-24) dates modernism from 1789-1989, or from the French Revolution until the crumbling of communism depicted by the tearing down of the Berlin wall. Stanley J. Grenz ("Star Trek and the Next Generation: Postmodernism and the Future of Evangelical Theology," in *Challenge of Postmodernism*, 76) sees modernism as far back as the decay of the Middle Ages and extending into the early and middle portions of the twentieth century. Suffice it to say that many writers on the subject of postmodernism find strong postmodern thought since the 1970s.

[5]Mohler, "Integrity of the Evangelical Tradition," 54.

of truth, morality, and interpretive frameworks.[6] Postmodernism, therefore, dismisses the Christian worldview because of its stance on objective truth and morality. Thus, postmodernism and Christianity are in direct disagreement, and people today are questioning the theological underpinnings of preaching as never before.

Another difficulty in discussing postmodernism lies with its various strands. Critics of postmodernism have labeled its strands as hard and soft postmodernism, destructive and constructive postmodernism, and even deconstructive, liberationist, constructive, and conservative or restorationist postmodernism.[7] The harder views want to strip meaning from any and every text, including the Scriptures. The softer views, while not quite as dogmatic, are, nevertheless, still dangerous.

Postmodernism's own pluralistic worldview explains such diverse understandings within postmodernism (and, for this study, its theology). David Wells claims that "there is little agreement as to what it means to be a postmodern in theology, precisely because pluralism is at the center of it."[8] One may best characterize postmodern theology as the following four strands: Karl Barth's confessional theology, the existential-hermeneutical theology, theological deconstruction, and process theology.[9] Several of the neo-orthodox theologians of the mid-twentieth century represent the former two, and the latter two are gaining grounds, even among those who claim to be evangelical.[10] Before discussing the relationship between

---

[6]David S. Dockery, "The Challenge of Postmodernism," in *Challenge of Postmodernism*, 11.

[7]See Millard J. Erickson, *Postmodernizing the Faith: Evangelical Responses to the Challenge of Postmodernism* [Grand Rapids: Baker Books, 1998], 19; Carl F. H. Henry, "Postmodernism: The New Spectre?" in *Challenge of Postmodernism*, 38-40; Dockery, "The Challenge of Postmodernism," 14-16.

[8]David F. Wells, *No Place for Truth, or Whatever Happened to Evangelical Theology?* (Grand Rapids: Eerdmans, 1993), 66.

[9]Diogenes Allen, *Christian Belief in a Postmodern World: The Full Wealth of Conviction* (Louisville: Westminster John Knox Press, 1989).

[10]Perhaps the most outspoken, and often quoted, evangelical open to postmodernism is Stanley J. Grenz. For understanding his approach, see his works: *Revisioning Evangelical Theology: A Fresh Agenda for the 21st Century* (Downers Grove, IL: InterVarsity, 1993); *Theology for the Community of God* (Nashville: Broadman & Holman, 1994); *A Primer on Postmodernism* (Grand Rapids: Eerdmans, 1996); "Star Trek and the Next Generation: Postmodernity and the Future of Evangelical Theology," in *Challenge of Postmodernism*, 75-89;

postmodernism and evangelicalism, it is beneficial to see how postmodern thought has affected preaching.

The Failure of the New Homiletic

Along with the rise of postmodernism in the 1970s came a new wave of preaching in America. Starting with Fred Craddock's *As One without Authority* in 1971, this movement has become known as the New Homiletic.[11] Offering to the contemporary audience a new and "exciting" kind of preaching, New Homileticians dismiss propositional claims—especially doctrinal ones—in favor of simply telling the story via narrative preaching. Both the characteristics and the shortcomings of this movement are of special importance here.

In step with postmodernism, the New Homiletic does not offer one unified approach to preaching but numerous avenues. While virtually each adherent of the New Homiletic has his/her own unique blend of what preaching should look like, Mark Howell summarizes the movement along a couple of shared characteristics. First, the New Homiletic rejects propositional preaching.[12] The reason for such a rejection appears to be

---

Renewing the Center: Evangelical Theology in a Post-Theological Era (Grand Rapids: Baker Academic, 2000). For a summary and critique of Grenz's views, see Erickson, *Postmodernizing the Faith*, 83-102; Mohler, "Integrity of the Evangelical Tradition," 64-67; Carson, "Domesticating the Gospel," 82-97.

[11]Fred B. Craddock, *As One without Authority* (Enid, OK: Phillips University Press, 1971). Other important works in this movement include Craddock, *Overhearing the Gospel* (Nashville: Abingdon Press, 1978); Richard Eslinger, *A New Hearing: Living Options in Homiletic Method* (Nashville: Abingdon Press, 1987); Eugene L. Lowry, *The Sermon: Dancing the Edge of Mystery* (Nashville: Abingdon Press, 1997); idem, *The Homiletical Plot: The Sermon as Narrative Art Form*, rev. ed. (Louisville: Westminster John Knox Press, 2001); Charles Rice, *Interpretation and Imagination: The Preacher and Contemporary Literature* (Philadelphia: Fortress Press, 1970); David Buttrick, *Homiletic: Moves and Structures* (Philadelphia: Fortress Press, 1987); Henry Mitchell, *The Recovery of Preaching* (San Francisco: Harper & Row, 1977); Lucy Atkinson Rose, *Sharing the Word: Preaching in the Roundtable Church* (Louisville: Westminster John Knox Press, 1997).

[12]Mark A. Howell, "Preaching at the Dawn of the 21st Century: Is There New Hope for a New Homiletic?" (Ph.D. colloquium paper, The Southern Baptist Theological Seminary, 2000), 11-16. For a complete analysis of this movement, see Howell, "Hermeneutical Bridges and Homiletical Methods: A Comparative Analysis of the New Homiletic and Expository Preaching Theory 1970-1995" (Ph.D. diss., Southeastern Baptist Theological Seminary, 1999).

two-fold. One reason is that there is "a conviction that the old rationalist paradigm for preaching is no longer effective; and second, a primary emphasis on the creation of an experience for the audience."[13]

Second, the New Homiletic focuses on the narrative quality of the Bible.[14] These adherents favor a storyline plot rather than any deductive argumentation a passage might present. Representative of postmodernism's community-based understanding the New Homiletic pushes for sermon structure to adhere to the biblical language that "is 'plotted' by the interaction between an intentional writer and the intersubjective consciousness of an intended audience."[15] Whether described in terms of movement, plot, or story, proponents of this movement stress preaching as narrative.

Thus, the use of story without any propositions is the highlighting feature of the New Homiletic. In summarizing his research on this movement, Howell states, "Authentic preaching, then, involves the meeting of two stories: The story of Scripture and the stories of life. If the preacher desires to bridge the distance between the biblical world and the contemporary world he must do so through the vehicle of story."[16]

In light of the New Homiletics' features, it is necessary to point out its weaknesses for preaching,[17] especially for doctrinal exposition (part 5 integrates some of its positive features). First, there is the big question of authority. The New Homiletic has followed in line with its postmodern underpinnings by shifting the authority away from the biblical text to the listener—going beyond the individual to the audience-community approach. This movement rejects biblical authority and theological substance in favor of accommodating to all the listeners. Not surprisingly, more recent advances among the New Homiletic argue for preaching as a "roundtable,"[18] where there is *no authority* but a gathered community on *equal footing*. Without objective truth, anything and everything becomes fair game for understanding the Bible.

---

[13] Howell, "Preaching at the Dawn," 5.

[14] Ibid., 16-18.

[15] David Buttrick, "On Doing Homiletics Today," in *Post Critical Studies in Preaching*, ed. Richard L. Eslinger (Grand Rapids: Eerdmans, 1994), 95.

[16] Howell, "Preaching at the Dawn," 18.

[17] For an expansion of these weaknesses, see Howell, "Preaching at the Dawn," 21-26.

[18] See Rose, *Sharing the Word*.

Second, the New Homiletic fails to declare the whole canon. Proponents prefer the narrative and parabolic sections of the Old Testament, Gospels, and Acts over the deductive sections of Scripture. Although these homileticians rightly remind preachers to avoid squeezing every biblical passage into a deductive outline, the New Homiletic becomes guilty of selecting from only a portion of the Scriptures. *Finding* the story to preach is more accurate of the New Homiletic than *telling* the story.[19]

Third, the issues of history, meaning, and truth are problematic for the New Homiletic. A growing number of preachers within this movement neglect the historical background of a text in favor of the text's form. Furthermore, any objective meaning tied to the text's historical surroundings is questionable because of the denial of authorial intent. Without authorial intent, no one can determine meaning absolutely, and if meaning is not absolute, then any notion of absolute truth must be impossible. No preacher can uphold the unchanging truth of Scripture, for it will entail determinant meaning. With regard to such truth, Eugene Lowry writes, "Propositional truth delivered through discursive language has a way of sounding more eternally true than it really is, even after we have researched the matter. Somehow, the mystery loses its awe."[20] What the New Homiletic (and postmodernism) really wants to claim is "We are absolutely sure that there is no such thing as absolute truth!"

In the end the New Homiletic walks in the footsteps of postmodernism and its rejection of normative truth in favor of individual, subjective, and even community-specific, intersubjective categories. That is to say, postmodernism's remedy for modernism's individualism is communitarianism or socialism. Such a notion of community or audience, however, is suspect. Mohler warns, "Communal meaning can quickly devolve into an oxymoron."[21]

Based on this assessment, the New Homiletic clearly fails to provide any certain hope for a not-so-certain culture. As a preaching method, its rejection of biblical authority and propositional preaching in favor of storytelling leave the "new" sermon as little more than cotton candy—an interesting taste without any substance. Moreover, its denial and dismissal of history, meaning, and truth leave more *questions* about preaching than *answers* to preaching. Without unchanging meaning and absolute truth, there is absolutely no point in preaching at all, let alone doing theological exposition. The New Homiletic is not preaching that builds bodies, but

---

[19]Eslinger, *A New Hearing*, 55.

[20]Lowry, *The Sermon*, 45.

[21]Mohler, "Integrity of the Evangelical Tradition," 71.

preaching that makes bodies flabby!

The Changing Face of Evangelicalism, or Neo-Evangelicalism?

The rise of postmodernism has not only affected preaching in particular but also evangelicalism in general. Indeed, "this postmodern world becomes the new challenge for the evangelical church."[22] Evangelicals have responded in a number of different ways to postmodernism—ignorance, indifference, dismissal, engagement, and acceptance.[23]

At the same time that evangelicals can respond to postmodernism, however, an identity crisis exists among evangelicalism because of the rising influence of postmodernism. The philosophical and theological strands of postmodernism have crept into the evangelical camp. The changing face of evangelicalism makes it harder to define than ever before, so much that it may be appropriate to label certain strands as neo-evangelical.[24]

Iain Murray has traced the changes in American and English evangelicalism over the last fifty years.[25] He argues that from the nineteenth century until the middle of the twentieth century to be evangelical meant to

---

[22]Dockery, "Challenge of Postmodernism," 12.

[23]For words of caution about ignoring postmodernism, see Thomas R. Schreiner, "The Perils of Ignoring Postmodernism," *The Southern Baptist Journal of Theology* 5, no. 2 (2001): 2-3. Mohler ("Integrity of the Evangelical Tradition," 70) writes, "In one respect, postmodernism may well represent a new evangelistic moment; an opportunity to transcend the corrosive elements of the older modern ideologies and to restate Christian truth in terms faithful to the biblical revelation and the Christian tradition, and yet addressed to a new consciousness."

[24]Elsewhere, some scholars define neo-evangelicalism as "the classification given particularly to a movement of North American Christians that arose initially in the 1940s. Neo-evangelicals were initially interested in proclaiming not only the personal but also the social dimensions of the gospel" (Stanley J. Grenz, David Guretzki, and Cherith Fee Nordling, *Pocket Dictionary of Theological Terms* [Downers Grove, IL: InterVarsity, 1999], 48). The term did not really stick in the mid-twentieth century, with many opting the more common term "evangelical." I use the term "neo-evangelical" to refer to those who have gotten away from the theological nature of the term in favor of a mere sociological connection. While not denying a sociological factor, there must also be a theological factor in identifying evangelicals.

[25]Iain H. Murray, *Evangelicalism Divided: A Record of Crucial Change in the Years 1950 to 2000* (Carlisle, PA: The Banner of Truth Trust, 2000).

be united on certain doctrinal issues. The last few decades, however, have witnessed a doctrinal demise within evangelicalism. Murray traces the origin of this demise to Friedrich Schleiermacher (1768—1834) and his *On Religion* (1799). Schleiermacher, often labeled the founding father of liberal Protestantism, was the first to argue "that religion is primarily not a matter of doctrine but rather of feeling, intuition and experience."[26]

Throughout the nineteenth and twentieth centuries, Schleiermacher gained a larger following. Still, during this same timeframe, evangelicalism had a strong sense of identity. Men such as Carl F. H. Henry and Harold J. Ockenga, along with an institution like Fuller Seminary, represented the "new evangelicals" of the mid-twentieth century. Some considered this "new evangelical" movement to be nothing more than fundamentalism at its best.[27] The best days of this movement, however, were short-lived.

Since the 1970s, more and more liberal Protestants have joined themselves to evangelicalism. Part of the reason for this marriage, Murray correctly asserts, has to do with the acceptance of Billy Graham around the world. Graham realized that his mass evangelistic crusades could draw greater numbers if the help of planning and preparation were shared with the liberal denominations. William Martin, a Graham biographer, observes that Graham

> doubtless intended to keep himself and his crusades free from Modernist contamination, but success weakened his resolve. . . . At first Graham was uneasy with non-Evangelical support but soon convinced himself that as long as no one tried to tell him what he could or could not preach, there could be no real harm in accepting the assistance and encouragement of people whose beliefs differed from his own at some points. After all, a key part of New Evangelical strategy was to gain a hearing for Evangelical doctrine in mainline denominations.[28]

Elsewhere, Murray employs a few of Martin's quotations in evaluating the role of the Billy Graham Evangelistic Association in weakening evangelicalism. He states,

> The reason why the BGEA decided to co-operate with liberals

---

[26]Ibid., 5.

[27]Ibid., 31. See note 98 in this chapter as well as David F. Wells, "Introduction: The Word in the World," in *The Compromised Church: The Present Evangelical Crisis*, ed. John H. Armstrong (Wheaton: Crossway Books, 1998), 26.

[28]William Martin, *A Prophet with Honor: The Billy Graham Story* (New York: Quill William Morrow, 1991), 218.

and other non-evangelicals was never set out in terms of principle. The fact is that the policy was seen as a necessary expedient designed sincerely for the best end, namely, to gain a wider hearing for the gospel. Crusades depended upon crowds and in the Graham story there is an almost ever-present concern for maintaining and increasing numbers. 'Keeping a customary eye for maximum public impact' and 'trying always for the largest possible crowds' was a settled part of the Billy Graham Association's strategy.[29]

Although Graham is not the only factor in the shift of American evangelicalism (both positively and negatively), one should not overlook his significant role.

By the latter half of the twentieth century, experiential unity became the rallying cry of many associated with evangelicalism. This recently-formed "Experience Party" holds debate with the traditional "Doctrine Party," those which see evangelicalism based on certain doctrinal essentials.[30] Even though each group wants to claim historical evangelicalism as its roots, history clearly stands on the side of the doctrinal group.

Perhaps no current historian has articulated the doctrinal decline within evangelicalism more than David Wells. His numerous writings have convincingly shown evangelicalism to be doctrinal throughout all but the most recent years of its history.[31] Insisting that evangelicalism includes orthodoxy, Wells writes,

> The stream of historic orthodoxy that once watered the evangelical soul is now damned by a worldliness that many fail to recognize as worldliness because of the cultural innocence with which it presents itself. To be sure, this orthodoxy never

[29]Murray, 58-59. The quotations are from Martin, *Prophet with Honor*, 251, 458. Richard V. Pierard also observes Graham's role in changing evangelicalism ("Evangelicalism," in *Evangelical Dictionary of Theology*, ed. Walter A. Elwell [Grand Rapids: Baker Books, 1984], 382).

[30]Mohler, "'Evangelical': What's in a Name?" in *The Coming Evangelical Crisis: Current Challenges to the Authority of Scripture and the Gospel*, ed. John H. Armstrong (Chicago: Moody Press, 1996), 32.

[31]See Wells, *No Place for Truth*; idem, *God in the Wasteland: The Reality of Truth in a World of Fading Dreams* (Grand Rapids: Eerdmans, 1993); idem, *Losing Our Virtue: Why the Church Must Recover Its Moral Vision* (Grand Rapids: Eerdmans, 1998); idem, *Above All Earthly Pow'rs: Christ in a Postmodern World* (Grand Rapids: Wm B Eerdmans, 2005).

was infallible, nor was it without its blemishes and foibles, but I am far from persuaded that the emancipation from its theological core that much of evangelicalism is effecting has resulted in greater biblical fidelity. In fact, the result is just the opposite. We now have less biblical fidelity, less interest in truth, less seriousness, less depth, and less capacity to speak the Word of God to our own generation in a way that offers an alternative to what it already thinks. The older orthodoxy was driven by a passion for truth, and that was why it could express itself only in theological terms. The newer evangelicalism is not driven by the same passion for truth, and that is why it is often empty of theological interest. . . .

. . . by substituting for its defining, confessional center a new set of principles (if they can appropriately be called that), evangelicals are moving ever closer to the point at which they will no longer meaningfully be able to speak of themselves as historic Protestants.[32]

Certainly, the term "evangelical" carries the notion of concern for the evangel, or good news in Jesus Christ. Therefore, wherever Christianity is void of Christian orthodoxy and the unique Person and work of Christ, one cannot consider it to be evangelical by definition. Simply put, evangelical preaching must necessarily be doctrinal preaching. Thus, gospel preaching is the normal exercise routine in building spiritual bodies.

An Answer to This Dilemma:
Doctrinal Expository Preaching for the Twenty-First Century

God has always called Christian preachers, especially those who serve as pastors, to declare the whole counsel of God (cf. Acts 20:27-28). Preachers can best accomplish this extremely awesome and weighty task through doctrinal expository preaching, for expository preaching goes through the biblical text in an organized, systematized fashion and doctrinal preaching declares the larger framework of the text's nuts and bolts. Furthermore, doctrinal exposition is most valuable whenever preaching equally concerns itself with the Scriptures' message and the listeners' understanding of that message. Thus, the preacher's logos will be both biblically faithful and contextually applicable. This does not mean that preachers need to jettison the Bible's terminology, but they must work harder now more than ever to explain the Bible's message to an audience ignorant of the theology of the Scriptures. Preaching in the twenty-first century demands that preachers be both theologically attuned and culturally aware.

---

[32]Wells, *No Place for Truth*, 11-12, 101-02.

Although preaching in the past has tended to favor either doctrine *or* exposition, most homileticians failed to stress the union between the two disciplines. This work argues, therefore, that an integration of theology *and* biblical exposition is a possible, and even necessary, approach to preaching. In the face of a meltdown of truth and morality, anything less than a return to doctrinal preaching will cause Christianity and its gospel claims to limp along through the course of the twenty-first century. The recent interest in biblical theology (along with the value of systematic theology) coupled with the growth of expositional preaching greatly anticipates a theological-biblical kind of preaching which is both faithful to the text and fruitful in the lives of today's people. Such preaching can provide stability to shaky pulpits and unsettled pews. May ministers of God return to God's firm foundation of Christ and His Word and practice a preaching that builds bodies!

Part 2: Definitional Clarity for Doctrinal Exposition

CHAPTER 5
DEFINING THE PARTS OF DOCTRINAL
EXPOSITION: STRETCHING OUT

The definitional clarity of many commonly used terms is often blurred in the twenty-first century. Although the ordinary speech and slang of each new generation will give some words secondary meanings, it seems that the postmodern intersubjective-interpretive approach has impacted the current era so much that some people make up the rules of grammar and language as they go. Sadly enough, preachers, with their heavy schedules of public speaking, have contributed to this demise, resulting in something of a different standard for grammar in preaching (split infinitives, ending sentences with prepositions, etc.). The rise in cellphone texting has also undoubtedly contributed to language malfunction. As chapter 4 argues, individuals who characterize themselves nowadays as evangelical without further defining what they mean bring confusion to evangelicalism. Similar uncertainty arises with the use of *expository* preaching. Nearly every proponent of preaching wants to claim expository preaching for his own view of preaching. Though not everyone agrees with him, Harold Bryson honestly claims, "No homiletical term has received as many definitions with an apparent authoritative definiteness as *expository preaching*. Each definition seems to be correct. Because of the variety of definitions, ambiguity abounds about a clear, authoritative, workable definition of expository preaching."[1] Because of this definitional vagueness, this work defines and

---

[1] Harold T. Bryson, *Expository Preaching: The Art of Preaching through a Book of the Bible* (Nashville: Broadman & Holman, 1995), 15. Bryson categorizes the advocates of expository preaching into three groups: etymological, morphological, and substantive. Groups one and three are virtually the same, so Bryson's distinction between groups one and two is the most significant. The etymological definition focuses merely on the explanation

explain its use of expository preaching, which in turn, will help define doctrinal exposition. With this definition in hand, efforts at combining the disciplines of doctrine and expository preaching will highlight the ways others have viewed this matter. Finally, since Scripture is the basis for both preaching and doctrine, a discussion of the doctrinal prerequisites of an expositor as they relate to Scripture will conclude this chapter.

One of the reasons this entire study is so crucial is due to the lack of information on doctrinal expository preaching and the need for a clear definition. This definition needs to include the basic tenets of both expository and doctrinal preaching. This section gives four of the leading and most precise definitions of exposition, followed by a working definition of doctrinal preaching. Integrating these definitions result in doctrinal exposition.

The best fitness instructors explain the value of stretching out before getting into serious exercise. Such explanation brings clarity to the bodybuilder's routine. Spiritual stretching-exercises help bring clarity to the preacher's goals.

The Use of Adjectives in Discussing Preaching

Many people, especially those in the pew, have nothing to do with adjectives when discussing preaching. To them, it matters little whether homileticians label preaching as topical, textual, expository, or any other type. They think that anything which declares Christ in some way falls under the large umbrella of preaching. Of course, adjectives, by definition, describe nouns, and students understand preaching better when adjectives are applied.

One needs only to turn to Broadus's seminal work to see the tremendous difficulty others have had in labeling different types of sermons. He writes,

> Various elaborate and unsuccessful attempts have been made to classify sermons. From the nature of the case no exact or scientific classification is possible; the various kinds will overlap and mingle in every conceivable way. . . . There are, however, two distinct principles or bases upon which these imperfect classifications may be made. One of these relates to the subject-matter of the sermon, including subjects, occasions, and materials. . . . The other basis of classification has regard to what may be called the *homiletical structure*

---

of the text, while the morphological definition involves issues such as length of passage, treatment of passage, and a connected series of sermons (ibid., 15-25). The morphological distinction plays a part in my view of exposition (see below).

of the sermon.[2]

Broadus's second group is of importance here. Even though common characteristics exist between different kinds of preaching, Broadus distinguishes three types based on the sermon structure. He calls these three "subject-sermons, text-sermons, and expository sermons."[3] A brief look at these is in order.

Evidently what Broadus calls "subject-sermons" is the same as today's topical sermons, for "subject-sermons are those in which the divisions are derived from the subject, independently of the text."[4] In this kind of preaching, preachers

> draw from the text a certain subject, usually stating it in the form of a proposition, and then the text, having furnished the thought, has no further part as a formative force in the plan of treatment pursued in the sermon, but the subject is divided and treated according to its own nature, just as it would be if not derived from a text.[5]

A modern description of topical preaching could hardly be more fitting. Such topical preaching begins with an idea or theme in the preacher's mind. Moreover, each aspect of the sermon flows from the topic. Many professors of preachers label this kind of preaching as "an idea in search of a text."

Broadus describes text-sermons in much the same way as expository sermons. The divisions of the text-sermon, like expository preaching, come from the Scriptures. One way in which textual preaching and expository preaching differs, however, is in "the *proper handling of the details.* If we simply take the topic and the heads which the passage affords, and proceed to discuss them in our own way, that is not an expository sermon, but a text-

---

[2]John A. Broadus, *A Treatise on the Preparation and Delivery of Sermons*, ed. Edwin Charles Dargan (Cambridge: University Press, 1898; reprint, New York: A. C. Armstrong and Son, 1906), 306. D. Martyn Lloyd-Jones argues for content *and* form in expository preaching in *Preaching & Preachers* (Grand Rapids: Zondervan, 1971), 58. See also his related discussion of the sermon's shape (ibid., 205-23).

[3]Broadus, *Preparation and Delivery of Sermons*, 307.

[4]Ibid.

[5]Ibid., 308. Broadus cites popular preachers as Robert Hall, Richard Fuller, and Charles H. Spurgeon as those who, at times, preached topical or subject-sermons (ibid., 309-11).

sermon."[6] Thus, textual preaching, though it springs from a passage, does not directly connect with the passage as much as with the preacher.

Expository preaching, defined below, aims at properly handling the details of the Scriptural passage, i.e., it rightly divides the word of truth (2 Tim 2:15). Because so many writers differ in their understanding of expository preaching, this work details what is meant.

Is Not All Preaching Expository?

Some argue that expository preaching is preaching which *exposes* the text—whether it be a passage of Scripture, a sentence, a phrase, or even a word.[7] Such a definition oversimplifies expository preaching and is far too broad, for nearly any kind of preaching exposes, or explains, something in the text, even if it may be a *poor* explanation.

Others argue that expository preaching is virtually synonymous with biblical preaching. Robert Smith, Jr. defines preaching in vein with John R. W. Stott's use of "expository preaching."[8] At the same time, however, Smith claims, "There is only one authentic type of preaching—biblical preaching. Biblical preaching must be defined by its substance and not by its shape—by its content and not by its contours—by its facts and not by its forms."[9] As stated before, this work presupposes exposition to be the most biblical kind of preaching. Expository preaching is distinctive from other forms such as topical, thematic, and narrative preaching.

---

[6]Ibid., 329.

[7]See, for example, Millard J. Erickson and James L. Heflin (*Old Wine in New Wineskins: Doctrinal Preaching in a Changing World* [Grand Rapids: Baker Books, 1997], 171), who claim that expository preaching "allows the preacher to take as a text (then explain and apply) any portion of Scripture, whether a word, phrase, verse, two verses, or extended portion exceeding two or three verses." How simply explaining a word or phrase accurately reflects the author's intention within a given context is difficult to see.

[8]Robert Smith, Jr., "Interview: Robert Smith, Jr.," *Vocatio* 10, no. 2 (1998): 8.

[9]Ibid., 10. See Charles Bugg, "Back to the Bible: Toward a New Description of Expository Preaching," *Review & Expositor* 90, no. 3 (1993): 414-15; Graeme Goldsworthy, *Preaching the Whole Bible as Christian Scripture* (Grand Rapids: Wm. B. Eerdmans, 2000), 119-21. Donald L. Tucker ("Biblical Preaching: Theology, Relevance, Empowerment," *Paraclete* 25 [Summer 1991]: 23) sees a close connection between biblical preaching and the biblical text, defining it as "speaking in a religious context to listeners wanting to hear about the actions and purposes of the God of the Bible."

On the other hand, certain extremists for expository preaching believe it to be the only kind of preaching. Anything that is not expository is not real preaching. One such proponent states,

> Exposition of Scripture, exposition worthy of its name, is of the very essence of preaching. It follows that it is a serious error to recommend expository preaching as one of several legitimate methods. Nor is it at all satisfactory, after the manner of many conservatives, to extol the expository method as the best. All preaching must be expository. Only expository preaching can be Scriptural.[10]

These statements are quite dogmatic, to say the least. These assertions are either based on broad definitions of expository preaching—including countless preachers throughout church history as expositors—or they reject such men as Spurgeon, Edwards, Whitefield, and Wesley as being something other than genuine preachers.

Why Focus on Expository Preaching?
Although this work falls short of viewing expository preaching as an "inerrant" method, one of its presuppositions is that expository preaching is the most biblical method of preaching. While methods such as topical, thematic, or narrative preaching are not necessarily unbiblical, exposition rightly allows the Scriptures to have the full authority in structure and substance.[11]

A Working Definition of Expository Preaching
In order to understand doctrinal expository preaching—preaching for

---

[10]R. B. Kuiper, "Scriptural Preaching," in *The Infallible Word*, 3rd ed., ed. Paul Woolley (Philadelphia: Presbyterian and Reformed, 1967), 253. See also A. Duane Litfin, "Theological Presuppositions and Preaching: An Evangelical Perspective" (Ph.D. diss., Purdue University, 1973), 169-70.

[11]This does not mean that expository preaching has a particular style or format. Roy Clements argues, "Expository preaching is not a matter of style at all. In fact, the determinative step which decides whether a sermon is going to be expository or not takes place, in my view, before a single word has been actually written or spoken. First and foremost, the adjective 'expository' describes the method by which the preacher decides what to say, not how to say it" (*The Cambridge Papers*, 1998, quoted in Alistair Begg, *Preaching for God's Glory* [Wheaton: Crossway Books, 1999], 28). Additionally, York and Decker write, "Expository preaching is defined not by a style nor by a particular methodology, but by the end result of explaining and applying the meaning of the text" (*Preaching with Bold Assurance*, 33).

bodybuilding—one needs to begin with a working definition of expository preaching. Such a definition, coupled with doctrinal preaching, can clarify the meaning of doctrinal exposition.

Perhaps the classic definition of expository preaching is Robinson's. He writes,

> Expository preaching is the communication of a biblical concept, derived from and transmitted through a historical, grammatical, and literary study of a passage in its context, which the Holy Spirit first applies to the personality and experience of the preacher, then through the preacher, applies to the hearers.[12]

Robinson's argument for expository preaching over the last thirty years owes a great deal to Broadus. Most professors of preaching consider Broadus's *A Treatise on the Preparation and Delivery of Sermons* to be the classic text on homiletics. Thus, one needs to consider what he had to say about this subject. He states,

> An expository discourse may be defined as one which is occupied mainly, or at any rate very largely, with the exposition of Scripture. It by no means excludes argument and exhortation as to the doctrines or lessons which this exposition develops. It may be devoted to a long passage, or to a very short one, even part of a sentence. It may be one of a series, or may stand by itself. We at once perceive that there is no broad line of distinction between expository preaching and common methods, but that one may pass almost insensible gradations from textual to expository sermons.[13]

Simply put, Broadus states that expository preaching has as its goal the explanation of a portion of the Scriptures.

In addition to the explanation of the Scriptures, some scholars define exposition morphologically in terms of the length of the biblical passage and/or the sermon's structure and substance. Walter Kaiser, Jr. says,

> Expository preaching is that method of proclaiming the Scriptures that takes as a minimum one paragraph of Biblical text (in prose narrative or its equivalent in other literary genre) and derives from that text both the shape (i.e., the main points and subpoints of the sermon) and the content (i.e., the substance, ideas, and principles)

---

[12]Haddon W. Robinson, *Biblical Preaching*, 2nd ed. (Grand Rapids: Baker Academic, 2001), 21.

[13]John A. Broadus, *A Treatise on the Preparation and Delivery of Sermons* (Philadelphia: Smith, English, 1870; reprint, New York: A. C. Armstrong & Son, 1891), 303. As stated above, this work argues that expository preaching includes more than "part of a sentence."

of the message itself.[14]

Mohler also argues along these same lines. He states, "As the Word of God, the text of Scripture has the right to establish both the substance and the structure of the sermon."[15] Wayne McDill concurs, "A biblical sermon is one in which the text shapes the sermon. The purpose, the theme, the structure, and the development of the sermon are to reflect the text."[16]

Furthermore, one scholar observes that

> the great strength of expository preaching is that it reinforces the authority and centrality of scripture in the life of the church. It is a homiletical method that teaches scripture and enhances the knowledge and understanding of the Bible for both the preacher and congregation. More than any other genre of preaching, expository preaching honors the desire of the hearer to understand and claim the meaning of the scriptures for life in today's world.[17]

Expository preaching is, therefore, the only method of preaching which upholds the full authority of the Scriptures. As John MacArthur claims,

---

[14]Walter C. Kaiser, Jr., "The Crisis in Expository Preaching Today," *Preaching* 11, no. 2 (1995): 4. Others who argue for a similar minimal length of the biblical passage include W. A. Criswell, *Criswell's Guidebook for Pastors* (Nashville: Broadman Press, 1980), 42; Faris D. Whitesell, *Power in Expository Preaching* (Westwood, NJ: Fleming H. Revell, 1967), vi-vii.

[15]R. Albert Mohler provided this definition in a D.Min. course on expository preaching as cited in Daniel L. Akin, "The Ministry of Proclamation: Book 1," section 4, "What Is Christian Preaching?" (The Southern Baptist Theological Seminary, 2002), 13. Mohler provides a much more complex definition of expository preaching in Mohler, *He Is Not Silent: Preaching in a Postmodern World* (Chicago: Moody Publishers, 2008), 65. Several writers within the New Homiletic movement argue that the Scriptures should provide the pattern for shaping the sermon; see Don M. Wardlaw, ed., *Preaching Biblically: Creating Sermons in the Shape of Scripture* (Philadelphia: The Westminster Press, 1983). The main problem with these writers is that they deliberately avoid certain biblical genres, such as the Epistles, in favor of narrative passages from the Old Testament, Gospels, or Acts.

[16]Wayne McDill, *The 12 Essential Skills for Great Preaching* (Nashville: Broadman & Holman, 1994), 14.

[17]John S. McClure, "Expository Preaching," in *Concise Encyclopedia of Preaching*, ed. William H. Willimon and Richard Lischer (Louisville: Westminster John Knox Press, 1995), 132.

The only logical response to inerrant Scripture, then, is to preach it *expositionally*. By expositionally, I mean preaching in such a way that the meaning of the Bible passage is presented *entirely* and *exactly* as it was intended by God. . . . inerrancy demands exposition as the only method that preserves the purity of Scripture and accomplishes the purpose for which God gave us His Word.[18]

This direct relationship between biblical authority and preaching emphasizes a point made in chapter 1—when biblical authority declines, preaching's decline must naturally follow. The only way for preaching to recover the necessary mixed ingredients of doctrine and exposition completely is to maintain a high view of the Scriptures. Then, and only then, can doctrinal expository preaching have any lasting and significant value.

Returning to the substance of expository preaching, one finds Stephen and David Olford's definition to be a bit more comprehensive. They write,

> Expository preaching is the Spirit-empowered explanation and proclamation of the text of God's Word with due regard to the historical, contextual, grammatical, and doctrinal significance of the given passage, with the specific object of invoking a Christ-transforming response.[19]

What these authors add to this discussion of expository preaching is the role of God in preaching, both as Anointer and Harvester. Moreover, the doctrinal significance of the text is of fundamental importance in preaching.

From these leading definitions of expository preaching, a synthetic definition follows. This definition will help establish the foundation for understanding doctrinal expository preaching. This work argues that

> expository preaching is the Spirit-empowered communication of at least one paragraph (or its literary equivalent) of the biblical text with special concern for interpreting the text in light of the historical, contextual, grammatical, syntactical, and doctrinal significance of that text, deriving from that text the shape and the substance of the message so that the message is experienced by and

---

[18]John MacArthur, Jr., "The Mandate of Biblical Inerrancy: Expository Preaching," in *Rediscovering Expository Preaching: Balancing the Science and Art of Biblical Exposition*, ed. Richard L. Mayhue (Dallas: Word, 1992), 23-24. Alistair Begg argues that "the absence of expository preaching is directly related to an erosion of confidence in the authority and sufficiency of Scripture" (*Preaching for God's Glory*, 18).

[19]Stephen F. Olford and David L. Olford, *Anointed Expository Preaching* (Nashville: Broadman & Holman, 1998), 69.

applied to the preacher and then to the hearers.

Along with this definition comes an analysis. First, expository preaching should include a limitation on the text's length to a minimum of one paragraph of biblical text. Kaiser's point is to differentiate expository preaching from what others might label as topical, textual, or thematic. While these preaching styles can be biblical, the expository method which handles at least one paragraph of the biblical text allows Scripture and its divisions to shape the message, and thus, could very well be the most biblical form of preaching.

Second, both the main idea and the minor ideas (serving the main one) of the message, i.e., the substance, should come from the primary text. Although references to other Scripture may emerge (by using systematic and/or biblical theology), and may be necessary for explaining an idea via the analogy of Scripture, the leading thought(s) of the sermon flow(s) from the main text. This form of expository preaching preserves each biblical author's intent and method. Therefore, even the way in which the Scriptures were written contribute to biblical authority, which stands over a preacher's own craftiness in a sermon.

Third, application is both an important and a necessary aspect of expository preaching.[20] The Holy Spirit's ministry of illumination helps the preacher both to understand the biblical text and to apply the meaning of that text to his audience.[21] The basic role of application is connecting the message of the ancient Scriptures to the contemporary world.

Fourth, expository preaching focuses upon Scripture like no other form of preaching, for exposition takes into account the passage's historical, contextual, literary, grammatical, and *theological* situations. Put simply, no other kind of preaching hinges on the biblical text like expository preaching. Furthermore, it has as part of its foundation the doctrinal significance of the passage. Therefore, expository preaching *includes* doctrine—such preaching feeds hearers to build them up in the faith. One may object,

---

[20]Scott Blue argues convincingly for application's necessary inclusion in expository preaching in "Application in the Expository Sermon: A Case for Its Necessary Inclusion" (Ph.D. diss., The Southern Baptist Theological Seminary, 2001). For ways in which applying doctrine can be made in a postmodern setting, see chapter 14 below.

[21]God's role in preaching should go without saying, but one must not forget that unless He governs the preacher's preparation and delivery, the preacher's message will have no lasting effect. For more on God's role in preaching, see John Piper, *The Supremacy of God in Preaching* (Grand Rapids: Baker Books, 1990), 17-46.

"Then what is the point of this work?" The answer lies in the many proponents of expository preaching who fail to address the doctrinal element.

An Understanding of Doctrinal Preaching

Doctrinal preaching, unlike expository preaching, offers few definitions. Many take for granted that preaching the Bible is doctrinal preaching. Unless one argues that weak doctrine and heretical doctrine falls under the category of doctrinal preaching, however, few examples of this type of preaching appear today.

Most agree that preaching doctrine should be both biblical and applicable.[22] Robert Smith defines doctrinal preaching as "*the escorting of the hearers into the presence of God for the purpose of transformation.*"[23] Moreover, an assumption of this work is that

> the test of good theology is that it is preachable. . . . [And] the converse is also true. The test of good preaching is that it is theological, rooted in the Scriptures and the theology behind the Scriptures and the theology distilled from the Scriptures.[24]

Thus, while some people may criticize doctrinal preaching as boring, the purest doctrinal preaching is biblically-saturated and interesting.

Perhaps the best working definition of doctrinal preaching is "Christian preaching grounded in the biblical witness to Jesus Christ; it starts with text, doctrine, or cultural question, but tends to focus on one or more Christian doctrines regardless of its starting point."[25] Theological

---

[22]Donald M. Ballie, "The Preaching of Christian Doctrine," in *The Theology of the Sacraments and Other Papers* (New York: Charles Scribner's Sons, 1957), 147-55.

[23]Robert Smith Jr., *Doctrine That Dances: Bringing Doctrinal Preaching and Teaching to Life* (Nashville: B&H Academic, 2008), 25.

[24]R. Alan Day, "Theology and Preaching," *The Theological Educator*, no. 57 (Spring 1998): 104. See also Heinrich Ott, *Theology and Preaching: A Programme of Work in Dogmatics, Arranged with Reference to Questions 1-11 of the Heidelberg Catechism*, trans. Harold Knight (Philadelphia: Westminster Press, 1965), 19-41. Ott views theology as a systematization of the whole picture while preaching focuses on a specific situation. Both of these disciplines "resemble each other and cohere with each other in the fact that they unfold and amplify one and the same truth" (Ott, *Theology and Preaching*, 55).

[25]William J. Carl III, *Preaching Christian Doctrine* (Philadelphia: Fortress Press, 1984), 8-9. Carl claims that the teaching sermon and the doctrinal sermon are basically synonymous (ibid., 30, 60, 104). Others who follow this

preaching, in this light, shares several elements common to expository preaching. The biblical text, the doctrine of the text, and/or a cultural concern of a text can be met with sound doctrinal preaching.[26]

One will recognize, of course, the claim that doctrinal preaching is "grounded in the biblical witness to Jesus Christ." Although some scholars prefer to interpret the Old Testament apart from Jesus Christ and the New Testament, Christian preaching by its very nature must ground itself in the Person and work of Jesus Christ. Graeme Goldsworthy claims that the gospel as the Person and work of Jesus Christ is both the hermeneutical key and the theological center of all the Scriptures.[27] Furthermore, "while there is much in the Bible that is strictly speaking not the gospel, there is nothing in the Bible that can be truly understood apart from the gospel."[28]

D. A. Carson agrees with such a definition, even applying it to expository preaching. He writes that expository preaching "draws attention to inner-canonical connections that inexorably move toward Jesus Christ and the gospel."[29]

This movement toward Christ rings loud in the following:

If our doctrinal preaching does not induce, and indeed force, men

---

thinking include James Earl Massey, *Designing the Sermon* (Nashville: Abingdon Press, 1980), 61-74; John W. Westerhoff, "The Pastor as Preacher-Teacher," *Homiletic* 18, no. 2 (1993): 3-4. Ronald J. Allen (*The Teaching Sermon* [Nashville: Abingdon Press, 1995], 35-36) believes doctrinal sermons are merely a subcategory of teaching sermons.

[26]Carl believes all true Christian preaching is doctrinal and biblical (*Preaching Christian Doctrine*, 5-6).

[27]Graeme Goldsworthy, *Preaching the Whole Bible*, 32-33, 84-86, 113. Few writers have argued so convincingly for this approach of redemptive preaching focused in Christ as Bryan Chappell, *Christ-Centered Preaching: Redeeming the Expository Sermon*, 2nd ed. (Grand Rapids: Baker Books, 2005), 79-80, 277-80.

[28]Goldsworthy, *Preaching the Whole Bible*, 95.

[29]"The *SBJT* Forum: Profiles of Expository Preaching," *The Southern Baptist Journal of Theology* 3, no. 2 (1999): 95. Similarly, Peter F. Jensen writes, "The goal of 'preaching the whole Bible' is attained when we so preach Christ that every part of the Bible contributes its unique riches to his gospel" ("Preaching the Whole Bible: Preaching and Biblical Theology," in *When God's Voice Is Heard: Essays on Preaching Presented to Dick Lucas*, ed. Christopher Green and David Jackman [Leicester: Inter-Varsity Press, 1995], 64).

to close with Christ, to learn to know him more and more, better and better, as the years slip by, as their Friend to whom they can go freely and with utter frankness, as their King whose word for them is law, as the Judge before whom, and by whom, the value of their lives will be assessed, as the Saviour in whom lies their only hope, our preaching, doctrinal or no, has missed its object, and not reached its end.[30]

Sinclair Ferguson argues for this same Christocentric view of preaching, especially expository preaching. He claims that the cross of Christ must shape the message and personalities of preachers, who

are called to be cruciformed (shaped by the cross), Christophers (bearing the Christ of the cross), and Christplacarders (setting Christ and Him crucified on display, cf. Galatians 3:1) in [their] preaching as [they] 'try to persuade men' (2 Corinthians 5:11).[31]

When the preacher follows this advice, he cannot preach any biblical passage without interpreting it sooner or later within the Christological framework. At this point preaching must identify itself with Jesus Christ in order to be distinctively *Christian* preaching—the type of preaching which aims to build listeners into the image of Christ.

---

[30] Arthur John Gossip, "The Whole Counsel of God: The Place of Biblical Doctrine in Preaching," *Interpretation* 1, no. 3 (1947): 334.

[31] Sinclair B. Ferguson, "Preaching to the Heart," in *Feed My Sheep: A Passionate Plea for Preaching*, ed. Don Kistler (Morgan, PA: Soli Deo Gloria, 2002), 217. Elsewhere in this book, John Armstrong asserts that all "preaching must be theological preaching" ("Preaching to the Mind," 169).

CHAPTER 6
DEFINING THE WHOLE OF DOCTRINAL
EXPOSITION: WARMING UP

Once a person has stretched her muscles, she is wise to begin her exercise by warming up. Without slowly building up to a serious workout, she will not maximize her routine. Preachers must take time to warm up and prepare themselves for the serious spiritual exercise of doctrinal exposition.

Blending the definitions of expository and doctrinal preaching from the previous chapter leads to doctrinal expository preaching, which I define as

> the Spirit-empowered communication of a biblical doctrine derived from at least a paragraph of Scripture (or its literary equivalent) with regard to the text's historical, grammatical, syntactical, and contextual significance interpreted through the larger Christological-redemptive theme of the Bible, first experienced by and applied to the preacher and, then, to his hearers with the goal of obedient behavior in light of the theological truth of the text.

This work argues for this kind of understanding of doctrinal expository preaching. In incorporating doctrinal exposition, Jerry Oswalt states that a planned approach to preaching doctrine in an expositional fashion will allow the preacher to be both comprehensive and balanced on theological issues in the Scriptures. This type of systematic preaching best accomplishes the preacher's task of declaring "the whole counsel of God" (Acts 20:27).[1] Doctrinal exposition can bring clarity where confusion has stood. It must also be relevant to the times of the twenty-first century.

---

[1] Jerry E. Oswalt, *Proclaiming the Whole Counsel of God: Suggestions for Planning and Preparing Doctrinal Sermons* (New York: University Press of America, 1993), 1.

Ultimately, this focus on theological exposition should help reinforce what biblical preaching really is. Indeed, doctrinal exposition is preaching that strengthens the lives of its listeners.

Efforts at Combining Theology and Exposition in Preaching

In order to be fair, the reader should be aware that at least a *few* writers have made efforts at combining theology and expository preaching. The reader must view their offerings as the groundwork to implementing these disciplines. What follows is meant to "give credit where credit is due," while also highlighting the void that remains.

Millard Erickson and James Heflin devote a single chapter to "Expository Doctrinal Preaching" in *Old Wine in New Wineskins*.[2] This chapter, however, deals more with defining and understanding the different genres of expository preaching rather than explaining a how-to integration of doctrine and exposition. To the authors' credit, their main objective is to show the need for doctrinal preaching today. That they devote four chapters to ways doctrinal preaching can be done signifies the need for preaching doctrine (in some form). This section of the book leaves much to be desired, however, for even their treatment of expository doctrinal preaching focuses more on the different sub-categories of expository preaching rather than on how to preach doctrine expositionally.

In addition to the chapter mentioned above, Erickson and Heflin discuss doctrinal preaching forms as topical doctrinal, narrative doctrinal, and dramatic doctrinal.[3] They obviously want to appeal to numerous preachers who favor various forms of preaching styles. Homiletics does not need to compartmentalize each of these preaching forms, however. In discussing the "how" of doctrinal exposition, this study will explain how doctrinal expository preaching may borrow elements from the narrative and dramatic forms.

Other than this treatment by Erickson and Heflin, some notable figures from the past have touched on this subject of blending theology and exposition. More than a century ago, John A. Broadus commented upon the inclusion of theological content with preaching. He wrote,

> Doctrine, i.e., teaching, is the preacher's chief business. Truth is the lifeblood of piety, without which we cannot maintain its vitality or support its activity. And to teach men truth, or to quicken what

---

[2]Millard J. Erickson and James L. Heflin, *Old Wine in New Wineskins: Doctrinal Preaching in a Changing World* (Grand Rapids: Baker Books, 1997), 167-82.

[3]Ibid., 183-239.

they already know into freshness and power, is the preacher's great means of doing good. The facts and truths which belong to the Scripture account of Sin, Providence, and Redemption, form the staple of all Scriptural preaching. But these truths ought not simply to have place, after a desultory and miscellaneous fashion, in our preaching. The entire body of Scripture teaching upon any particular subject, when collected and systematically arranged, has come to be called the doctrine of Scripture on that subject, as the doctrine of Sin, of Atonement, of Regeneration, etc.; and in this sense we ought to preach much on the doctrines of the Bible.[4]

At the same time that Broadus urged preachers to teach doctrine, he also lamented the decline of doctrinal preaching. He added,

> We all regard it as important that the preacher should himself have sound views of doctrine; is it not also important that he should lead his congregation to have just views? In our restless nation and agitated times, in these days of somewhat bustling religious activity, there has come to be too little of real doctrinal preaching.[5]

If the premier teacher of preachers decried doctrine-less exposition in his day, one may only surmise what his opinion would be of twenty-first century preaching!

Long before Broadus entered the scene, William Perkins proposed certain elements of expository preaching within a doctrinal-thematic approach. His work is most succinct in his own summary, where he stated,

> Preaching involves:
> 1. Reading the text clearly from the canonical Scriptures.
> 2. Explaining the meaning of it, once it has been read, in the light of the Scriptures themselves.
> 3. Gathering a few profitable points of doctrine from the natural sense of the passage.
> 4. If the preacher is suitably gifted, applying the doctrines thus explained to the life and practice of the congregation in

---

[4]John A. Broadus, *A Treatise on the Preparation and Delivery of Sermons,* ed. Edwin Charles Dargan (Cambridge: University Press, 1898; reprint, New York: A. C. Armstrong and Son, 1906), 76-77. A few years before Broadus' work, Francis Wayland observed the importance of expounding doctrine, but he differentiated between doctrinal preaching and expository preaching (*Notes on the Principles and Practices of Baptist Churches* [New York: Sheldon, Blakeman & Co., 1856], 284-87, 293-94).

[5]Broadus, *Preparation and Delivery of Sermons,* 77.

straightforward, plain speech.[6]

Clearly, both the explanation and application of a biblical text and its doctrine lies at the heart of Perkins's view of preaching.

Moreover, D. Martyn Lloyd-Jones, one of the great expositors of the late-twentieth century, has submitted the necessary inclusion of theological substance within exposition. He believed that

> to expound is not simply to give the correct grammatical sense of a verse or passage, it is rather to set out the principles or doctrines which the words are intended to convey. True expository preaching is, therefore, *doctrinal* preaching, it is preaching which addresses specific truths from God to man.[7]

Elsewhere he wrote that preaching "is theology on fire."[8] Also, "preaching must always be theological, always based on a theological foundation" and "a sermon should always be expository."[9] Thus, for Lloyd-Jones, theological preaching and expository preaching are, for the most part, overlapping disciplines.

Not only did Lloyd-Jones argue for theological, expositional preaching, he also warned against misusing Scripture in preaching doctrine. He wrote,

> It is wrong for a man to impose his system violently on any particular text; but at the same time it is vital that his interpretation of any particular text should be checked and controlled by this system, this body of doctrine and of truth which is found in the Bible. The tendency of some men who have a systematic theology, which they hold very rigidly, is to impose this wrongly upon particular texts and so to do violence to those texts. In other words they do not actually derive that particular doctrine from the text with which they are dealing at that point. The doctrine may be true but it does not arise from that particular text; and we must always

---

[6]William Perkins, *The Art of Prophesying; with The Calling of the Ministry* (Cambridge: J. Legatt, 1592; reprint, Carlisle, PA: The Banner of Truth Trust, 1996), 79.

[7]Iain H. Murray, *D. Martyn Lloyd-Jones: The Fight of Faith 1939-1961* (Edinburgh: The Banner of Truth Trust, 1990), 261. Idem, *Evangelical Divided: A Record of Crucial Change in the Years 1950-2000* (Edinburgh: The Banner of Truth Trust, 2000), 81.

[8]D. Martyn Lloyd-Jones, *Preaching & Preachers* (Grand Rapids: Zondervan, 1971), 97.

[9]Ibid., 64-65, 71. For his discussion on the roles of biblical and systematic theology in preaching, see Lloyd-Jones, *Preaching & Preachers*, 64-80.

be textual. That is what I mean by not 'imposing' your system upon a particular text or statement. The right use of systematic theology is, that when you discover a particular doctrine in your text you check it, and control it, by making sure that it fits into this whole body of biblical doctrine which is vital and essential.[10]
Heeding such a warning will keep preachers from preaching un-biblically.

A couple of modern noteworthy preachers touch on the need for expository preaching to be doctrinal. Alistair Begg laments the contemporary pulpit as one void of "the kind of expository preaching that is Bible-based, Christ-focused, and life-changing—the kind that is marked by doctrinal clarity, a sense of gravity, and convincing argument."[11] He also cites the *Westminster Directory for Public Worship* for three principles for biblical exposition:

1. The matter we preach should be true; that is, in light of general doctrines of Scripture.
2. It should be truth contained in the text or passage we are expounding.
3. It should be truth preached under the control of the rest of Scripture.[12]

Thus, according to Begg, biblical doctrine and exposition go hand-in-hand.

John MacArthur also observes the theological content needed in preaching expositionally. He writes,

Preaching an expository sermon involves more than merely repeating the technical results of one's Bible study. True expository preaching involves transforming technical details into principles or doctrines so that the expositor preaches theologically with appropriate applications.[13]

---

[10]Ibid., 66-67.

[11]Alistair Begg, *Preaching for God's Glory* (Wheaton: Crossway Books, 1999), 11.

[12]Ibid., 31. The quotation is adapted from *A Directory for the Publique Worship of God throughout the Three Kingdoms of England, Scotland, and Ireland: Together with an Ordinance of Parliament for the Taking Away of the Book of Common-Prayer and for Establishing and Observing of This Present Directory throughout the Kingdom of England and Dominion of Wales* (London: printed for Evan Taylor, Alexander Fifield, Ralph Smith, and John Field, 1644), 29-30.

[13]John MacArthur, Jr., "Moving from Exegesis to Exposition," in *Rediscovering Expository Preaching: Balancing the Science and Art of Biblical Exposition*, ed. Richard L. Mayhue (Dallas: Word Publishing, 1992), 288.

While defining expository preaching as including theological elements, MacArthur laments much of the doctrine-less preaching taking place today. He cries,

> One of the things that grieves my heart is we have had weak preaching and weak pulpits in America for a long time and we have people in Christian leadership who have almost non-existent theology. . . . They don't have any theological foundation on which to build their activities, as noble as their efforts and as true as their hearts might be to these things.[14]

Moreover, contemporary theologians have spoken on the overlapping disciplines of theology and biblical exposition. Walter Kaiser, Jr., a leading proponent for biblical theology, sees the need for careful theological analysis in the realm of sermon preparation. Articulating the preparation stages of expository preaching, Kaiser describes biblical exegesis as the foundation to biblical preaching. Such exegesis includes contextual, syntactical, verbal, theological, and homiletical analyses. Thus, biblical theology necessarily falls within the preparation stage of expository preaching.[15]

Timothy George similarly writes, "Every doctrinal sermon must be contextually rooted in sound exegesis; and every expository or biblical sermon should place a given passage in the widest theological framework possible."[16] Such a statement forms the heart of this study, and part 3 will propose how the preacher can integrate biblical and systematic theology in expository preaching.

A few select places in books and journal articles also address theology and exposition. For example, one recent writer laments the all-too-common-divorce of doctrine and exposition by claiming that expository

[14]John MacArthur, Jr., *E. Y. Mullins Lectures on Preaching: Question and Answer Luncheon* (Louisville: The Southern Baptist Theological Seminary, 2002), videocassette.

[15]Walter C. Kaiser, Jr., *Toward an Exegetical Theology: Biblical Exegesis for Preaching and Teaching* (Grand Rapids: Baker Books, 1981), 69-163, cf. especially 131-40.

[16]Timothy George, "Doctrinal Preaching," in *Handbook of Contemporary Preaching*, ed. Michael Duduit (Nashville: Broadman Press, 1992), 96; cf. W. E. Sangster, *The Craft of Sermon Construction* (Philadelphia: Westminster Press, 1951), 42-45. From a theologically moderate position, John S. McClure lists several subcategories of expository preaching, one of which is "exposition of scripture in relation to confessional statements or doctrines" ("Expository Preaching," 131).

preaching often neglects doctrine, but systematic exposition needs to be theological, especially Christological.[17] This perception supports the need for a thorough wrestling with this issue.

Within a forum on expository preaching and related disciplines, Carl F. H. Henry speaks of the close connection between systematic theology and exposition:

> If Christian preaching is indifferent to the legitimacy of and the need for systematic theology, it will inevitably be penalized by disorderly exposition. And if theology is not preachable, one had better take a second look.[18]

Henry, at the very least, advocates both an explanatory form and an applicatory form of preaching doctrine.

The Founders Journal, edited by Tom Ascol, often includes articles pertaining to doctrine and preaching. How one can blend doctrine and exposition, however, is never handled in a holistic way. Writers of this journal uphold expository preaching as the biblical model, often emphasizing its practice during the Reformation. Additionally, re-enforcing doctrine and providing models of theological instruction are among the central features of this quarterly journal. After reading through a number of issues, I am under the impression that Ascol and the other contributors simply assume that highlighting doctrine within preaching means practicing doctrinal *expository* preaching.[19] Rather than remain an underlying assumption, however, someone needs to provide an explicit and extensive discussion of the necessary union between theology and biblical exposition.

Timothy Warren sees the need for blending theology and exposition, too, claiming "genuine expository preaching communicates theological

---

[17]Sinclair B. Ferguson, "Preaching to the Heart," in *Feed My Sheep: A Passionate Plea for Preaching*, ed. Don Kistler (Morgan, PA: Soli Deo Gloria, 2002), 213.

[18]"The *SBJT* Forum: Profiles of Expository Preaching," *The Southern Baptist Journal of Theology* 3, no. 2 (1999): 91.

[19]All of the issues of this journal are at founders.org/ journal/. Articles of special interest to this study include Tom Ascol, "Systematic Theology and Preaching," no. 4 (1991); "The Pastor as Theologian," no. 43 (2001); Tom J. Nettles, "The Transforming Power of Theological Preaching—Part 1," no. 21 (1995); idem, "The Transforming Power of Theological Preaching—Part 2," no. 22 (1995); idem, "Doctrinal Preaching: The Central Task of the Christian Minister," no. 65 (2006); Ernest Reisinger, "The Priority of Doctrinal Preaching," no. 23 (1996).

meaning and significance."[20] Moreover, he states that "although the study of theology comprises a substantial portion of most seminarians' curriculum, most, if not all, of that study has not been specifically and practically related to the preaching task."[21]

As part 4 argues below, both systematic theology and biblical theology are beneficial to this view of doctrinal expository preaching. Peter Adam pushes for the incorporation of biblical theology in expository preaching,

> for both imply commitment to Scripture as a whole. Expository preaching implies commitment to the literary extent of Scripture, and biblical theology to its theological depth. The preacher who is using both will be a true preacher of Jesus Christ.[22]

Clarence Roddy assumes the inclusion of theology within exposition. He claims that one may be certain that "it is impossible to expound the Word apart from the preaching of doctrine."[23] Moreover, William Houser insists that every sermon be biblical and "give a proper interpretation (exegesis) of the text which includes the teaching of pure doctrine."[24]

From all of these treatments, one begins to see that homileticians have not *completely* neglected the integration of doctrine and exposition. At the same time, however, these discussions fall short of the definitional clarity and substantive depth needed in incorporating these disciplines.

Contributions from the New Homiletic

Before concluding this section, a few words about the contribution of the New Homiletic in combining doctrine and preaching are in order. A growing number of preachers in this camp advocate a union between theology and preaching. For instance, David Buttrick calls for preaching to

---

[20]Timothy S. Warren, "The Theological Process in Sermon Preparation," *Bibliotheca Sacra* 156, no. 623 (1999): 337.

[21]Ibid., 356.

[22]P. J. H. Adam, "Preaching and Biblical Theology," in *New Bible Dictionary of Biblical Theology: Exploring the Unity & Diversity of Scripture,* ed. T. Desmond Alexander and others (Downers Grove: InterVarsity Press, 2000), 108-09.

[23]Clarence S. Roddy, "On the Preaching of Theology," *Christianity Today* 3, no. 23 (1959): 7.

[24]William G. Houser, "Puritan Homiletics: A Caveat," *Concordia Theological Quarterly* 53, no. 4 (1989): 266.

make "a turn to theology."[25] William D. Thompson, preferring the term *biblical* preaching to *expository* preaching, articulates the proper method of interpreting a text, noting particularly the significance of theological exegesis as a foundation for biblical preaching.[26] Gerhard O. Forde believes that even though systematic theology and preaching are different, "they are necessarily correlated: one is impossible without the other."[27]

Listening to this advice, Ronald Allen writes that "a conversational model of relating scripture, systematic theology, and preaching encourages conscientious, critical engagement."[28] Allen also writes that expository preaching can, and should, make adaptations to preaching systematic theology.[29] Moreover, he defines doctrinal preaching as the "systematic theological exposition of Christian belief which takes account of Scripture, tradition, experience, and reason."[30]

Additionally, Robert Hughes and Robert Kysar write, "Sound biblical preaching is always theological, and sound theological preaching is always

---

[25]David Buttrick, *A Captive Voice: The Liberation of Preaching* (Louisville: Westminster John Knox Press, 1994), 110-12. See also Edward Farley, "Preaching the Bible and Preaching the Gospel," *Theology Today* 51 (April 1994): 90-103; idem, "Toward a New Paradigm for Preaching," in *Preaching as a Theological Task: World, Gospel, Scripture*, ed. Thomas G. Long and Edward Farley (Louisville: Westminster John Knox Press, 1996), 176-88.

[26]William D. Thompson, *Preaching Biblically: Exegesis and Interpretation* (Nashville: Abingdon Press, 1981), 23-26, 33-35.

[27]Gerhard O. Forde, *Theology Is for Proclamation* (Minneapolis: Fortress Press, 1990), 3-4. While Forde argues that theology leads to proclamation, others in this camp claim that *"proclamation is for theology"* (Robert G. Hughes and Robert Kysar, *Preaching Doctrine: For the Twenty-First Century* [Minneapolis: Fortress Press, 1997], 20). Gerhard Ebeling probably states this inter-dependent relationship best: "Theology without proclamation is empty, proclamation without theology is blind" (*Theology and Proclamation* [London: Wm. Collins Son and Co., 1966], 20).

[28]Ronald J. Allen, *Preaching Is Believing: The Sermon as Theological Reflection* (Louisville: Westminster John Knox Press, 2002), 50. See also Ronald J. Allen, *The Teaching Sermon* (Nashville: Abingdon Press, 1995).

[29]Allen, *Preaching Is Believing*, 82.

[30]Allen, *The Teaching Sermon*, 36.

biblical."[31] Paul Scott Wilson poetically states, "Like strands of one rope, doctrine, preaching, and theology braid a lifeline through history."[32]

Such advice from these spokesmen looks good at the surface, but a serious flaw exists in the underlying foundation of these men—doubts exist in the truthfulness of Scripture. Continually rejecting the claims of Scripture, Allen presupposes various theologies at work in the Bible, often containing "contradictory elements."[33] Likewise, Hughes and Kysar want to call into question the soundness of a text's theology, even calling others to sometimes preach against the text![34]

Furthermore, Buttrick sneers, "For the better part of the twentieth century, preaching and the Bible have been wrapped up in a kind of incestuous relationship."[35] With such a low view of Scripture, one wonders how "a turn to theology" can ever be meaningful, if there is no confidence in the source of that theology. Surely the foundation and framework of the New Homiletic have serious defects that true biblical preaching must avoid in order to warm up for an effective workout!

---

[31]Hughes and Kysar, *Preaching Doctrine*, 36.

[32]Paul Scott Wilson, "Doctrine in Preaching: Has It a Future?" in *Preaching on the Brink: The Future of Homiletics*, ed. Martha J. Simmons (Nashville: Abingdon Press, 1996), 84.

[33]Allen, *Preaching Is Believing*, 44. See especially his comments throughout 37-62.

[34]Hughes and Kysar, *Preaching Doctrine*, 45-46.

[35]Buttrick, *A Captive Voice*, 171.

CHAPTER 7
THE DOCTRINAL PREREQUISITES OF AN EXPOSITOR: WATCHING YOUR DIET TO MAXIMIZE YOUR WORKOUT

In order to avoid the pitfalls of the New Homiletic, the preacher should think long and hard through some doctrinal issues so that he has confidence in preaching. Like the most serious students of exercise watch their diet closely, so must the doctrinal expositor.

This diet speaks to a preacher's theological prerequisites, or commitments. Since preaching explains and applies the Bible, a theological book, expositors will need to tackle certain doctrinal issues before actually being able to declare the whole counsel of God. Rust said it well:

> The truth is that no man can be an effective preacher of the Gospel unless his preaching is undergirded by solid dogmatic affirmations and unless it is illuminated and made intelligible by some sound theological thinking.[1]

It should be clear that every preacher—even every Christian—is a theologian, albeit good or bad. In order to be a faithful expositor of God's Word, one must also be a serious theologian. This does not mean that theology is all that a preacher should read, but it does presume that theology will be a staple in the preacher's study. Throughout the history of the church, people assumed that preachers should be sound in biblical truth.[2] Such an assumption is no longer true, for many contemporary

---

[1] E. C. Rust, "Theology and Preaching," *Review and Expositor* 52, no. 2 (1955): 146. Preachers must be "knowledgeable in theology and in the Bible" (John H. Leith, *From Generation to Generation* [Louisville: Westminster/John Knox Press, 1990], 89).

[2] See Tom J. Nettles, "Basil Manly: Fire from Light: The Transforming

preachers have little to do with theology and even think it unnecessary or an obstacle to effectiveness.

John MacArthur correctly claims that theology should drive preaching, even stating that

> the heart of my preaching is my theology . . . I am driven by, I am shaped by, I am conformed to my understanding of divine truth. . . . [Moreover], the heart of all preaching is the love of the truth—the love of the truth at such a level that it yields the discipline of discerning that truth.[3]

Furthermore, certain doctrines are necessary for a solid theological foundation for preaching.

The Doctrine of Scripture

The most important of these is the doctrine of Scripture.[4] If the preacher fails to wrestle with bibliology, all other doctrinal issues will rest on a faulty foundation. Several facets of this doctrine are significant.

The Doctrine of Revelation

The theological expositor must first come to grips with the doctrine of revelation. God has revealed Himself and His plan for His creation specifically through the Christian Scriptures. Beginning with Abraham and the Old Testament patriarchs through the prophets and the New Testament apostles and believers, God's plan of redemption has been revealed in a progressive fashion. There also exists an order to God's revelation, so that God's redemptive plan makes sense.[5]

Specific to this doctrine is a high view of Scripture as the perfect revelation of God. Every expositor—because he is textually driven by definition—will uphold the full authority of the Bible. Hershael York and Bert Decker define what this view looks like: "A high view of Scripture

---

Power of Theological Preaching, Part 1," *The Founders Journal*, no. 21 (1995); founders.org/FJ21/article3.html.

[3]John MacArthur, Jr. *2002 E. Y. Mullins Lectures on Preaching* (Louisville: The Southern Baptist Theological Seminary), videocassette.

[4]Ibid. MacArthur also includes the doctrines of election (divine sovereignty), identification (substitution of the believer being in Christ), and sanctification (purification). Though each of these is important in theology, their specific relationship to expository preaching is hard to see.

[5]Merrill F. Unger, *Principles of Expository Preaching* (Grand Rapids: Zondervan, 1955), 77-79.

means that the Bible *is* what God says, and what God says is what we must say when we preach. . . . A high view of Scripture is the *sine qua non* of exposition."[6]

The Doctrine of Inspiration
Related to the divine revelation of the Bible is the divine inspiration of the Bible. Belief in the divine revelation of the Scriptures is simply not enough. One must also trust that God has kept His Word free from error.[7] York and Decker describe this as "a commitment to the profitability of all Scripture," noting that "even though all Scripture is equally inspired, it is not all equally profitable."[8] Because all Scripture is profitable, it is necessary to preach all of it in declaring the whole counsel of God.

The Doctrine of Illumination
A third associated doctrine of Scripture concerns the divine illumination of the Bible. This speaks of the Holy Spirit's role in bringing understanding to the mind and heart of the expositor.[9] Although it is possible an unbeliever can dissect and diagram a biblical text as well as a committed expositor, the former can never truly comprehend the meaning of the biblical passage apart from the illuminating ministry of the Spirit (1 Cor 2:10-16).

Furthermore, one needs to believe that he can attain the accurate interpretation of the Bible.[10] The notion of authorial intent comes into play here. While the task of getting into the mind of the author is impossible, it is possible through grammatical, syntactical, historical, and contextual study

---

[6]Hershael W. York and Bert Decker, *Preaching with Bold Assurance: A Solid and Enduring Approach to Engaging Exposition* (Nashville: Broadman & Holman, 2003), 19. Closely related to Unger's prerequisites of an expositor, York and Decker list five commitments of an expositor (ibid., 18-31). They credit Duane Litfin in an endnote for his contributions to these commitments.

[7]Unger, *Principles of Expository Preaching*, 79-82.

[8]York and Decker, *Preaching with Bold Assurance*, 19, 22.

[9]Unger, *Principles of Expository Preaching*, 82-83. See also Greg Heisler, *Spirit-Led Preaching: The Holy Spirit's Role in Sermon Preparation and Delivery* (Nashville: B&H Academic, 2007), and J. Kent Edwards, *Deep Preaching: Creating Sermons That Go Beyond the Superficial* (Nashville: B&H Academic, 2009).

[10]Unger, *Principles of Expository Preaching*, 83-84. See also York and Decker, *Preaching with Bold Assurance*, 28-31.

to determine what the biblical author meant in any given passage of Scripture. Without confidence in this possibility, there remains little, or no, reason for declaring the Scriptures.

A High View of Proclamation

A final related doctrine to this discussion is a belief that the expositor should also commit to a high view of preaching.[11] That is, since Scripture is the Word of God, declaring that Word is extremely important. Preaching involves the Spirit of God working through the preacher in communicating the Bible. In light of this entire discussion, one may summarize this commitment to revelation and Scripture as follows: God has spoken (revelation), and what He has spoken was written in Scripture (inspiration), and what has been written can be understood by His Spirit's aid (illumination), therefore, a need remains to preach the Word (proclamation).[12]

These doctrinal prerequisites will enhance the expositor's preaching. In regards to the Bible, his confidence will be sure and steadfast. In relationship to preaching, the preacher will stand both humbly and authoritatively. Such commitments will give the preacher a solid foundation from which to preach.

This section has aimed at providing definitional clarity to doctrinal expository preaching. It has considered what others have done in this field and has offered theological commitments important to doctrinal exposition. Now that this groundwork of dieting commitments is in place, one is ready to observe the biblical basis of preaching for bodybuilding.

---

[11]See York and Decker, *Preaching with Bold Assurance*, 22-23. These writers claim that an expositor must also be committed to thinking about the Scriptures, its application, and how people receive such preaching (ibid., 24-28). While in full agreement with their discussion, this area does not directly fall under my umbrella of doctrinal prerequisites.

[12]See Peter Adam, *Speaking God's Words* (Downers Grove: InterVarsity Press, 1998), 15-56. For a summary of this teaching, see Peter Adam, "Preaching and Biblical Theology," in *New Bible Dictionary of Biblical Theology: Exploring the Unity & Diversity of Scripture*, ed. T. Desmond Alexander and others (Downers Grove: InterVarsity Press, 2000), 104-05; cf. also R. Albert Mohler, Jr., "A Theology of Preaching," in *Handbook of Contemporary Preaching*, ed. Michael Duduit (Nashville: Broadman Press, 1992), 13-20.

Part 3: Biblical Bases for Doctrinal Exposition

CHAPTER 8
THE SEMANTIC DOMAIN FOR DOCTRINE AND PREACHING: STARTING WITH THE BASICS

The integration of theology and expository preaching has a long history. Peter Adam writes, "Preaching depends not only on having a God-given source, the Bible, but also a God-given commission to preach, teach and explain it to people and to encourage and urge them to respond."[1] This statement reflects the inherent relationship between teaching and exposition in the act of preaching. Even though both doctrinal preaching and expository preaching have not always occurred simultaneously, preachers from different eras—even in Bible times—have implemented the two disciplines. The Scriptures are the focus of this chapter—both its terms and its models. A study of the Scriptures should underscore the *biblical* bases of doctrinal expository preaching. Before someone can become a serious weightlifter, he must begin with the basics.

The Bible is rich with descriptions of the proclamation of God's Word. The terminology includes both preaching and teaching. A brief lexical study will help set up a more detailed look at the preaching content and habits of the Bible's expositors.

When considering the meaning of biblical words, the concept of semantic domains comes into play. Moisés Silva admits

> that the past two decades have seen considerable progress in the proper use of language for biblical interpretation, but [one] must not fall under any delusion that linguistics and exegesis have been genuinely integrated in modern scholarship. And beyond that, modern linguistics—and semantics in particular—continues to develop at a very fast pace.[2]

---

[1] Peter Adam, *Speaking God's Words: A Practical Theology of Expository Preaching* (Downers Grove: InterVarsity Press, 1996), 37.

[2] Moisés Silva, *Biblical Words and Their Meaning: An Introduction to*

More specifically,

> modern linguistic theory teaches that the meaning of a given word is not located in the word per se but in the relationship a word has to other words in the context of a given occurrence and in contrast to other words which share its semantic domain.[3]

With respect to preaching, words which describe the preaching event are important in this study (see Tables 1 and 2 in the Appendices). This kind of "word study" approach at biblical interpretation, however, has its fair share of critics. Silva observes,

> It has become customary in articles and books dealing with biblical topics to begin the discussion with an examination of "the terminology." Occasionally, the author may even think that a study of the relevant terms completes his research of the topic.
>
> Such an approach is inadequate. When a discussion depends primarily or solely on the vocabulary, one may conclude either that the writer is not familiar with the contents of Scripture or that Scripture itself says little or nothing on the subject.[4]

Of course, conservative evangelicals holding to propositional revelation rightly emphasize the meaning of words. Philip Hughes acknowledges the importance of words, but "only in combination. Words isolated from their context have lost their significance and are not sacrosanct. What is essential is the truth which the words unitedly reveal."[5]

In order to uphold propositional revelation, this chapter employs tables of key terms to underscore meaning in a general way. At the same time, however, a closer look at some of these words in different contexts

---

Lexical Semantics, rev. and exp. ed. (Grand Rapids: Zondervan, 1994), 21-22.

[3]Karen H. Jobes, "Distinguishing the Meaning of Greek Verbs in the Semantic Domain for Worship," *Filologia Neotestamentaria* 4, no. 8 (1991): 183-84. Louw and Nida place preaching, teaching, and similar words under the domain of communication. These writers contend, "The basis for the various semantic domains and subdomains consists of three major classes of semantic features: shared, distinctive, and supplementary" (Johannes P. Louw and Eugene A. Nida, eds., *Greek-English Lexicon of the New Testament Based on Semantic Domains*, 2nd ed., vol. 1 (New York: United Bible Societies, 1989), vi.

[4]Silva, *Biblical Words and Their Meaning*, 22. Silva argues against the misuse of lexicography, for even his own book "is intended to encourage the study of words" (ibid., 28-29).

[5]Philip E. Hughes, "The Reformers' View of Inspiration," in *The Word of God and Fundamentalism* (London: Church Book Room, 1961), 99.

helps avoid the criticism of "word studies."

Even though both the Old Testament and New Testament fall within this study, a few words are in order of the latter's multi-faceted view of preaching. Kittel's *Dictionary* claims, "The New Testament uses thirty-three verbs to express the activity of preaching."[6] One way of classifying these words is as follows:

> *Words of information*: teach, instruct, point out, make known, remind.
>
> *Words of declaration*: preach, proclaim, cry out, testify, bear witness, declare, write, read, pass on, set forth.
>
> *Words of exhortation*: call, denounce, warn, rebuke, command, give judgment, encourage, appeal, urge, ask.
>
> *Words of persuasion*: explain, make clear, prove, guard, debate, contend, refute, reason, persuade, convince, insist, defend, confirm, stress.
>
> *Words of conversation*: say, speak, talk, answer, reply, give answer.[7]

The most common terms for preaching in the NT—κηρυσσω and ευαγγελιζω—are of special concern. The former occurs more than seventy times and refers to proclaiming or heralding an announcement. The latter means to bear good news and occurs over forty times. The two words are "essentially similar . . . for both expressions may refer to the content of the gospel. This does not mean, however, that the meaning of the two expressions is precisely identical."[8] One sees the close association between these terms in Luke 8:1, where Jesus' ministry is described as "preaching (κηρυσσων) and proclaiming the gospel (ευαγγελιζομενος) of the kingdom of God."

Kerygma and Didache

Before looking at this terminology in different contexts, it is necessary to address the relationship between *kerygma* (preaching) and *didache* (teaching). Some have argued for a clear distinction between the two while others see them as overlapping. The mid-twentieth century produced writers on both sides of the debate. A brief look at the main arguments from both sides follows.

---

[6]Gerhard Friedrich, "κηρυσσω," in *Theological Dictionary of the New Testament* [*TDNT*], vol. 3, ed. Gerhard Kittel, trans. Geoffrey W. Bromiley (Grand Rapids: Eerdmans, 1965), 703. See Adam, *Speaking God's Words*, 76, for the multi-faceted descriptions of New Testament preaching.

[7]Adam, *Speaking God's Words*, 76.

[8]Louw and Nida, *Greek-English Lexicon*, s. v. "preach, proclaim."

C. H. Dodd, the pioneer of this discussion, argues for a clear-cut distinction between *kerygma* and *didache*,

> The New Testament writers draw a clear distinction between preaching and teaching. The distinction is preserved alike in Gospels, Acts, Epistles, and Apocalypse, and must be considered characteristic of early Christian usage in general. Teaching (*didaskein*) is in a large majority of cases ethical instruction. Occasionally it seems to include what we should call apologetic, that is, the reasoned commendation of Christianity to persons interested but not yet convinced. Sometimes, especially in the Johannine writings, it includes the exposition of theological doctrine. Preaching, on the other hand, is the public proclamation of Christianity to the non-Christian world. The verb *keryssein* properly means "to proclaim". . . . Much of our preaching in Church at the present day would not have been recognized by the early Christians as *kerygma*. It is teaching, or exhortation (*paraklesis*), or it is what they called *homilia*, that is, the more or less informal discussion of various aspects of Christian life and thought, addressed to a congregation already established in the faith.[9]

Though Dodd labels *didache* as "ethical instruction" here, he also defines it as "a traditional body of ethical teaching given to converts from paganism to Christianity."[10] As proof to this clear-cut distinction between *didache* and *kerygma*, Dodd goes to great links to show that *kerygma* always relates to some element of the gospel.[11] He defines the pre-Pauline, and hence, primitive, *kerygma* as "a proclamation of the death and resurrection of Jesus Christ, in an eschatological setting from which those facts derive

---

[9]C. H. Dodd, *The Apostolic Preaching and Its Developments: Three Lectures with an Appendix on Eschatology and History* (London: Hodder & Stoughton, 1936), 7-8.

[10]C. H. Dodd, *Gospel and Law: The Relation of Faith and Ethics in Early Christianity* (Cambridge: University Press, 1951), 15.

[11]Dodd summarizes the *kerygma* in six elements. First, it is the dawning of the age of fulfillment. Second, this age has come through Jesus' ministry, death, and resurrection. Third, Jesus' exaltation at God' right hand makes Him the Messianic head of the new Israel. Fourth, the Holy Spirit is the sign of Christ's presence. Fifth, the Messianic age will soon consummate in Christ's return. Finally, the *kerygma* always ends with an appeal for repentance, which includes forgiveness of sins, the offer of the Holy Spirit, and the promise of salvation (*Apostolic Preaching*, 21-24). See also Dodd, *Apostolic Preaching*, 17.

their saving significance."[12] The writings of Paul and John, because of their later dates, represent the most significant developments of the *kerygma* in the NT.[13]

Dodd's followers on this distinction label contemporary preaching under two categories. First, missionary preaching directed at unbelievers focuses on the *kerygma*. Second, congregational preaching which addresses believers handles *didache*.[14] Many in this camp argue that much of what people call preaching today is nothing more than teaching, or instructing believers.

D. Martyn Lloyd-Jones appears to follow Dodd on this view. Lloyd-Jones sees two main sections within the Bible's message. The first he calls

> the message of salvation, the *kerygma*, that is what determines evangelistic preaching. The second is the teaching aspect, the *didache*, that which builds up those who have already believed—the edification of the saints. Here is a major division which we must always draw . . .[15]

Because of Dodd's work, others have examined preaching and teaching more closely from a biblical perspective. Robert Mounce and others disagree with Dodd's conclusions, noting that they find some distinctions between *kerygma* and *didache*, but also a great deal of overlap (see below). In agreement with Mounce, Klaas Runia writes,

> It is impossible to make a clear-cut distinction between the two terms. In the first place, the terms are often used together. Again and again we read of 'teaching and preaching' (Matt 4:23; 9:35; 11:1; Luke 20:1; Acts 4:1-2; 5:42; 15:35; 28:30-31). Apparently, the two activities are inseparable, and the various passages clearly show that teaching was not restricted to believers but was aimed at any one who listened in the various places where teaching took place. Even in describing the missionary activity of the disciples and apostles both words are used. They are apparently used interchangeably.[16]

---

[12]Ibid., 24.

[13]Ibid., 73.

[14]See Klaas Runia, "What Is Preaching according to the New Testament?" *Tyndale Bulletin*, no. 29 (1978): 13-16.

[15]D. Martyn Lloyd-Jones, *Preaching & Preachers* (Grand Rapids: Zondervan, 1971), 62.

[16]Runia, "What Is Preaching?" 14. For an excellent analysis and critique of Dodd's work, see Robert C. Worley, *Preaching and Teaching in the Earliest*

Observing two verses from the list above, Donald Tucker comments,

Acts 4:2 links *didache* with *katangeleo*, to preach or to proclaim. Acts 15:35 links *didache* with *evangelize*. Both are addressed to either believers or unbelievers depending on who is present. Both appeal to Scripture for authority. Both present the message and work of Christ. Both call for repentance and conversion and faith in God. Both demand a decision.[17]

On a similar note, while admitting that "teaching is usually in the synagogue, whereas proclamation takes place anywhere in the open," Kittel's *Dictionary* observes that "the NT also speaks of a κηρυσσειν in the synagogue."[18] Likewise, although noting that *kerygma* and *didache* are not completely equal, Mounce asserts,

Kerygma is foundation and *didache* is superstructure; but no building is complete without both. It is only when they are ideally conceived that teaching and preaching can be taken as entirely distinct. In actual practice they overlap, and may be so intermingled that one can hardly ever say, "Now this is preaching," or, "This, on the other hand, is teaching." All *didache* is based on *kerygma*, and it may be seriously doubted whether any *kerygma* ever stands without some measure of explanatory *didache*.[19]

Mounce argues that the *kerygma* has a significant amount of theological substance. Whether the focus is on the vicarious atonement of Christ (see 1 Cor 15:3) or the Lordship of Jesus the Messiah (see 2 Cor 4:5; 1 Cor 8:6; Col 2:6; Phil 2:6-11), the *kerygma* passed down to Paul was full of doctrinal substance.[20] E. C. Rust considers the theological nature of the gospel as a given when he writes,

You cannot preach this Gospel and not preach theology, and everytime you do preach it, as the early church preached it, you are making certain basic theological affirmations. That is why the New Testament is full of doctrine.[21]

Church (Philadelphia: Westminster Press, 1967).

[17]Donald L. Tucker, "Biblical Preaching: Theology, Relevance, Empowerment" *Paraclete* 25 (Summer 1991): 29.

[18]Friedrick, *TDNT*, s. v. "κηρυσσω."

[19]Robert H. Mounce, *The Essential Nature of New Testament Preaching* (Grand Rapids: Eerdmans, 1960), 42-43.

[20]Ibid., 103-08.

[21]E. C. Rust, "Theology and Preaching," *Review and Expositor* 52, no. 2

James Cox agrees with this assessment,

> Preaching is teaching. What one declares calls for explanation, perhaps for argumentation. . . . In fact, teaching is necessary as preparation for the proper hearing of the good news, as part of the proclamation of the good news, and as follow-up of the good news. We can make no absolute distinction between gospel proclamation and Christian teaching.[22]

Ultimately, Mounce argues that people should not think of the *kerygma's* development in terms of lineal progression,

> but in terms of theological and ethical expansion. It is not that the *kerygma* undergoes any significant alteration, but that the unique event which by [sic] it is interpreted for missionary purposes, also carries vast implications for Christian living, and the drawing out of these implications constitutes the development which we find in the New Testament.[23]

These expansions can be seen as three concentric circles around Christ's death, resurrection, and exaltation (see Figure 1 in the Appendices). The inner circle includes the *kerygma* and explains these events in order to bring people to saving faith. The middle circle provides theological explanation for believers to understand God's larger purposes. The outer circle consists of the ethical or practical element, addressing the Christian how to live daily in light of the inner truths.[24]

The conclusions one reaches in this study of *kerygma* and *didache* reveal a couple of truths. First, a difference does exist between the two, for the former often deals with the gospel to unbelievers while the latter unfolds the gospel's implications for believers. Second, even though a difference exists, it is not a *complete* distinction. The *kerygma* can include doctrinal elements and *didache* often restates the gospel in linking it to larger theological issues. Each biblical context is thus the determining factor as to how one should understand both preaching and teaching. Understanding these integrated issues helps in seeing just how common doctrinal exposition is in the Scriptures.

(1955): 150.

[22]James W. Cox, *Preaching: A Comprehensive Approach to the Design and Delivery of Sermons* (Nashville: Seminary Extension, 1993), 8. Cox believes one "cannot draw a sharp line between *kerygma* and *didache*" (ibid., 12-13).

[23]Mounce, *Essential Nature of NT Preaching*, 133.

[24]Ibid.

CHAPTER 9
THE BIBLICAL PRACTITIONERS OF DOCTRINAL EXPOSITION: RUNNING THE RACE TO BUILD YOUR HEART

More important than merely seeing the Scriptures' word usage on preaching and teaching is discerning how the Bible employs these terms. Certain individuals stand out in both the Old and New Testaments as spokesmen for God. Although dozens of preachers populate the pages of Scripture, those who integrated doctrine and exposition serve as the subjects of this study. They serve as models as we follow them in running the race to strengthen our own hearts as we prepare to strengthen those of our hearers.

Old Testament Doctrinal Expositors
The Old Testament is not as well-known as the New for its strong preachers. Historically speaking, one could say that Enoch (Gen 5:18-19, 21-24) was the earliest preacher, for the New Testament describes him as one who "prophesied" (Jude 14). Furthermore, Scripture calls Noah "a preacher of righteousness" (2 Pet 2:5) and labels Abraham "a prophet" (Gen 20:7). Although no one knows the full extent of these men's preaching and teaching, these preachers preceded the greatest doctrinal expositor of OT history—Moses.

Moses
The great prophet and law-giver Moses is a portrait of all future preachers in Israelite history. He speaks for God, writes down the words of God, reads the words of God, and expounds the words of God. At least two different texts provide insight in understanding Moses' preaching.

First, Exodus 19-24 reveals several aspects of Moses as preacher. Once God addressed Moses about the covenant, Moses "set before [the people] all [the] words which the LORD had commanded him" (19:7). This statement, along with its preceding verses, appears to be a summary of chapters 19-24. A similar summary occurs in 24:3-8. Some interpreters rightly label these summaries as sermons. Of course, the reader will notice that

> nothing is expressly said in Exodus 24:1-11 about preaching. It is the reading of the Law that figures in this story. We can perhaps draw from this that the reading of Scripture is primary in worship and that the place of the sermon is therefore to make that reading meaningful. The modern biblical scholar, however, will want to point out that the book of the covenant found in Exodus 21-23 is in fact an interpretation of the Law, so that for those who read Exodus at that level the passage at least suggests both reading the Law and interpreting the Law. Indeed, even in these earliest records one finds that the reading of the Scriptures entails their preaching.[1]

Simply put, reading the Law led to an explanation of the Law.

In Exodus 19, Moses' sermon relays God's covenant with the people. The message begins with words of remembrance—Israel's holy history (v. 4). Moses then admonishes Israel to obey God and keep His covenant (v. 5). Moreover, Moses assures Israel of the promise of God's covenantal blessing (vv. 5-6). Hughes Oliphant Old is on target when he states, "Surely the sermon included an exposition of exactly what the stipulations of that covenant were."[2]

As to the doctrinal elements in this preaching, three stand out. First, the commandment to "remember the Sabbath day, to keep it holy" (20:8) teaches both the doctrinal and practical aspects related to creation (v. 11). Israel was to remember that the God she served was the Creator of all and

---

[1] Hughes Oliphant Old, *The Reading and Preaching of the Scriptures in the Worship of the Christian Church*, vol. 1, *The Biblical Period* (Grand Rapids: Wm. B. Eerdmans, 1998), 24. The expositional element may also be seen in the piel imperfect form of דָּבַר, meaning "speak, recount, even speak again and again" (John I. Durham, *Exodus*, Word Biblical Commentary, vol. 3 [Waco: Word Books, 1987], 257).

[2] Old, *The Biblical Period*, 27. One sees the notion of exposition in the piel of סָפַר, "recount, rehearse, declare" (William Gesenius, *The New Brown-Driver-Briggs-Gesenius Hebrew and English Lexicon: with an Appendix Containing the Biblical Aramaic*, ed. and trans. Francis Brown, S. R. Driver, and Charles A. Briggs [*BDBG*] [Peabody, MA: Hendrickson Publishers, 1979], s. v. "סָפַר"). On a related note, even if one does not argue for Mosaic authorship of the Pentateuch, it is clear that much of Exodus through Deuteronomy reveals God's instructions to and through Moses to Israel.

that a day of rest each week honored God's creative work. Second, the significance of the use of זכר ("to remember") in the commandment to "remember the Sabbath day" may very well imply the notion that God was Israel's Redeemer. This implication is drawn from 12:14, where the act of God redeeming Israel from Egypt becomes a memorial (זכרון). Furthermore, the explanation of this same commandment in Deuteronomy 5:15 grounds the Sabbath rest in God's redemption of Israel. Third, the notion of covenant is an important theme in this message, for Moses declares Yahweh to be a God of grace (cf. 19:4) and then applies this covenant by means of sprinkling the blood of the sacrifice on the people (24:3-8).

In the end Exodus 19-24 portray Moses speaking God's words to the people, writing the words down, and applying the message through sprinkling the people with blood. Additionally, Moses' message includes doctrinal elements about the One True God. Thus, both explanation and doctrine appear to be present in Moses' preaching.

In addition to the text in Exodus, Deuteronomy contains at least three distinct sermons of Moses.[3] Although space does not permit a full treatment of each sermon here, the reader should see some shared features. First, the authority of Moses' spoken word as the revealed Word of God stands out. The use of דבר; shows this fact, for Moses spoke God's words to Israel so that they might heed them (1:1; 4:1-2, 12-13). These passages show that God's spoken דבר became Moses' preached דבר.

Exposition of God's Word is the second characteristic of Moses' preaching, for "Moses undertook to expound" God's law (1:5). The verb באר, meaning "explain, expound," emphasizes the careful instruction of Moses' preaching. Moreover, διασαφεω in the LXX, meaning "explain," or "tell plainly, in detail, report," highlights such a meaning.[4]

Closely related to exposition is the teaching element of Moses' sermons, the third noteworthy feature. Without a doubt Moses viewed his own expositional practice largely as teaching because he describes his own ministry of the Word as one of "teaching" (למד, 4:1, 14).[5] His doctrinal

---

[3]Though somewhat debated, many accept the textual divisions of the sermons as 1:6-4:40; 5:1-28:68; and 29:1-30:20 (see Jeffrey H. Tigay, *Deuteronomy*, The JPS Torah Commentary [Philadelphia: The Jewish Publication Society, 1996], xii).

[4]The idea of "distinct" or "plain" for באר appears also in Deut 27:8.

[5]The LXX's use of διδασκω here would become even more prominent in the ministries of Jesus and the Apostles. Moses' constant reference to torah ("instruction, teaching") may also pinpoint his role as teacher (cf. Tigay,

teaching included sin, sacrifice, atonement, worship, God's judgment, His covenant of grace, the Law, and much more.

The fourth feature of Moses' preaching involves the application of the law to the congregation of Israel (5:1) and the exhortation of the people to obey the law (4:1; 6:13; 8:1; 10:12-13; 27:1; 29:9; 30:15-20). Moses clearly believed God's Word could only truly be heard if people practiced it. Moreover, the purpose of reading and preaching God's Law is so that one may hear it, learn it, fear and obey God from it, and have life (see 17:18-20). For life to come from the Word, one must first preach it and apply it.

Summarizing Moses' ministry, Peter Adam writes that one sees "the main ingredients of the ministry of the Word—the servant who hears God's words, the writing down and reading out aloud of God's words, and the preaching of God's words by means of exposition, application, and exhortation."[6] Moses' preaching is so significant that Peter Adam names him "the paradigm prophet in the Bible" (Deut 18:15-19),[7] one who is both a preacher and a teacher without any major distinction between the two. Furthermore, one should see the various ways in which prophets and priests in Jewish history carried out God's Word as springing from Moses' ministerial role.[8]

Ezra

As one of the most skilled scribes in Jewish history, Ezra both learned and taught God's Word (cf. Ezra 7:6, 11, 25). He even "set his heart to seek the law of the LORD and to practice *it*, and to teach statutes and ordinances in Israel" (7:10). Mervin Breneman sees here

> the secret of Ezra's impact. He loved God's Word and God's people. He had 'devoted himself' to the three things mentioned,

---

Deuteronomy, 5). Such teaching should also characterize each family, as parents instructed the children in the Torah (6:4-9).

[6]Peter Adam, *Speaking God's Words: A Practical Theology of Expository Preaching* (Downers Grove: InterVarsity Press, 1996), 40. Gerhard von Rad argues that the components of remembrance, interpretation with elaboration and application, and exhortation are central to the sermons in Deuteronomy (*Studies in Deuteronomy*, trans. David M. G. Stalker [Chicago: Henry Regnery, 1953], 11-24).

[7]Adam, *Speaking God's Words*, 40.

[8]See Adam , *Speaking God's Words*, 40. He defines Moses' role as the origin for six groups of ministers: prophets, priests, wise men and women, writers of history, writers of songs, and leaders.

but not as a hobby or pastime activity. He had devoted himself to the 'study' of God's law, to its 'observance,' and to 'teaching' it.[9] Similarly, David Deuel claims that Ezra "had a deep desire to exposit God's Torah, 'i.e. to learn and interpret' Genesis through Deuteronomy, particularly the legal portions although not excluding the narratives."[10]

Several elements stand out in Ezra's ministry of the Word. First, it revealed an in-depth nature as seen in the use of דרשׁ, meaning "seek with application, study, follow, practise."[11] Careful exegesis was the groundwork of Ezra's preaching and teaching. Second, it focused on application—he wanted to carry out (literally, "observe") what was written. Third, the Bible labels his ministry of the Word as "teaching" (למד). He desired to learn what God's Law said and to instruct God's people in it. With these commitments Ezra "must now present the fruit of his labor. In Augustine's terminology he must offer his 'sacrifice.' In the simplest terms, he must read and 'expose' the Word of God."[12]

Furthermore, one may describe Ezra's preaching as expository, for Ezra and other scribes "explained the law to the people . . . . They read from the book, from the law of God, translating to give the sense so that they understood the reading" (Neh 8:7-8). While some debate exists about the exact meaning of פרשׁ, whether it has to do merely with translation or an element of interpretation, it seems that the context of these verses clearly show that careful explanation occurred.[13] Breneman comments,

> The leaders helped the people understand by "making it clear" (or translating) and by "giving the meaning." All translations, however, are to some degree "interpretation." But beyond that the exposition helps students of the Word understand the overall

---

[9]Mervin Breneman, *Ezra, Nehemiah, Esther*, The New American Commentary, vol. 10 (Nashville: Broadman & Holman, 1993), 129. Ezra must have been an effective teacher, because certain people, having heard him, "trembled at the words of the God of Israel" (9:4). Moreover, a revival broke out as a result of his reading and exposition (Walter C. Kaiser, Jr., *Quest for Renewal: Personal Revival in the Old Testament* [Chicago: Moody Press, 1986], 135).

[10]David C. Deuel, "An Old Testament Pattern in Expository Preaching," *The Master's Seminary Journal* 2, no. 2 (1991): 131.

[11]Gesenius, *BDBG*, s. v. "דרשׁ."

[12]Deuel, "Old Testament Pattern," 135.

[13]See Old, *The Biblical Period*, 98; Breneman, *Ezra, Nehemiah, Esther*, 226.

message and the implications of the text for doctrine and practice.[14] Likewise, Deuel correctly observes,

> Few other passages in either the OT or the NT depict expositional preaching in such detail for what it truly is, i.e., 'exposing' the written Word of God to the community of faith so that the people hear with a view to learning, learn with a view to fearing, and fear with a view to practicing godliness, as Moses had instructed (Deut 31:12). In short, exposition assists the reading process whether the written Word is read individually or corporately, as was the case here. . . . [Ezra] expounded clearly only what he read in God's Word and based his exposition on what he had learned through careful study. . . .
>
> But this is not where the teaching/preaching stopped. Ezra also had a ministry of teaching among the heads of the households, the priests, and the Levites, i.e., the other teachers (Neh 8:13).[15]

Such preaching was obviously effective, for everyday for one week the people "gathered to Ezra the scribe that they might gain insight into the words of the law" (v. 13; cf. v. 18). Once the people heard God's Word they sought to learn more about its teachings.

Deuel summarizes Ezra's contribution to preaching,

> While on the one hand Ezra's proclamation is not a Sunday sermon delivered to a local church, it does manifest a timeless and universal quality as regards the nature of exposition. Ezra models *an expositor's commitments—studying, practicing godliness, and teaching—* which leads him to perform *an expositor's task—reading distinctly* and *explaining* the Scriptures so that his congregation may hear with a view to learning, learn with a view to fearing, and fear with a view to practicing godliness.
>
> To the encouragement of expositors, God's people still repent and rejoice as they did in Ezra's day when a well-prepared teacher helps them understand Scripture.[16]

Thus, one can describe Ezra's ministry in terms of careful exegesis of God's Word, clear exposition of it, faithful doctrine out of it, and helpful application of it to the people.[17] His role was such that one could not

---

[14]Breneman, *Ezra, Nehemiah, Esther*, 226.

[15]Deuel, "Old Testament Pattern," 138-39.

[16]Ibid., 140.

[17]Bryan Chapell describes Ezra's proclamation as the presentation, explanation, and exhortation of the Word. The New Testament preaching of Jesus and Paul also reflects this ministry (*Christ-Centered Preaching: Redeeming*

distinguish between his preaching and teaching. His ministry of both exposition and doctrine were evident and effective. Ezra as learner and teacher of God's Word is a great model for doctrinal exposition, for the best bodybuilders not only exercise, but they train others to exercise.

The Prophets

While the number of prophets who could receive ample treatment is beyond the scope of this paper, completely omitting them would fail to realize their contribution in this arena. Each of the prophets served as God's mouthpiece throughout Israel's history, for, to them, God revealed His secrets (Amos 3:7).

Some of the outstanding prophets in Jewish history include Samuel, Elijah, Isaiah, Jeremiah, Ezekiel, and Amos, to name but a few. Not only did these men speak God's word, they also handled important theological themes.[18] Their preaching incorporated the doctrines of God's holiness, majesty, faithfulness, and justice, as well as doctrines such as God's redemption of Israel and the coming Messiah. Although it is difficult to label each prophet as an expositor in a narrow sense of explaining a particular section of Scripture, the fact that they spoke the words of God and explained His actions certainly fits a broader view of exposition. Moreover, their explanations of Moses' Law were often exhortations to get Israel to turn from idolatry to the one true God.

The Qoheleth on preaching

In addition to the Nehemiah 8 passage above, Ecclesiastes 12:9-10 serves as a helpful and succinct model for Old Testament preaching. Solomon, identified as the Preacher, or Qoheleth, "taught the people knowledge; and he pondered, searched out and arranged many proverbs. . . . [and] sought to find delightful words and to write words of truth correctly."[19] A brief look

---

the Expository Sermon [Grand Rapids: Baker Books, 1994)] 86-88).

[18]For the prophets' preaching and some distinct messages within their writings, see Old, *The Biblical Period*, 41-84. Old claims that the OT priests also had both a teaching and preaching ministry. The argument comes largely from 2 Chr 15:3—"For many days Israel was without the true God and without a teaching priest and without law." Old writes, "The ministry of the Word is essential to true priesthood. It had been a cardinal function of the priesthood ever since Moses established the Levitical priesthood and entrusted to it the tablets of the Law" (ibid., 32).

[19]Although debate surrounds the authorship of Ecclesiastes, I, nevertheless, follow the traditional arguments in favor of Solomon (see Duane

at this passage should make clear that Solomon mixed both theology and exposition in his message.

First, Solomon meticulously searched for the right wording in composing his message as though he wanted to explain in especially clear language. His proverbs were both "weighed" (אזן) and thoroughly examined (חקר). [20] Moreover, he selected "delightful words" to communicate clearly with his audience. His preaching showed

> a deliberateness and care that merited his audience's most serious attention. There was a careful composing, investigating, and arranging of the proverbs and lessons he wrote. This was no haphazard spouting of negative thoughts in negative language. On the contrary, Solomon deliberately searched for 'pleasant words,' or 'words of grace' (12:10).[21]

Second, Solomon exhorted his audience to obey God's commandments (vv. 12-13) and he taught God's word as "words of truth" (v. 10). When connected with what is said above, it is clear that Solomon taught the truth of God in words the people could understand. Such a description of preaching should fit every gospel minister.

When looking at these doctrinal expositors from the Old Testament, several characteristics stand out in their preaching. Adam summarizes these common elements of the ministry of the Word:

> These include the acceptance of the written or spoken Word as coming from God, the role of 'Scripture', the place of public reading and explanation, encouragement to the right response, and the effect of the ministry on the people.[22]

To these one must add the doctrinal element, which, although not as full and descriptive as New Testament doctrine, is still quite prevalent. Hence, Old Testament preaching often consisted of theological exposition.

New Testament Doctrinal Expositors

It is not hard to find preachers in the New Testament. Moreover, little difficulty exists in trying to find elements of exposition and doctrine intermixed in the declaration of the Word. Beginning with Jesus Christ and

---

A. Garrett, *Proverbs, Ecclesiastes, Song of Songs*, The New American Commentary, vol. 14 [Nashville: Broadman & Holman, 1993], 257-66).

[20]Gesenius, *BDBG*, s. v. "אזן" and "חקר" respectively.

[21]Walter C. Kaiser, Jr., *Ecclesiastes: Total Life* (Chicago: Moody Press, 1979), 123.

[22]Adam, *Speaking God's Words*, 41.

certain apostles, NT preaching is many-sided.

Jesus Christ

The greatest preacher and teacher of all-time is, without question, Jesus Christ of Nazareth. As the God-Man, Jesus never uttered a single falsity. Furthermore, He had an advantage that no other preacher has ever had—He knew exactly what people were thinking and how they received His message. Although some preachers may have an idea of what their listeners are thinking, no one knows with precision except Jesus. For these reasons alone, today's preachers should not emulate certain aspects of Jesus' preaching, i.e., they should not speak in parables and leave people wondering.[23] At the same time, however, it is important to preach the gospel as Jesus did and to see the NT description of Jesus' preaching ministry.

As to Jesus' practice of preaching, the Gospels label Him both a Prophet (John 4:19, 44; 6:14; etc.) and a Teacher (11:28; 13:13-14; etc.),[24] emphasizing the ministries of preaching and teaching. Likewise, both preaching and teaching are evident in Jesus' first message. While Luke describes His ministry generally as teaching (διδασκω, 4:15), Matthew shows Him to be both "teaching in [the] synagogues and proclaiming (κηρυσσω) the gospel of the kingdom" (Matt 4:23; cf. 9:35; 11:1).[25] Jesus says He specifically came to preach the gospel (ευαγγελιζω) and "to proclaim (κηρυξαι) the favorable year of the Lord" (Luke 4:18-19). The text implies careful explanation and application because the people spoke well of Him and wondered at His "gracious words" (v. 22). Old comments,

---

[23]For more on avoiding some of Jesus' practices in preaching, see Hershael W. York and Bert Decker, *Preaching with Bold Assurance: A Solid and Enduring Approach to Engaging Exposition* (Nashville: Broadman & Holman, 2003), 15-17.

[24]For more on the doctrinal preaching of Jesus, see Ernest Reisinger, "The Human Will and Doctrinal Decline," *The Founders Journal*, no. 26 (1996) [journal on-line]; accessed 2 April 2003; available from founders.org/FJ26/article2_fr.html.

[25]The other Synoptic writers' summaries of Christ's Galilean ministry reveal that they understood, at least in part, teaching within preaching—Mark claims that Jesus went into the synagogues "preaching" (1:39) as does Luke (4:44). On another note, the Synoptic writers also summarize Jesus' ministry in terms of the numerous healings he performed, but such a focus is outside the scope of this work.

JOEL BREIDENBAUGH

As Luke presents the sermon, extensive use is made of the principle that Scripture is to be interpreted by Scripture. When Jesus preached in the synagogue on the Sabbath he was an expository preacher. His sermon was an interpretation of Scripture.

. . .

. . . The sermon is thoroughly expository and yet at the same time takes up into it the concerns, capacities, and interests of the congregation. It is an interpretation of Scripture and also an interpretation of the congregation.[26]

The fact that Jesus preached on Isaiah 61 emphasizes that the doctrinal content was Christological. People were beginning to see the fulfillment of Isaiah's prophecy about God's Anointed One. Additionally, the use of κηρυσσω in the Greek version of Isaiah 61:1 provides

the proper transition between the Old and New Testaments, for Jesus maintained that His ministry was the fulfillment of this prophetic portion (Luke 4:21). Sent by God and anointed by the Spirit, He was to 'proclaim liberty to the captives and recovery of sight to the blind.' Herein lies a uniqueness that characterizes New Testament heralding: while it proclaims, it brings to pass its proclamation. The proclamation of liberty at the same time frees. The preaching of sight opens blind eyes.[27]

Not only do Matthew and Luke portray Jesus as both preaching and teaching, but Mark does also, even employing the terms interchangeably. Old writes,

The words 'teach' and 'preach' seem to be synonymous in the Gospel of Mark. While we might want to draw some clear distinctions between preaching and teaching elsewhere in the New Testament, these distinctions are probably not applicable here.[28]

---

[26]Old, *The Biblical Period*, 132-33. Stein states that 4:21 "is best understood as a summary of Jesus' sermon" (Robert H. Stein, *Luke*, The New American Commentary, vol. 24 [Nashville: Broadman & Holman, 1992], 157). Synagogue sermons at the beginning of the Christian era involved translating the Hebrew into Aramaic and preaching a sermon. The sermon included a learned interpretation of the Scripture passage and an application to the audience. The sermon aimed "to teach, admonish, inspire and comfort the congregation" (Old, *The Biblical Period*, 103).

[27]Robert H. Mounce, *The Essential Nature of New Testament Preaching* (Grand Rapids: Eerdmans, 1960), 18.

[28]Old, *The Biblical Period*, 118. The fact that Mark uses κηρυσσω and διδασκω synonymously seems clear from Jesus' commission for them

Furthermore, Mark's use of διδασκω in 4:1-2 "seems to make it clear that the preaching ministry of Jesus put an emphasis on teaching and had a strong teaching content."[29]

Many of the verses above from the Synoptics highlight the overlap between *didache* (διδασκω) and *kerygma* (κηρυσσω). Furthermore, since κηρυσσω and ευαγγελιζω are nearly synonymous (see Luke 9:2, 6), the fact that Jesus "was teaching (διδασκοντος) the people in the temple and preaching the gospel (ευαγγελιζομενου)" (Luke 20:1) shows His integration of doctrine and preaching on a regular basis.[30]

One of Jesus' greatest sermons was the Sermon on the Mount (Matt 5-7).[31] Whether this passage is *one* of Jesus' actual sermons or a *compilation* of various sermons, these chapters are clearly sermonic material. The sermon is Matthew's way of fleshing out Jesus' preaching and teaching (4:23, cf. v. 17), showing Him to be the fulfillment of the prophet like Moses (Deut 18:15-18). Although Jesus gives much ethical instruction, the doctrines of inerrancy and the full authority of the Scriptures also stand out (5:17-19).

The elements of exposition and doctrine are also especially clear in Jesus' preaching in the temple (Matt 21:23-23:39; Mark 11:27-12:44; Luke 20:1-47). Luke introduces this sermon to the religious leaders and crowds as "one of the days while He was teaching the people in the temple and preaching the gospel" (20:1). In this sermon Jesus uses texts like Psalm 118, Exodus 3, Deuteronomy 6, Leviticus 19, and Psalm 110, explaining them in a number of question and answer sessions.[32] The doctrines of Christ and the resurrection stand out in these teaching sessions. Furthermore, the way

---

κηρυσσειν (3:14; cf. 6:12) and their later report to Him of all which they εδιδαξαν (6:30).

[29]Ibid., 127.

[30]See also Luke 24:47-48 where proclamation (κηρυσσω) is equated with being a witness (μαρτυς).

[31]For a thorough treatment of this sermon, see Craig L. Blomberg, *Matthew*, The New American Commentary, vol. 22 (Nashville: Broadman & Holman, 1992), 93-135.

[32]Commenting on the NT authors' quotation of Psalms, Henry M. Shires writes, "Often the use of the verse indicates that the Christian authors had in mind not simply the particular verses utilized but also their setting and even the entire psalm" (*Finding the Old Testament in the New* [Philadelphia: The Westminster Press, 1974], 131).

in which Jesus often had to confront people's misunderstanding of Scripture highlights His focus on doctrine. Peter Adam writes that Jesus

> frequently prefaced his explanation of their error with the question 'Have you not read?' On one level this was simply a way of reminding them of the *content* of Scripture, and of pointing out to them that the truth would be found in that Scripture. On another level the question 'Have you not read?' challenged them to question their understanding of the *meaning* of Scripture.[33]

The climax of Jesus' preaching takes place after His resurrection. Alongside two disciples on the road to Emmaus, Jesus clearly expounds (διερμηνευω) every Messianic text of the Old Testament (Luke 24:27; cf. v. 44). The roles of doctrine and expository preaching blend here in Jesus' ministry like never before, because He declares Christology in an expositional manner.

Not only can Jesus' practice of preaching be beneficial, but His precepts for preaching are also insightful for this study. Reading through the Gospels, one sees Jesus commanding His disciples to preach (κηρυσσω) (Mark 3:14; 6:12) and giving them authority to do so (Matt 16:19; 28:18-20).[34] Specifically, they are to preach the kingdom of heaven/God (Matt 10:7; Luke 9:2), or the gospel (Luke 9:6).

Jesus' climactic charge to His followers occurs just before His ascension. In the Luke-Acts account, He charges His disciples to be "witnesses" (μαρτυρες) of Him (Luke 24:48; Acts 1:8). Their witness is "to proclaim" (κηρυχθηναι) the doctrine of Christ throughout the Scriptures as well as repentance for the forgiveness of sins (24:44-47). Ultimately, Christ wants His people to explain the Scriptures the way He did.

Similarly, Matthew shows Jesus commanding His followers to "make disciples of all the nations" (28:19). Jesus defines the imperative μαθητευσατε in two ways. First, Christians are to make disciples by baptizing them in the name of the Triune God (v. 19). This element assumes conversion through the gospel message. Second, Christians must make disciples by teaching (διδασκω) the new converts to keep all of

---

[33]Peter J. H. Adam, "Preaching and Biblical Theology," in *New Dictionary of Biblical Theology: Exploring the Unity and Diversity of Scripture*, ed. T. Desmond Alexander and others (Downers Grove: InterVarsity, 2000), 106.

[34]The authority handed down to the apostles is evident in Titus 1:5, 9; 1 Tim 3-4; and 2 Tim 4 (Samuel T. Logan, Jr., "The Phenomenology of Preaching," in *The Preacher and Preaching: Reviving the Art in the Twentieth Century*, ed. Samuel T. Logan, Jr. [Phillipsburg, NJ: Presbyterian and Reformed Publishing, 1986], 151).

Christ's commands (v. 20). That is, new believers need to have doctrine applied to their lives. Here, it is quite clear that both *kerygma* and *didache* are essential elements in the Christian message—whether it be by way of preaching or teaching. Old concludes,

> In the light of a text like this it is rather hard to drive a wedge between preaching the gospel of salvation and teaching the Christian way of life. Obviously according to this text Christian preaching is to do both. At times the Church has understood this passage as the charter of evangelistic preaching, and at other times as the charter of catechetical preaching. The least we can say is that in regard to the apostolic ministry it puts a high priority on preaching.[35]

Indeed, it puts a high priority on preaching doctrinally!

In summary of Jesus' ministry of the Word, Adam writes,

> By his preaching and teaching he both announced and extended the kingdom, called people to faith, refuted error, rebuked those who taught error, encouraged the weak, trained his disciples, explained the Scripture, rebuked sinners and summoned all to faith and obedience.[36]

In the end one recognizes Jesus to be both the greatest preacher and the greatest theologian ever. Doctrine filled His preaching, and His teaching had its roots in the gospel message. Those who followed Him closest preached in like fashion. The best listeners to Jesus' message constructed their spiritual lives on His sacrifice and sermons.

The Apostle Paul

Although Jesus was the greatest preacher ever, the Apostle Paul's preaching clearly reached more people. Even though Jesus addressed thousands of Jews in Israel and only a handful of Gentiles, Paul's ministry encountered thousands of both Jews and Gentiles, even striving for "the remotest part of the earth" (Acts 1:8). Paul's all-encompassing preaching integrated both doctrine and exposition.

Scholars often say that Paul's preaching focused on "Jesus Christ and Him crucified" (1 Cor 2:2; cf. 1:23). One must see this focus, however, as primary but not exclusive. That is, Paul preached both the cross of Jesus Christ and the doctrinal, as well as ethical, implications of the cross. In his letter to the Colossians, he described his own preaching, "We proclaim Him, admonishing every man and teaching every man with all wisdom, so

---

[35] Old, *The Biblical Period*, 152.

[36] Adam, *Speaking God's Words*, 47.

that we may present every man complete in Christ" (1:28). Paul viewed his own proclamation (καταγγελλω) as including admonition (νουθετεω) and teaching (διδασκω). Such preaching is found in the message of Acts and Paul's own writings.[37]

As one studies Acts, he finds Paul (earlier called Saul) both preaching and teaching the Scriptures. Just days after his conversion, Saul preached (κηρυσσω) Jesus as the Son of God, proving (συμβιβαζω) Him to be the Christ (9:20, 22).[38] Later, on his first mission, Paul announced (καταγγελλω, 13:5, 38) the Word of God in the synagogues with words of exhortation (παρακλησις, v. 15), explanation (vv. 17-41), and proclamation (ευαγγελιζω, v. 32). Paul's preaching was "a biblical-theological exposition,"[39] which covered "the whole history of salvation from Moses to Christ," explaining such messianic passages as Psalm 2, Isaiah 55, and Psalm 16.[40] Moreover, Paul's final stop in Antioch consisted of "teaching and preaching" (διδασκοντες και ευαγγελιζομενοι) God's Word (15:35).

During the second mission in Acts 17, Paul continues blending preaching and teaching. He traveled to Thessalonica and "reasoned to [the Jews] from the Scriptures" (διελεξατο αυτοις απο των γραφων),

---

[37]One should be careful with theological interpretation in Acts due to its literary genre of narrative history (see chapter 11 below for more on theological interpretation in various genres). Acts summarizes the actions of the apostolic church as do the Gospels with Jesus' life. At the same time, however, readers can learn much about Paul's ministry by studying Acts because its honest reporting accurately represents the actions of the early church (see Luke 1:1-4). For the elements of history and theology in Acts, see John B. Polhill, *Acts*, The New American Commentary, vol. 26 (Nashville: Broadman & Holman, 1992), 50-55.

[38]Polhill observes that συμβιβαζω "means to *join* or *put together* and seems to picture [Paul's] assembling Old Testament texts to demonstrate how Christ fulfilled them" (ibid., 239).

[39]Graeme Goldsworthy, *Preaching the Whole Bible as Christian Scripture: The Application of Biblical Theology to Expository Preaching* (Grand Rapids: Wm. B. Eerdmans, 2000), 58.

[40]Old, *The Biblical Period*, 175. In emphasizing the expository nature of Paul's message, Old adds that Paul's sermon may possibly have been "based on Deuteronomy 4:25-26 for the lesson from the Law and II Samuel 7:6-16 for the lesson from the prophets" (ibid.). See also Polhill, *Acts*, 298.

proclaiming (καταγγελλω) Jesus as the Christ through opening (διανοιγω) the Scriptures and laying them before (παρατιθημι) them (17:1-3). In Athens Paul used both theological and philosophical argumentation in "preaching Jesus and the resurrection" (vv. 18ff). Though straying from his normal practice of Old Testament exposition and then application, Paul's preaching in Athens began with Old Testament theology, moved to the resurrection of Christ, and finally ended with application.[41]

Testifying (μαρτυρεω, 18:5) about Jesus as the Christ and "teaching the Word of God" (διδασκων τον λογον του θεου, v. 11) characterized Paul's eighteen month stay in Corinth. His follow-up letters to the Corinthian church may best convey his practice of doctrinal exposition among those believers—something like a series of sermons. Paul's voice is loud and clear on a number of doctrines, including ecclesiology—the Lord's Supper (1 Cor 11:17-34) and worship (14:26-40), pneumatology—the Spirit's illumination (2:10-16) and spiritual gifts (12:1-31; 14:1-25), and eschatology—the Lord's return and the resurrection of the dead (15:1-58), as well as a theology of preaching (1:17-2:5) and ministry (2 Cor 2:14-6:10).

Paul's third mission began in Ephesus where his message consisted of reasoning (διαλεγομαι) and persuading (πειθω) people about the kingdom of God (19:8). This disciplined approach to teaching Scripture took place daily (vv. 9-10). His departure from Ephesus most certainly reveals Paul's preaching habits (see below).

Paul's preaching in Acts also includes his speeches, or what is known as his defense (απολογια, 22:1; cf. 24:10; 26:1) of preaching the gospel of Christ (cf. 22:3-21; 24:10-21; 26:2-29). Though some may question viewing these speeches as sermons, it seems clear "that the early Christian preachers were happy to present their message in any situation or in any form which presented itself."[42] Although his audiences were much smaller, Paul continued to witness about Jesus and do so from a clear argument.

The Book of Acts closes with Paul in Rome doing what he had always done—preaching and teaching the gospel of Jesus Christ. The elements of exposition (εκτιθημι, 28:23), testimony (διαμαρτυρομαι, v. 23), and persuasion (πειθω, vv. 23-24) were in full play. As a matter of fact, Luke can best summarize Paul's time in Rome as "preaching the kingdom of God and teaching concerning the Lord Jesus Christ" (κηρυσσων την βασιλειαν του θεου και διδασκων τα περι του κυριου Ιησου Χριστου) (28:31).

---

[41]Adam, *Speaking God's Words*, 86.

[42]Old, *The Biblical Period*, 179.

The clearest moment in Luke's account where Paul's preaching implemented both doctrine and exposition comes in his departure from Ephesus. Speaking to the elders of the church, Paul summarized his ministry among them. It contained elements of declaration (αναγγελω, 20:20, 27), doctrine (διδασκω, v. 20), witness (διαμαρτυρομαι, vv. 21, 24, 26), preaching (κηρυσσω, v. 25), and admonition (νουθετεω, v. 31). Only such solid and multifaceted preaching as this could fulfill his goal of declaring "the whole counsel of God" (20:27).

As to the message Paul preached, he labels it as the gospel, Christ, and even the kingdom of God. The reader should understand these descriptions synonymously, i.e., to preach the gospel is to preach Christ and to preach Christ is to preach the kingdom (cf. 1 Cor 1:23; 15:12; 2 Cor 1:19; 4:5; Acts 28:31; Rom 1:16).[43] The fact that the gospel of grace could both save the sinner and sanctify the saint makes it a message for unbelievers and believers.

In the end, Paul's preaching handles primarily the doctrines of salvation and Christ. The soteriological aspect of Paul's message discusses themes of redemption (Eph 1:7), justification (Rom 3:21-4:25; Gal 2:14-4:11), and reconciliation (2 Cor 5:18-21).[44] The Christological element reveals Jesus to be the last Adam (1 Cor 15:45ff), the Son of David (Rom 1:3), the wisdom of God (1 Cor 1:24, 30), the new Torah (Rom 10:6ff), and the pre-existent Agent of creation (Col 1:15-20).[45] Even preaching has an important place in God's plan of salvation, for after a thorough exposition of the doctrine of justification by faith, Paul makes a direct connection between preaching the gospel and expressing faith in Christ (see Rom 10:14-17). Paul's clear practice in his writings is doctrinal exposition.[46]

---

[43]For the replacement of the kingdom of God with the gospel of Christ, see Mounce, *Essential Nature of NT Preaching*, 52-53.

[44]Although many would contend that we should not label the NT epistles as preaching, it seems clear that they were understood largely as sermonic material in the fact that they were often read out loud to the assembled church (Col 4:16; Rev 2-3; cf. 1:3). See also Sidney Greidanus, *The Modern Preacher and the Ancient Text: Interpreting and Preaching Biblical Literature* (Grand Rapids: Wm. B. Eerdmans, 1988), 313-14.

[45]Ibid., 137-42.

[46]Paul's style of explaining doctrine as the basis for duty is a common observation. That is to say, the doctrine of many letters (e.g. Rom 1-11; Eph 1-3; Gal 1-4; 2 Thess 1:5-2:12; Col 1-2) gives reason for the duty that follows (e.g. Rom 12-16; Eph 4-6; Gal 5-6; 2 Thess 2:13-3:15; Col 3-4).

Just as one can make a connection between Jesus' preaching practice and precepts, so a similar relationship exists in Paul's preaching. His Pastoral Epistles provide instructions about preaching and are tremendously significant in discussing the integration of doctrine and exposition. Paul's precepts to Timothy and Titus, like his own practice, emphasize that preaching needs to be both doctrinal and expositional.

Paul, who identifies himself as a preacher (κηρυξ) and teacher (διδασκαλος) in faith and truth (2:7; 2 Tim 1:11), commands Timothy to "give attention to the *public* reading of *Scripture*, to exhortation and teaching" (1 Tim 4:13).[47] The αναγνωσις is most surely the public reading of Scripture in a book-by-book approach. Παρακλησις includes both exhortation and application of the Scriptures.[48] Additionally, διδασκαλια focuses on the doctrinal substance needed in every expository sermon, for Kelly states, "*teaching* signifies catechetical instruction in Christian doctrine."[49] For Paul, "the ministry of the Word includes the proclaiming of the message of salvation and the teaching of the Christian way of life."[50]

Timothy also receives instruction about elders who work hard at "preaching and teaching" (λογω και διδασκαλια, 5:17). Furthermore, he must "teach and exhort" (διδασκε και παρακαλει) others in the "sound words" of Jesus Christ and "the doctrine (διδασκαλια) conforming to godliness" (6:2-3). Clearly, Paul expects preachers to apply exposition and doctrine regularly in the preaching event.

Likewise, Paul's words to Titus include staying true to the "teaching" (διδαχη), in order that he might be able "to exhort in sound doctrine" (παρακαλειν εν τη διδασκαλια τη υγιαινουση) (1:9). This teaching is a direct link to the "faithful word" (πιστου λογου), which most certainly is

---

[47]Of course, Paul's apostolic call is also important in his ministry (cf. 1 Tim 2:7; 2 Tim 1:11) but is not as significant for this study.

[48]George W. Knight III, *Commentary on the Pastoral Epistles*, New International Greek Testament Commentary (Grand Rapids: Wm. B. Eerdmans, 1992), 207-08.

[49]John N. D. Kelly, *A Commentary on the Pastoral Epistles: I Timothy, II Timothy, Titus* (New York: Harper & Row, 1963), 105. For a summary of these three aspects of ministry, see Old, *The Biblical Period*, 246-50. Paul's use of διδασκαλια throughout the Pastoral Epistles is nearly synonymous with διδαχη (see Old, *The Biblical Period*, 244).

[50]Old, *The Biblical Period*, 250.

the "proclamation" (κηρυγμα) of God's Word to Paul (cf. 1:3). Moreover, one may be able to relate this sound, or pure, doctrine (cf. 2:1, 7) to exposition because of the "faithful" word. Expositional teaching, like no other form of teaching, strives for faithfulness to the Word.

Many rightly consider the apostle's second letter to Timothy as his swan song. Here Paul lays out the challenge every preacher must face— "accurately handling the word of truth" (2:15). This word of truth is clearly none other than the "sacred writings" (ιερα γραμματα), also known as the God-breathed Scripture (γραφη θεοπνευστος) (3:15-16). This Scripture shaped the theological clarity needed for serving as an elder (cf. Tit 1:9). Furthermore, such Scripture is useful, first and foremost, for "doctrine" (διδασκαλια). Tom Ascol observes, "If the first profit of Scripture is doctrine, then doctrinal preaching is an essential ingredient for the growth and thorough equipping of Christian men and women."[51] Moreover, in light of the God-inspired Scriptures and the presence of God and Christ, preachers must "preach the Word" (κηρυξον τον λογον)! Exhortation (παρακαλεω) and instruction (διδαχη) are always needed, especially when people shun sound doctrine (υγιαινουσης διδασκαλιας) (4:2-3). The repetition of υγιαινω used to describe the teaching ministry underscores the importance Paul placed on doctrinal integrity (cf. 1 Tim 1:10; 6:3; 2 Tim 1:13; 4:3; Tit 1:9, 13; 2:1-2).

Paul undoubtedly provides a worthy model of implementing doctrine and expository preaching. His preaching has many flavors, including explanation, illustration, instruction, application, argumentation, and exhortation. Better yet, his ministry deals with preaching the gospel message of the cross of Christ, reminding believers of the gospel, explaining it theologically, and drawing implications from it. For Paul, then, exposition and doctrine are two sides of the same coin.

The Apostle Peter

Simon Peter serves as another example of one who implemented both theology and exposition in his preaching ministry.[52] One can trace the

---

[51] Tom Ascol, "Systematic Theology and Preaching," *The Founders Journal*, no. 4 (1991) [journal on-line]; accessed 20 January 2003; available from founders.org/FJ04/ editorial_fr.html.

[52] If Mark's Gospel is a compilation of Peter's preaching, then all that has been said above about Mark's use of the terms "preach" and "teach" has its origin in Peter's preaching. William Lane seriously considers this tradition from Papias in *The Gospel of Mark*, New International Commentary on the New Testament (Grand Rapids: Wm. B. Eerdmans, 1970), 8-12.

origin of his ministry of the Word to Jesus' command for Peter to "feed [Christ's] lambs" (John 21:15). Beginning at Pentecost in Acts 2, Peter practiced doctrinal exposition. Here one finds Peter explaining Joel 2 using the analogy of faith, i.e., Scripture is explained by Scripture. Peter quoted Psalms 16 and 110 to explain the death, burial, and resurrection of Jesus, proving Him to be the Christ. Peter concluded by commanding the people to repent to have their sins forgiven. His preaching included both testimony (διαμαρτυρομαι) and exhortation (παρεκαλεω) (v. 40). As soon as people received the message and were baptized, Peter and the other apostles taught them doctrine (διδαχη) (v. 42).[53]

Later, Peter explained the gospel message from the Law and the Writings (3:22, 25; cf. 4:11) with exhortation to repentance (3:19) and argumentation of the exclusivity of Jesus Christ (4:12). The likelihood that Acts 3 refers to the prophecies of Isaiah 52:13-53:12 further highlight the expositional nature of Peter's message.[54] Peter, commanded not to teach (μηδε διδασκειν) about Jesus (4:18), continued to instruct others about Him, nonetheless (5:28ff). Furthermore, Luke describes Peter and the apostles as "teaching and preaching" (διδασκοντες και ευαγγελιζομενοι) Jesus Christ (v. 42). Both gospel witness and doctrinal instruction are evident in this kind of ministry.

A person can make an argument that 1 Peter, although presented as a letter, is, in fact, "an epitome of the apostle's preaching."[55] When viewed in this light, 1:1-2:10 is actually theological exposition of the gospel. This gospel which Peter proclaimed is no less than the enduring Word of the Lord (1:24-25). Furthermore, the message of 2 Peter focuses on the doctrinal stability of the gospel (1:19-21), warning believers to hold fast to God's Word, the way of truth (2:2, 21). While this is not all that one sees of Peter's preaching (see Acts 10:34-43), the disciplines of exposition and theology were clearly part of his regular practice.

---

[53]The doctrine probably "included such subjects as [Christ's] resurrection, the Old Testament Scriptures, the Christian witness, and surely [the apostles'] own reminiscences of Jesus' earthly ministry and teachings" (Polhill, *Acts*, 119).

[54]For the possible allusions to Isaiah's Suffering Servant, see Polhill, *Acts*, 131-32; Old, *The Biblical Period*, 169-71.

[55]Old, *Reading and Preaching*, 237. For commonalities between 1 Peter and the primitive *kerygma*, see Mounce, *Essential Nature of NT Preaching*, 133-37.

Other Notables in Scripture

In addition to Jesus, Paul, and Peter, a few other doctrinal expositors may be found in the New Testament. The Apostle John was most certainly a doctrinal expositor. Though it is difficult to determine the content of his preaching from Acts, since he is usually portrayed alongside Peter (cf. 3:1ff; 4:19-20; 5:18ff; 8:14), 1 John appears to be a summary of John's message. Both "witness" (μαρτυρεω, 1:2) and "proclamation" (απαγγελλω, 1:2-3, 5) about various truths pertaining to the Trinity characterize his message. Even an admonition about false worship concludes John's message (5:21).[56]

Furthermore, if a preaching element underlies the Gospels, then John's prologue is an excellent example of doctrinal exposition. John shows Christ to be the eternal Logos made flesh (1:1, 14). Moreover, the Logos "has explained" (εξηγησατο) the unseen God (v. 18). The use of εξηγεομαι means that Jesus has literally "exegeted" the Father to believers.[57]

In addition to John, Apollos, who receives relatively little treatment in the Scriptures, showed elements of doctrinal exposition. He was an educated man who was "mighty in the Scriptures" (Acts 18:24). He "taught" (διδασκω) others about Jesus (v. 25), but after receiving full instruction about the way of God, Apollos clearly "demonstrated" (διακατελεγχομαι) Jesus to be the Messiah (v. 28). Such demonstration from the Scriptures must have included clear explanation and instruction. As F. F. Bruce comments, "Apollos's 'mastery of the scriptures' probably consisted both in his familiarity with the sacred text and in his skill in interpreting messianic prophecy in a Christian sense."[58]

Finally, the author of Hebrews provides one long sermon filled with doctrinal exposition. The author's closing words reveal the sermonic nature of the letter—"I urge you, brethren, bear with this word of exhortation" (13:22). By his use of παρακαλεω ("urge") and παρακλησις ("exhortation"), the writer viewed his letter as a sermon. On the use of these terms, David Peterson writes,

> Paraklesis . . . involved the proclamation of the mighty acts of God in Christ, often with some exposition of the O.T., and a drawing

---

[56]For more on John's teaching as an expansion of the apostolic church's *kerygma*, see Mounce, *Essential Nature of NT Preaching*, 145-50.

[57]Walter C. Kaiser, Jr., *Toward an Exegetical Theology: Biblical Exegesis for Preaching and Teaching* (Grand Rapids: Baker Books, 1981), 44.

[58]F. F. Bruce, *Peter, Stephen, James, and John: Studies in Early Non-Pauline Christianity* (Grand Rapids: Wm. B. Eerdmans, 1979), 68.

out of the practical implications for the audience in question—believers or unbelievers (*cf.* Acts 13:15-41). The terminology itself suggests that the activity had a summons to decision or an encouragement to persevere in the Christian way. Although systematic teaching was clearly involved, the address is not simply to the intellect but also to the affections and the will.[59]

The author explains in great detail some of the greatest theological truths about Christ. He continually uses Old Testament Scripture for both explanation and exhortation. The entire letter is doctrinal exposition at its best, for it continually explains, illustrates, and applies the OT with solid doctrinal teaching about the supremacy and sufficiency of the Person and work of Christ.[60] Moreover, the writer exhorts believers to pay attention to what they have heard (2:1), to hold fast to their confession of Christ (4:14), to encourage one another (10:24-25), and to cling to Christ and fix their eyes on Him (12:2).

All of these Old and New Testament examples help show the significance of doctrinal expository preaching. Both the semantic domain for preaching and preaching models in Scripture stress the *biblical* basis of doctrinal expository preaching. May preachers return to the Scriptures, and to its models, in declaring the whole counsel of God for spiritual bodybuilding among their audience!

---

[59]David Peterson, "The Ministry of Encouragement," in *God Who Is Rich in Mercy*, ed. P. T. O'Brien and D. G. Peterson (Homebush West, Australia: Lancer, 1986), 240; quoted in Adam, *Speaking God's Words*, 78-79.

[60]For Hebrews' distinctive contributions in developing the *kerygma*, see Mounce, *Essential Nature of NT Preaching*, 142-45.

Part 4: Theological Methods for Doctrinal Exposition

CHAPTER 10
THE THEOLOGICAL FRAMEWORK FOR
DOCTRINAL EXPOSITION: TONING MUSCLES

After providing a definition for doctrinal expository preaching and recognizing its biblical bases, the next task calls for implementation. This section offers a proposal on how the preacher can integrate both doctrine and exposition in an effective manner. Since a wellspring of manuals exists on how to do expository preaching, this study specifically focuses on theological exegesis and explanation within an expository framework. By the end of this section, the reader should see theology as "a hermeneutical arch that reaches from the text to the contemporary sermon."[1]

The last part of this work analyzed the biblical bases for doctrinal exposition—the Scriptures show its practice and prescription. This chapter begins by looking at the theological framework for doing doctrinal expository preaching. Timothy Warren states,

> Preaching that lacks solid theological footing also lacks authority. Students of preaching must become students of theology as well, developing skill in doing theology. Adopting a system of theology may provide an essential starting point, but preachers must also learn how to do theology, both biblical and systematic. To move from the contextualized exegetical meaning, dealing with a multitude of specifics, to the single universal statement of truth is a skill that is never learned or seldom demonstrated by many preachers. . . .
>
> The basic skills of studying theology—the theology of the book, the theology of the pericope within that book, and systematic

---

[1]John Warwick Montgomery, "The Theologian's Craft," *Concordia Theological Monthly* 37, no. 2 (1966): 79.

theology—cannot be ignored. The risks of misrepresenting and misapplying the text are great for the preacher who ignores or misunderstands the theological message of the particular text.[2] For the connection between theology and preaching, one needs to consider the distinct but related disciplines of biblical theology and systematic theology as twin pillars of implementing doctrinal exposition. Think in terms of weightlifting: toning your muscles while removing fatty tissue.

Biblical Theology

Biblical theology is quite possibly the most important realm of all the theological disciplines. It involves careful exegesis and hermeneutics, all-the-while incorporating the whole canon of Scripture.[3] In order to interpret biblical texts theologically, one needs to begin with biblical theology as a foundation to doctrinal exposition.

Some Definitions of Biblical Theology

Biblical theology is the

theological interpretation of Scripture in and for the church. It proceeds with

---

[2]Timothy S. Warren, "A Paradigm for Preaching," *Bibliotheca Sacra* 148, no. 592 (1991): 485. In light of this need to integrate theological study with preaching, Warren proposes a new preaching paradigm (ibid., 472-81). While a helpful paradigm, this paper focuses more on the theological and homiletical processes. See also John Koessler, "Why All the Best Preachers Are Theological," in *The Art & Craft of Biblical Preaching: A Comprehensive Resource for Today's Communicators*, eds. Haddon Robinson and Craig Brian Larson (Grand Rapids: Zondervan, 2005), 241-46. See appendix 7 for the exegetical, theological, and homiletical processes in doctrinal expository preaching.

[3]Brian S. Rosner states, "Because biblical theology is the fruit of exegesis of the texts of the various biblical corpora it has a logical priority over systematics and the other specialized types of theologizing. However, the mutuality of the disciplines can be seen in our coming to the task of exegesis with certain dogmatic presuppositions about the nature and authority of the Bible" ("Biblical Theology," in *New Dictionary of Biblical Theology: Exploring the Unity & Diversity of Scripture* [*NDBT*], ed. T. Desmond Alexander and others [Downers Grove: InterVarsity Press, 2000], 3). On a similar note, Tom Ascol argues for the necessity of both biblical and systematic theology; while the former deals with the diversity among various authors, the latter stresses the Scriptures' unity as a product of the divine hand ("Systematic Theology and Preaching," *The Founders Journal*, no. 4 (1991) [journal on-line]; accessed 20 January 2003; available from founders.org/FJ04/editorial_fr.html).

historical and literary sensitivity and seeks to analyse and synthesize the Bible's teaching about God and his relations to the world on its own terms, maintaining sight of the Bible's overarching narrative and Christocentric focus.[4] Geerhardus Vos defines it as "that branch of exegetical theology which deals with the process of the self-revelation of God deposited in the Bible."[5] Comprehensively, Goldsworthy asserts,

> Biblical theology is concerned with God's saving acts and his word as these occur within the history of the people of God. It follows the progress of revelation from the first word of God to man through to the unveiling of the full glory of Christ. It examines the several stages of biblical history and their relationship to one another. It thus provides the basis for understanding how texts in one part of the Bible relate to all other texts. A sound interpretation of the Bible is based upon the findings of biblical theology.[6]

Features of Biblical Theology

These definitions emphasize several features of biblical theology. First, biblical theology allows "the Bible to speak as a whole: as the one word of the one God about the one way of salvation."[7] Preachers should reject as invalid any employment of biblical theology which does not accept the unity of Scriptures. Edmund P. Clowney confesses, "Biblical theology is a contradiction in terms unless the Bible presents a consistent message. Its essential presuppositions are the principles of revelation and inspiration claimed and assumed in the Bible itself."[8]

---

[4]Rosner, "Biblical Theology," 10. The expression "biblical theology" may refer, in some places, to the movement of the 1940s-1960s. Brevard S. Childs documents this movement in *Biblical Theology in Crisis* (Philadelphia: Westminster, 1970).

[5]Geerhardus Vos, *Biblical Theology: Old and New Testaments* (Grand Rapids: Eerdmans, 1948), 13.

[6]Graeme Goldsworthy, *According to Plan: The Unfolding Revelation of God in the Bible* (Downers Grove: InterVarsity Press, 1991), 32.

[7]Graeme Goldsworthy, *Preaching the Whole Bible as Christian Scripture: The Application of Biblical Theology to Expository Preaching* (Grand Rapids: Wm. B. Eerdmans, 2000), 7.

[8]Edmund P. Clowney, *Preaching and Biblical Theology* (Grand Rapids: Wm. B. Eerdmans, 1961), 13. Similarly, Peter F. Jensen claims that an evangelical view of biblical theology entails the Bible's unity in origin and content, the Bible

Second, the goal of biblical theology is to understand the parts of Scripture in relation to the whole. Preachers attain such a goal when they *"so preach Christ that every part of the Bible contributes its unique riches to his gospel."*[9] D. A. Carson, borrowing from Hasel, says,

> In this sense it is canonical biblical theology, 'whole-Bible' biblical theology; i.e. its content is a theology of the whole Bible, not a theology that merely has its roots in the Bible, or merely takes the Bible as the place to begin.[10]

Third, biblical theology helps define that "the center and reference point for the meaning of all Scripture is the person and work of Jesus of Nazareth, the Christ of God."[11] Particularly speaking, even the Old Testament centralizes around Jesus Christ with numerous texts referring to Him.[12] John Bright declares, "Christ is indeed to us the crown of revelation through whom the true significance of the Old Testament becomes finally apparent."[13] Moreover, Clowney writes,

---

as God's self-revelation, and the Bible as its own interpreter ("Preaching the Whole Bible: Preaching and Biblical Theology," in *When God's Voice Is Heard: Essays on Preaching Presented to Dick Lucas*, ed. David Jackman and Christopher Green [Leicester: Inter-Varsity Press, 1995], 68). The assertion on unity is why Childs' view of biblical theology falls short. Ultimately, he is unable to come to grips with biblical authority by failing to uphold the biblical text as a product of divine revelation. Therefore, as helpful as his claims are, his theological system has nothing on which to stand (see Childs, *Biblical Theology in Crisis*).

[9]Jensen, "Preaching the Whole Bible," 64.

[10]D. A. Carson, "Systematic Theology and Biblical Theology," in *NDBT*, 100. See Gerhard F. Hasel, "Proposals for a Canonical Biblical Theology," *Andrews University Seminary Studies* 34, no. 1 (1996): 23-33.

[11]Goldsworthy, *Preaching the Whole Bible*, 16.

[12]Kaiser notes that as many as 456 OT texts refer to Christ (Walter C. Kaiser, Jr., *Preaching and Teaching from the Old Testament: A Guide for the Church* [Grand Rapids: Baker Books, 2003], 20). On a related note, Clowney believes the key for preaching the Old Testament "is the witness of the Scriptures to Christ" ("Preaching Christ from All the Scriptures," in *The Preacher and Preaching: Reviving the Art in the Twentieth Century*, ed. Samuel T. Logan, Jr. (Phillipsburg, NJ: Presbyterian and Reformed, 1986), 166.

[13]John Bright, *The Authority of the Old Testament* (Grand Rapids: Baker Book House, 1975), 112.

Biblical theology serves to center preaching on its essential message: Jesus Christ. [And thus,] preaching must be theological. Salvation is of the Lord, and the message of the gospel is the theocentric message of the unfolding of the plan of God for our salvation in Jesus Christ. He who would preach the Word must preach Christ.[14]

Likewise, Goldsworthy adamantly asserts,

Jesus Christ in his life, death and resurrection is the fixed point of reference for the understanding of the whole of reality. We must apply this fact to our doing of biblical theology. The gospel is the fixed point of reference for understanding the meaning of the whole range of biblical revelation.[15]

Evangelicals as a whole have even adopted this kind of hermeneutic. Article III of "The Chicago Statement on Biblical Hermeneutics" (1982) declares: "The person and work of Jesus Christ are the central focus of the entire Bible. We deny that any method of interpretation which rejects or obscures the Christ-centeredness of the Bible is correct."[16]

Fourth, biblical theology's Christocentric focus naturally leads one to find a main focal point for interpreting the Scriptures. Whether one can honestly argue for *the* central theme of the OT, NT, or even the Bible, it is still important to establish a focal point for organization and clarity. Paul House writes,

A focal point is valuable as long as it is true to Scripture and actually helps the theologian's analysis hold together. Attempting to argue a certain theme as the only major uniting idea can succeed only if all other motifs are proven secondary. . . . Surely such an argument would require an extended discussion before the theologian could begin.[17]

---

[14]Clowney, *Preaching and Biblical Theology*, 74. Ultimately, there should be "no distinction between preaching doctrine and preaching Jesus" (Robert B. Selph, *Southern Baptists and the Doctrine of Election* [Harrisonburg, VA: Sprinkle Publications, 1996], 14).

[15]Goldsworthy, *According to Plan*, 60; ibid., 23, 72.

[16]"The Chicago Statement on Biblical Hermeneutics," in *Hermeneutics, Inerrancy, and the Bible*, ed. Earl D. Radmacher and Robert D. Preus (Grand Rapids: Academie Books, 1984), 882.

[17]Paul R. House, *Old Testament Theology* (Downers Grove: InterVarsity, 1998), 56. See also Hasel, "Canonical Biblical Theology," 30-32. The role of biblical theology emphasizes certain themes to contribute to the understanding of the Bible's single, unified message (Goldsworthy, *According to Plan*, 77). For

Some of the central, unifying themes of the Bible are the kingdom of God, the covenants, creation—old and new, God's redemption plan for His people, and God's promise-line—the story of the Lord and His work. Underscoring the Bible's Christ-centered message strengthens any of these themes.

Finally, biblical theology is an engaging, theological interpretation of Scripture. Peter Stuhlmacher writes,

> A biblical theology . . . must attempt to interpret the Old and New Testament tradition as it wants to be interpreted. For this reason, it cannot read these texts only from a critical distance as historical sources but must, at the same time, take them seriously as testimonies of faith which belong to the Holy Scripture of early Christianity.[18]

These features describe biblical theology more fully, showing its concern for the Bible's message about God and Christ.

The Value of Biblical Theology for Doctrinal Exposition

In order to carry out doctrinal exposition most effectively, the expositor will want to implement biblical theology and exposition regularly. This implementation will prove valuable in a number of ways.

First, it sets the individual text in its larger contexts. Adam explains,

> To place a text in context we must identify its literary context in the book, its theological context in the writings of the author, and the historical context of the book. Then to place a text in the context of the whole biblical revelation will involve understanding its context in OT or NT theology, its context in God's progressive revelation within each period of salvation-history, and its context in biblical theology. In sum, context must be theological as well as literary, and context must include the whole biblical revelation, as

---

another argument for the Bible's unity and central themes, see Kaiser, *Preaching and Teaching from the OT*, 30-34. Much of NT theology concerns the more specific discipline of Pauline theology. It seems that those who view the major unifying themes of Christology and the gospel not only accurately depict Paul but the rest of the NT as well. See Thomas R. Schreiner, *Paul Apostle of God's Glory in Christ: A Pauline Theology* (Downers Grove: InterVarsity, 2001), 22; Joseph A. Fitzmyer, *Paul and His Theology: A Brief Sketch* (Englewood Cliffs, NJ: Prentice Hall, 1989), 37-38.

[18]Peter Stuhlmacher, *How to Do Biblical Theology* (Allison Park, PA: Pickwick, 1995), 1.

well as the book in which the text occurs.[19]
Similarly, Kaiser claims that good exegesis considers the whole context, whether the context is immediate, sectional, within in a book, or canonical (see figure 2 in the Appendices).[20]

Second, biblical theology for exposition is valuable because it helps readers "trace longitudinal themes from the Old Testament to the New."[21] Preachers will be able to interpret the OT in light of the NT message concerning Christ.

Biblical theology, then, is so significant that attempting expository preaching without it often leads to a lack of appreciation for the bigger story of the Scriptures and its relationship to Christian life.[22] At the same time, if one's view of biblical theology focuses solely on Scriptures' diversity without respect for its unity, then the preacher has to deal with the problem of discontinuity and even contemporary insignificance. Only a unified biblical theological approach can effectively relate the one (unity) to the many (diversity), bringing the role of systematic theology into play[23]—we now turn our attention to that discipline.

Systematic Theology

Not only is biblical theology important for doctrinal exposition, but systematic theology is also. While not necessarily inferior to biblical theology, systematic theology reaps the fruit of biblical theology's task.

Some Definitions of Systematic Theology

Systematic theology "is nothing other than the saving truth of God presented in systematic form."[24] More specifically, it "*is any study that answers*

---

[19]Adam, "Preaching and Biblical Theology," in *NDBT*, 107.

[20]Walter C. Kaiser, Jr., *Toward an Exegetical Theology: Biblical Exegesis for Preaching and Teaching* (Grand Rapids: Baker Books, 1981), 69-85.

[21]Sidney Greidanus, *Preaching Christ from the Old Testament: A Contemporary Hermeneutical Method* (Grand Rapids: Wm. B. Eerdmans, 1999), 267.

[22]Goldsworthy, *Preaching the Whole Bible*, 59.

[23]Ibid., 63-68.

[24]B. B. Warfield, *Selected Shorter Writings*, vol. 2, ed. John E. Meeter (Phillipsburg, NJ: Presbyterian and Reformed, 1973), 180.

the question, 'What does the whole Bible teach us today?' about any given topic."[25]

The Features of Systematic Theology

As to its features, systematic theology is, first of all, biblically thematic. It draws on biblical themes and the work of biblical theology. Second, systematic theology is comprehensive in that it looks to both the Bible and historical theology in the development of doctrine. Third, this discipline is normative, or prescriptive, of the Bible's teachings. Fourth, this theology is systematic; it presents biblical doctrine in an orderly manner. Fifth, systematic theology is contemporary, for it addresses current language and issues. While the truth does not change, how the preacher should articulate the truth in the face of new issues does change. Finally, systematic theology is practical, related to Christian living.[26] These features help describe systematic theology while pointing to its value in doctrinal exposition.

The Value of Systematic Theology for Doctrinal Exposition

Just as biblical theology is valuable for doctrinal expository preaching, systematic theology is as well. Lloyd-Jones speaks of the importance of systematic theology to preaching:

> To me there is nothing more important in a preacher than that he should have a systematic theology, that he should know it and be well grounded in it. This systematic theology, this body of truth which is derived from the Scripture, should always be present as a background and as a controlling influence in his preaching. Each message, which arises out of a particular text or statement of the Scripture, must always be a part or an aspect of this total body of truth. It is never something in isolation, never something separate or apart. The doctrine in a particular text, we must always remember, is a part of this greater whole—the Truth or the Faith. That is the meaning of the phrase 'comparing Scripture with Scripture'. We must not deal with any text in isolation; all our preparation of a sermon should be controlled by this background

---

[25]Wayne Grudem (*Systematic Theology: An Introduction to Biblical Doctrine* [Grand Rapids: Zondervan, 1994], 21) borrows this definition from John Frame. Systematics is synonymous with dogmatic theology.

[26]Samuel T. Logan, Jr., "Preaching and Systematic Theology," in *The Preacher and Preaching*, 248; Millard J. Erickson, *Christian Theology*, 2nd ed. (Grand Rapids: Baker Books, 1998), 23-24; David F. Wells, *No Place for Truth, or Whatever Happened to Evangelical Theology?* (Grand Rapids: Wm. B. Eerdmans, 1993), 97-106.

of systematic theology.[27]

Moreover, J. I. Packer writes,

> Theology helps the preacher as the coach helps the tennis player, grooming and extending his performance by introducing him to the range of strokes that can be made and drilling him in the art of making them correctly. As the coach is the embodiment of decades of experience in playing tennis, so theology is the embodiment of centuries of study, debate, and interpretative interaction as the church has sought to understand the Scriptures. One can play tennis after a fashion without ever having been coached, and one can preach from the Bible after a fashion without ever having encountered serious theology in a serious way. But, just as one is likely to play better with coaching, so one is likely to preach better—more perceptively, more searchingly, more fruitfully—when helped by theology; and so the preacher who is theologically competent will, other things being equal, be more use to the church.[28]

Even Jesus' Great Commission stresses the value of systematic theology for preaching. Within the command to make disciples of all the nations comes the task of teaching all of Christ's commands (Matt 28:19-20). Surely Christ's teachings include all of Scripture. As Wayne Grudem observes,

> The task of teaching all that Jesus commanded us is, in a broad sense, the task of teaching what the whole Bible says to us today. To effectively teach ourselves and to teach others what the whole Bible says, it is necessary to *collect* and *summarize* all the Scripture passages on a particular subject.[29]

Systematic theology is, therefore, valuable because it helps Christians carry out the Great Commission.

The Relationship between
Biblical Theology and Systematic Theology

It should be clear that a close relationship exists between biblical and systematic theology. One homiletician remarks on this connection:

> After the biblical theology has been discovered, but before the

---

[27]D. Martyn Lloyd-Jones, *Preaching & Preachers* (Grand Rapids: Zondervan, 1971), 66.

[28]J. I. Packer, "The Preacher as Theologian: Preaching and Systematic Theology," in *When God's Voice Is Heard*, 93.

[29]Grudem, *Systematic Theology*, 27.

theological product is articulated, the preacher must run his biblical theological conclusions through the lens of systematic theology in order to account for the theological truth of the passage in light of the progress of revelation.[30]

Furthermore, Rosner adds that

even if the Bible's storyline contains numerous subplots, its main story can be told, and often is with reference to major themes of *systematic theology* such as sin, salvation, and worship. Such topics act as centres around which the Bible's basic plot and message can be organized (emphasis mine).[31]

Simply put, biblical theology contributes to systematic theology and systematic theology borrows from biblical theology.

Contrast and comparison also highlights the relationship between these two disciplines. They differ in that systematic theology, unlike biblical theology, does not encourage the full exploration of the Bible's plot-lines. That is, biblical theology is a thematic approach to Scripture within biblical history and systematic theology is a topical approach to Scripture.[32] Moreover, systematic theology seeks to answer what Christians should believe *now* about some aspect of Christianity and results in Christian doctrine. Biblical theology, on the other hand, attempts to answer the process in which God *revealed* Himself and results in relating the whole Bible to the Christian life.[33] Further, systematic theology engages the culture with the Scriptures while biblical theology deals solely with the Scriptures. Finally, systematic theology is a culminating discipline and biblical theology is a bridge discipline.[34]

Even though these contrasts exist, one should be careful not to dismiss one of these disciplines in favor of the other, for there is a close connection. About this close relationship, Clowney claims that no opposition exists

between biblical theology and systematic or dogmatic theology, though the two are distinct. Systematic theology must draw from the results of biblical theology, and biblical theology must be aware of the broad perspectives of systematics. The two approaches

---

[30]Warren, "Paradigm for Preaching," 477.

[31]Rosner, "Biblical Theology," 9.

[32]Jensen, "Preaching the Whole Bible," 69.

[33]Goldsworthy, *According to Plan*, 30-32.

[34]Carson, "Systematic Theology and Biblical Theology," 103.

differ in the development of material. The development of systematics is strictly thematic or topical. . . . The development of biblical theology is redemptive-historical.[35]

This leads to the comparison of these two disciplines. Several view biblical theology and systematic theology as complementary, for biblical theology aims at exegesis of individual texts in light of the whole canon's doctrinal picture and systematic theology, working from the premise that the Scriptures are coherent, focuses on the main doctrines of the canon.[36] Both biblical and systematic theology also share the same authority base—the sacred Scriptures.[37] Furthermore, systematic theology builds on the work of biblical theology and, at times, even employs a biblical-theological method in analyzing doctrine's historical development. Ultimately, systematic theology aims at collecting all of the biblical data on a given subject (similar to biblical theology) in order to summarize the Scriptures' teaching.[38]

Consequently, employing both biblical and systematic theology enhances doctrinal expository preaching. Indeed, without one or the other, doctrinal exposition suffers from malnourishment. With both forces, however, doctrinal exposition seeks to divide the biblical text accurately (2 Tim 2:15)—biblical theology—and to declare its teachings comprehensively (Acts 20:27)—systematic theology. Now we are ready to take spiritual bodybuilding to another level.

---

[35]Clowney, *Preaching and Biblical Theology*, 16.

[36]"The reason why Grudem thinks it is possible to organize a systematic theology from almost any point is precisely because in his view the truth behind theology—which theology is meant to discover and expound—is so superbly coherent that the internal ties will eventually take you to the whole anyway" (D. A. Carson, "Domesticating the Gospel: A Review of Stanley J. Grenz's *Renewing the Center*," *The Southern Baptist Journal of Theology* 6, no. 4 [2002]: 96).

[37]Carson, "Systematic Theology and Biblical Theology," 102. For more on the contrasts between biblical and systematic theology, see Goldsworthy, *Preaching the Whole Bible*, 26. Allen's distinctions between systematic theology and doctrine appear to be between systematics and a mixture of biblical and historical theology (see Ronald J. Allen, *Preaching Is Believing: The Sermon as Theological Reflection* [Louisville: Westminster John Knox Press, 2002], 12-15).

[38]Grudem, *Systematic Theology*, 23.

CHAPTER 11
DERIVING DOCTRINE FROM A PASSAGE OF SCRIPTURE: DEVELOPING A REGULAR ROUTINE

Equipped with the tools of biblical and systematic theology, the preacher is ready to do some theological digging. The theological exegesis of a biblical text may possibly be the most neglected phase in the sermon preparation process. Due to factors ranging from theological disinterest to a lack in theological training to theological illiteracy, many preachers simply do not take the extra time to mine the biblical text for all of its rich resources, especially the doctrinal substance. Once the preacher resolves to put in the extra time, he can, with disciplined effort, derive doctrine from any passage of Scripture.[1] Rosner rightly claims, "Not to attend to theological interpretation is to stop short of interpretation, to ignore the interests of the texts themselves."[2] Furthermore, such theological interpretation is necessary because many commentaries are void of theological discussion, focusing instead on insignificant issues.[3] Both discipline and effort are essential in faithfully deriving doctrine from Scripture. Put simply, all of the exercises done up to this point may end up as vanity unless a regular routine for long-term growth occurs.

---

[1]Just as Merrill F. Unger argues that a preacher can expound any passage through proper exegesis (*Principles of Expository Preaching* [Grand Rapids: Zondervan, 1955], 237-52), so I argue that an expositor can preach any passage doctrinally with theological exegesis.

[2]Brian Rosner, "Biblical Theology," in *New Dictionary of Biblical Theology: Exploring the Unity & Diversity of Scripture* [*NDBT*], ed. T. Desmond Alexander and others (Downers Grove: InterVarsity Press, 2000), 4.

[3]See Brevard S. Childs, *Biblical Theology in Crisis* (Philadelphia: Westminster, 1970), 142-46.

General Principles for Theological Interpretation
As to biblical interpretation, the different literary genres affect meaning. At the same time, several *universal* principles stand out for interpreting any text theologically, regardless of genre. Theological interpretation is clearly an aspect of exegesis, as Stephen and David Olford contend:

> Study or investigation should take into account: (1) the historical and literary settings of the text; (2) the syntactical and verbal specifics of the text; and (3) the *doctrinal and theological significance* of the text (emphasis mine).[4]

Therefore, preachers would be wise to employ these principles early in their exegetical work.[5]

Observing the Redemptive-Historical Context
First, the theological interpretation "must always begin by finding the immediate theological horizon and then relating that to the broader biblical-theological perspectives."[6] This step helps place the text within the larger

---

[4]Stephen F. Olford and David L. Olford, *Anointed Expository Preaching* (Nashville: Broadman & Holman, 1998), 104.

[5]This theological process will yield a theological product, which serves as the basis for the homiletical process (see also appendix 1). For ways in which self-conscious attention to doctrine in sermon preparation contributes to preaching, see Mark Ellingsen, "Doctrine," in *Concise Encyclopedia of Preaching*, ed. William H. Willimon and Richard Lischer (Louisville: Westminster John Knox Press, 1995), 103-04. On a different note, an assumption of this section is that interpreters are already employing the basic rules of hermeneutics in light of the different genres. For basic guides to hermeneutics, see Gordon D. Fee and Douglas Stuart, *How to Read the Bible for All Its Worth: A Guide to Understanding the Bible*, 2nd ed. (Grand Rapids: Zondervan, 1993); Robert H. Stein, *A Basic Guide to Interpreting the Bible: Playing by the Rules* (Grand Rapids: Baker Books, 1994); Robert Plummer, *40 Questions about Interpreting the Bible* (Grand Rapids: Kregel, 2010). For a more technical, advanced approach, see Grant R. Osbourne, *The Hermeneutical Spiral: A Comprehensive Introduction to Biblical Interpretation* (Downers Grove: InterVarsity, 1991).

[6]Edmund P. Clowney, *Preaching and Biblical Theology* (Grand Rapids: Eerdmans, 1961), 92. Ibid., 89. See also Graeme Goldsworthy, *Preaching the Whole Bible as Christian Scripture: The Application of Biblical Theology to Expository Preaching* (Grand Rapids: Eerdmans, 2000), 69, 137. Ronald J. Allen offers similar criteria for theological interpretation, but his critical presuppositions leads him to dismiss any notion of absolute truth in the text (*Preaching Is Believing: The Sermon as Theological Reflection* [Louisville:

framework of redemptive history. Greidanus comments,

> Redemptive history is the mighty river that runs from the old covenant to the new and holds the two together. It is true, of course, that there is progression in redemptive history, but it is one redemptive history. It is true that there is an old covenant and a new covenant, but it is one covenant of grace. It is true that the sacrifice of Christ brought an end to Old Testament worship with its blood sacrifices, but Christians are still required to bring sacrifices to the same God. Progression in redemptive history takes place within the continuity of a single redemptive history.[7]

Related to this redemptive-historical approach is the Person and work of Jesus Christ—the link between the two testaments. T. C. Vriezen claims that Christ

> is the creator of the events of which the New Testament is full and thus the head of the new community of the Kingdom of God. In this way there is a fundamental connection between the two Testaments in the person of Jesus Christ.[8]

The role of Jesus Christ, thus, becomes a major interpretive principle for theological exegesis.

A common objection to this interpretive principle is that while the New Testament clearly revolves around the Person of Christ, the Old Testament has its own hermeneutical issues apart from the New Testament.[9] While there is great profit in understanding an OT text the way

---

Westminster John Knox Press, 2002], 51-58).

[7]Sidney Greidanus, *Preaching Christ from the Old Testament: A Contemporary Hermeneutical Method* (Grand Rapids: Eerdmans, 1999), 48. The groundwork for Greidanus' more recent works on the redemptive-historical approach to interpretation is his *Sola Scriptura: Problems and Principles in Preaching Historical Texts* (Kampen, Netherlands: J. H. Kok, 1970).

[8]T. C. Vriezen, *An Outline of Old Testament Theology*, rev. ed., trans. S. Neuijen (Oxford: Basil Blackwell, 1970), 123.

[9]Walter C. Kaiser, Jr. at times, leans toward a non-Christological approach in his discussions on interpreting an OT passage in its original setting, focusing on authorial intent without proper concern for the bigger picture of Authorial intent (see *Toward an Exegetical Theology: Biblical Exegesis for Preaching and Teaching* [Grand Rapids: Baker Books, 1981], 17-66). Elsewhere, however, Kaiser claims that the OT leads people to Jesus the Messiah (Kaiser, *Preaching and Teaching from the Old Testament: A Guide for the Church* [Grand Rapids: Baker Books, 2003], 20-23). For a clear Christocentric approach to OT interpretation, see Goldsworthy, *According to Plan: The Unfolding Revelation of*

a Jew might have in the ancient era, it seems contemporary *Christian* preaching must interpret the OT in light of Christ's completed work in redemptive history, otherwise today's preaching of the OT may quickly become Judaistic, legalistic, and futile.

This hermeneutical method of bringing out the Christ-centered message in the Bible is none other than the redemptive-historical approach to biblical interpretation. Perhaps no contemporary writer has articulated this position as well as Sidney Greidanus in *Preaching Christ from the Old Testament*. In describing his view of the "redemptive-historical christocentric method," Greidanus says,

> The christocentric method complements the theocentric method of interpreting the Old Testament by seeking to do justice to the fact that God's story of bringing his kingdom on earth is centered in Christ: Christ the center of redemptive history, Christ the center of the Scriptures.[10]

Employing this method, Greidanus offers seven ways to interpret and to preach Christ from the Old Testament. A summary of three of the most important of these methods follows.

First, and most important for this study, is the way of redemptive-historical progression. This approach

> sees every Old Testament text and its addressees in the context of God's dynamic history, which progresses steadily and reaches its climax in the life, death, and resurrection of Jesus Christ and ultimately in the new creation.[11]

This interpretive principle uses biblical theology well, for it "focuses on the core of redemptive history in Christ."[12]

Second, and closely related, is the way of promise-fulfillment. This way "is embedded in redemptive history, for God gives his promises at one stage of redemptive history and brings them to fulfillment in subsequent

---

God in the Bible (Downers Grove: InterVarsity Press, 1991), 49-51; idem, *Preaching the Whole Bible*, 1-7, 115-27.

[10]Greidanus, *Preaching Christ from the OT*, 227.

[11]Ibid., 237. For the complete treatment and examples from Scripture, see ibid., 203-25, 234-77. Besides the three approaches above, Greidanus labels the other four as the ways of analogy, longitudinal themes, contrast, and New Testament reference. See also David L. Larsen, *The Anatomy of Preaching: Identifying the Issues in Preaching Today* (Grand Rapids: Baker Book House, 1989), 166-67.

[12]Clowney, *Preaching and Biblical Theology*, 78.

stages."[13] Moreover, only when one interprets the promise structure of the OT as fulfilled in Christ can his preaching of the OT have theological depth.[14]

Third, the way of typology is a common interpretive method. Although some preachers take typology to the extremes, most agree that the Bible contains a typology structure which tracks God's work in history up through the work of Christ.[15] Expositors will find these methods helpful in theological interpretation of the OT.

Asking Theological Questions

In addition to setting a text within redemptive history, the preacher should also ask himself a number of questions of each passage, beginning with "What does the passage teach about God?" Haddon Robinson claims that "every passage has a vision of God, such as God as Creator or Sustainer."[16] Additionally, the interpreter needs to ask, "What is the depravity factor? What in humanity rebels against that vision of God?"[17] A more general question to ask is "what aspects of Christian doctrine does this text prompt [me] to consider?"[18] These questions are crucial in determining the

---

[13]Greidanus, *Preaching Christ from the OT*, 206. Kaiser prefers to call this interpretive method the promise-plan of God. He views 1 Peter 1:3-12 and the "so great a salvation" as the best substantial claim to this method. Moreover, the Scriptures everywhere attest to God carrying out His promises, much of which has roots in Genesis 12:3 (*Preaching and Teaching*, 31-33).

[14]Clowney, "Preaching Christ," 166-83.

[15]See Greidanus, *Preaching Christ from the OT*, 212-13; Goldsworthy, *According to Plan*, 59.

[16]Haddon W. Robinson, "The Heresy of Application," *Leadership* 18, no. 4 (1997): 24. See also Hershael W. York and Bert Decker, *Preaching with Bold Assurance: A Solid and Enduring Approach to Engaging Exposition* (Nashville: Broadman & Holman, 2003), 75.

[17]Robinson, "Heresy," 24. Answering these questions helps translate the exegetical idea into the homiletical idea via the theological idea (see Steven D. Mathewson, *The Art of Preaching Old Testament Narrative* [Grand Rapids: Baker Books, 2002], 83-84).

[18]Allen, *Preaching Is Believing*, 105. Cf. William Muehl, *Why Preach? Why Listen?* (Philadelphia: Fortress Press, 1986), 16. Similar advice comes from Robert G. Hughes and Robert Kysar, *Preaching Doctrine: For the Twenty-First Century* (Minneapolis: Fortress Press, 1997), 39-48. The main weakness in the

theological meaning of a text.

Other related questions to theological interpretation are what does the text say? What are the text's concerns? What do contemporary listeners have in common with the original audience? According to Bryan Chapell, the answers to these questions help determine the Fallen Condition Focus (FCF) of the passage, making sure the expositor grounds the sermon in the intent of the divine Author.[19]

Furthermore, a preacher needs to ask certain key theological questions of the text. Some of these questions include

> How does this text fit into the progressive revelation that God gives in the Bible? Is it related to any major biblical themes? Is its theme one in which there is significant development between the OT and NT? What relationship does it have to the gospel? How does the gospel form a context for it? How does it relate to the revelation of Jesus Christ, to the promise or the fulfillment? Is it used or interpreted elsewhere in the Bible? In which major theological category does it occur, e.g. promise, law, prophecy, wisdom, instruction, blessing, curse, people of God, gospel?[20]

Answering such questions helps keep the preacher focused on doctrinal content.

---

approach by Hughes and Kysar is their failure to see the authority of the Bible, for they note that the Bible may present "faulty theology," when preachers are then "called to preach *against a text*" (ibid., 45-46). Obviously, one may want to preach against the theology of (say) the Sadducees, but Hughes's and Kysar's proposal clearly takes issue with biblical authority.

[19]Bryan Chapell, *Christ-Centered Preaching: Redeeming the Expository Sermon* (Grand Rapids: Baker Books, 1994), 43. Chapell defines the FCF as "*the mutual human condition that contemporary believers share with those to or for whom the text was written that requires the grace of the passage*" (ibid., 42). For a more complete treatment of discerning the FCF within redemptive exposition, see Chapell, *Christ-Centered Preaching*, 263-312.

[20]Peter J. H. Adam, "Preaching and Biblical Theology," in *NDBT*, 108. With specific regard to Christ-centered interpretation, the preacher should ask himself about each text, "What does this passage mean in the light of Jesus Christ? And what does this passage reveal about Jesus Christ?" as well as specific questions concerning each of the seven ways of employing the Christocentric method (Greidanus, *Preaching Christ from the OT*, 232-33). See also Warren W. Wiersbe, *Preaching & Teaching with Imagination: The Quest for Biblical Ministry* (Grand Rapids: Baker Books, 1994), 248.

Observing the Inter-Canonical Relationship

A third general principle for theological interpretation concerns the relationship between the OT and the NT. If beginning with a NT theme, the student will do well to consider its relationship to the central tenets of the gospel. At the same time, if beginning in the OT, checking for direct quotations and allusions in the NT should enable interpretation.[21] Such an approach employs the entire focus of biblical theology.

The Analogy of Faith

Finally, the analogy of faith aids in interpreting Scripture theologically. Although one particular text may touch on a doctrine, other passages of Scripture may help in understanding it more fully. The Westminster Confession states,

> The infallible rule of interpretation of Scripture is the Scripture itself; and therefore, when there is a question about the true and full sense of any Scripture (which is not manifold, but one), it must be searched and known by other places that speak more clearly."[22]

When employing the analogy of Scripture, Kaiser claims that it is most valid to compare Scripture only with *antecedent* Scripture—thus, keeping the interpreter focused on the antecedent theology of a text. Clues to determining this antecedent theology include terms which have taken on special meaning, a reference or allusion to a prior event in progressive revelation, and references to a covenant or promise.[23]

Cox wisely comments on the significance of the analogy of faith: "Many heresies or occasions for controversy through the ages could have been avoided if every interpretation of scripture had been subjected to the test of total scripture."[24] On this note, Stephen and David Olford caution against forcing one's theology onto the text:

> One's theology will impact what is viewed as essential, significant, purposeful, intentional, and meaningful within the text. We grant

---

[21]Goldsworthy, *Preaching the Whole Bible*, 246. See also William Perkins, *The Art of Prophesying; With the Calling of the Ministry* (Cambridge: J. Legatt, 1592; reprint, Carlisle, PA: The Banner of Truth Trust, 1996), 26-29.

[22]"The Westminster Confession of Faith" 1.9, 57, in *Creeds of the Church*, in The Master Christian Library, version 5 [CD-ROM] (Albany, OR: AGES Software, 1997).

[23]Kaiser, *Toward an Exegetical Theology*, 136-37, 161-62.

[24]James W. Cox, *Preaching: A Comprehensive Approach to the Design & Delivery of Sermons* (Nashville: Seminary Extension, 1993), 66.

that. And yet, the careful exegetical-theological preacher will seek for *real indicators within the text* that express priority truths and emphases. These textual emphases need to be viewed in order to express the doctrine and theology of the text, rather than simply imposing a theological framework on the text. The goal is exposition of the truth(s) that is intrinsic to and intentionally expressed by the text.[25]

When comparing Scripture with Scripture, the interpreter would do well to practice the following guidelines (the first four are general and the last is specific):

1. An obscure passage gives way to a clear one.
2. The most secure doctrines are those which are treated often in and throughout various parts of Scripture.
3. Even though an apparent contradiction of two biblical doctrines exists, one should accept both.
4. Lengthy and systematic passages of a particular doctrine should clarify brief passages of the same doctrine, especially if it is an allusion.
5. The NT is the norm for interpreting the OT.[26]

In addition to these basic hermeneutical guidelines for theological exegesis, one needs to consider the form of the biblical text. Although the preacher can extract doctrine from any portion of Scripture, the literary genre of each passage will most certainly affect the means by which it is extracted. Therefore, principles for theological interpretation of the various biblical genres are in order.

Observing Specific Literary Genre

As argued in chapter 5, expository preaching allows the Bible to have both the first and final say in the message. For preaching to be as closely connected to the Bible as possible, the Scriptures must determine both the substance and the shape of the sermon. Don Wardlaw's *Preaching Biblically* in 1983 grabbed the attention of many homileticians to consider a sermon's shape.[27] Similarly, Fred Craddock argues for variety in sermon presentation,

---

[25]Olford and Olford, *Anointed Expository Preaching*, 127.

[26]The origin of these guidelines came from a classroom lecture by Roy Zuck as noted in Daniel Akin, "The Ministry of Proclamation: Book 1" (The Southern Baptist Theological Seminary, 2002), sec. 14, 19-21. See also Olford and Olford, *Anointed Expository Preaching*, 126-38.

[27]Don M. Wardlaw, ed., *Preaching Biblically: Creating Sermons in the Shape of Scripture* (Philadelphia: Westminster Press, 1983).

> Why should the multitude of forms and moods within the Biblical literature and the multitudes of needs in the congregation be brought together in one unvarying [preaching] mold, and that copied from Greek rhetoricians of centuries ago? An unnecessary monotony results, but more profoundly, there is an inner conflict between the content of the sermon and its form.[28]

Likewise, well-known expositor Warren Wiersbe states that biblical preaching "means much more than to preach the truth of the Bible accurately. It also means *to present that truth the way the biblical writers and speakers presented it.*"[29]

Greidanus may argue this point most clearly:

> When the text is a narrative, we should seriously consider using a narrative form that follows the story line of the text rather than the standard didactic form which imposes its own structure on the text. Or when the text is a lament Psalm, we should consider following the form of the Psalm through its various moves from calling upon God, to description of distress, to complaint against God, to petitions to God for help, to professions of trust, to final praise. Or when the text aims to teach, we should consider following its major affirmations to its conclusion to convey its meaning. The point is, in expository preaching we should not only expose the meaning of the text but also the form and structure that convey this meaning.[30]

The Scriptures' shape varies among numerous literary genres. Since genre affects interpretation and interpretation affects preaching, the literary genres of the Bible demand a closer look. Not only is the Bible the result of God's revelation to some forty different human authors, but it also consists of several literary genres. Some of the most common genres are narrative, poetry, prophecy, wisdom, didactic, and apocalyptic. This section will observe the interpretative guidelines needed for deriving doctrine from a particular kind of biblical text. To follow the analogy of preaching for bodybuilding, you can think of the following areas as using different kinds

---

[28]Fred B. Craddock, *As One without Authority: Essays on Inductive Preaching* (Enid, OK: Phillips University Press, 1971), 25-26. Ibid., 45.

[29]Warren W. Wiersbe, *Preaching and Teaching with Imagination: The Quest for Biblical Ministry* (Grand Rapids: Baker Books, 1994), 36.

[30]Greidanus, *Preaching Christ from the OT*, 290. See also Greidanus, *The Modern Preacher and the Ancient Text: Interpreting and Preaching Biblical Literature* (Grand Rapids: Wm. B. Eerdmans, 1988), 141-56. For a more recent treatment of this issue, see Jeffrey D. Arthurs, *Preaching with Variety: How to Re-create the Dynamics of Biblical Genres* (Grand Rapids: Kregel, 2007).

of weights.

Narrative

Without a doubt, the most common genre in the Bible is narrative. Kaiser writes, "According to one way of counting, narrative could make up half of the corpus of both testaments."[31] Other, more conservative, estimates attribute one-third of the Scriptures to narrative.[32] Either way, the narrative sections of God's Word are so frequent that anyone trying to avoid preaching on them is like a driver attempting to dodge potholes on a country road in desperate need of re-pavement—sooner or later the two will meet!

In order to understand narrative for doctrinal exposition, preachers should follow a few guidelines in deriving doctrine from a narrative text.[33] First and foremost, the interpreter must seek to determine the narrative's teaching about God. Goldsworthy contends, "The story is never complete in itself and belongs as part of the one big story of salvation culminating in Jesus Christ."[34] This argument is important, because narrative genre can become anthropocentric rather than theocentric, if one is not careful. Fee and Stuart observe,

> Bible narratives tell us about things that happened—but not just any things. Their purpose is to show God at work in his creation and among his people. The narratives glorify him, help us to understand and appreciate him, and give us a picture of his providence and protection.[35]

This theocentric purpose of narratives runs throughout all the Old Testament as the following quotation supports:

> A striking feature of all the historical books proper is that they emphasize the activity of the Lord in bringing about His divine purpose: He punished those who disobey Him and blesses those who worship Him (Deut.), if people pray to Him and trust in Him

---

[31]Kaiser, *Preaching and Teaching*, 63.

[32]David C. Deuel, "Suggestions for Expositional Preaching of Old Testament Narrative," *The Master's Seminary Journal* 2, no. 1 (1991): 47.

[33]For a more detailed approach to this task, see Millard J. Erickson and James L. Heflin, *Old Wine in New Wineskins: Doctrinal Preaching in a Changing World* (Grand Rapids: Baker Books, 1997), 124-31.

[34]Goldsworthy, *Preaching the Whole Bible*, 150.

[35]Fee and Stuart, *How to Read the Bible*, 79.

their enemies are virtually impotent (Chronicles, Ezra-Nehemiah), what the prophets preach, happens (Kings) and what Yahweh promises (to the patriarchs or David) is fulfilled (Genesis-Joshua and Samuel).[36]

Second, readers will need to observe the author's purpose for the history. Certain details may be important here, such as Ruth's inclusion in the canon as a time of transition from the period of judges to the hopeful reign of David, or John's Gospel account as a selection of Jesus' signs in order to get people to believe Jesus is the Messiah, the Son of God, so that they might have life in Him. Such details can provide clues to theological interpretation.[37]

Third, one must identify each key character and determine whether he is a believer or unbeliever. This identification will help put the theological teaching in the proper perspective. Fourth, when dealing with God's action, one should ask what presupposes that action. God's wrath being poured out on people presupposes ongoing sin, and His redemption presumes His grace and election. Fifth, readers ought to see how the characters within the passage interpret the event. They may have special insight or they may be completely unaware of the bigger picture.

Sixth, the preacher can refer to the rest of Scripture to see if it provides an interpretation or analysis of the story elsewhere. A New Testament epistle may shed light on the doctrinal significance, such as Paul's explanation of Abraham's seed in Galatians 3-4. Seventh, discernment of divine approval or disapproval, if possible, may underscore actions to emulate or avoid. Finally, the interpreter needs to make sure he distinguishes between timeless principles and culture-specific principles. The best way to determine the timeless principle is to consider the entire development of the story-line.[38]

---

[36]I. H. Eybers, "Some Remarks Concerning the Composition of the Historical Books of the Old Testament," in *De Fructu Oris Sui: Essays in Honor of Adrianus Van Selms*, ed. I. H. Eybers and others (Leiden, Netherlands: E. J. Brill, 1971), 45. For related purposes in preaching narrative, see Greidanus, *Modern Preacher*, 220.

[37]Eugene H. Merrill, "History," in *Cracking Old Testament Codes: Interpreting the Literary Genres of the Old Testament*, ed. D. Brent Sandy and Ronald L. Giese, Jr. (Nashville: Broadman & Holman, 1995), 91, 104-06. Although much of the Bible's narrative history springs from the OT, the Book of Acts fits this category from the NT (Fee and Stuart, *How to Read the Bible*, 108-12).

[38]Deuel, "Suggestions for Expositional Preaching," 53. See also note 83 in

Torah

Torah stands out in certain sections of the Pentateuch. Intermixed with historical narrative, Torah provides instructions for Israelite living. In certain cases, Torah remains a part of the Christian life.

To interpret Torah theologically, one should begin by relating the law to God's promise and personal faith. Since God's promises (see Gen 3:15; 9:27; 12:1-3) preceded the law, one should interpret any response to the law in the larger context of God's promise-plan. Furthermore, the Pentateuch's focus on individual faith and obedience may highlight the purpose of the law as instruction toward faith rather than a strict keeping of the law.[39]

Second, one needs to note the style of the law. Recognizing the features of apodictic and casuistic law aids the preaching of law. The former is unconditional, imperative, and general (such as the Ten Commandments). The latter is conditional, declarative, and specific (such as certain civil laws). Third, preachers should check to see if the New Testament repeats the law in a way that is binding on the Christian.[40] While ceremonial and civil laws do not necessarily carry over from the OT to the Christian, the moral law is certainly still in effect.[41]

Poetry

Poetry often consists of either praise or lament, so the interpretation of poetry in general applies to each. Concerning praise one should distinguish between descriptive and declarative praise. The former praises God for who He is and the latter for what He does.[42] Furthermore, if possible, the reader should try to set the psalm in its historical setting, which may shed light on the reason the psalmist offered the praise. Psalm 51, for example, makes much more sense in light of David's sin with Bathsheba. Finally, identifying spiritual principles that apply to all times and settings will help the homiletical task.[43]

---

chapter 5 below.

[39]Kaiser, *Preaching and Teaching*, 140-44.

[40]Richard E. Averbeck, "Law," in *Cracking OT Codes*, 130-31.

[41]For a more complete treatment of the Law and the Christian, see Mark F. Rooker, *Leviticus*, The New American Commentary, vol. 3a (Nashville: Broadman & Holman, 2000), 65-77.

[42]Kaiser, *Preaching and Teaching*, 153.

[43]Kenneth L. Barker, "Praise," in *Cracking OT Codes*, 225-28.

Interpreting the lament needs to consider the specific theological teaching of the lament, especially what it teaches about God or people's relationship to Him.[44] Moreover, the reason for the lament is usually found in the *ki*-clause, providing the focal point and main lesson of the lament.[45] The main lesson should clue the interpreter in on the doctrinal teaching.

Wisdom

Most interpreters divide this genre into two groups—Proverbs and non-proverbial wisdom. The reader must first distinguish between proverb and promise. Proverbs tend to be the general rule of thumb rather than ironclad promises. Second, preachers need to bear in mind the entire Old Testament context, especially the context of the wisdom literature. Creation, human experience, and immorality are common themes in the wisdom tradition, pointing readers to the theological meaning. Third, one should look for the particular truth of the proverb by looking for pairs or strings of proverbs. Although the arrangement of many proverbs is non-thematic, many concepts occur elsewhere in wisdom literature. Comparing proverbs on the same subject can shed light on the theological meaning.[46]

Prophecy

Two main subgenres of prophecy are oracles of salvation and announcements of judgment. For theological interpretation, the reader should, first of all, check to see if the prophetic words are unconditional or conditional.[47] This evaluation will prove valuable for the sermon. Second, noting any assurances of promise or blessing to God's earlier revelation will help determine the universal principle. Third, the preacher should evaluate the whole issue of prophecy and fulfillment. He will want to explain those prophecies which have been fulfilled in the falls of Israel and Judah, in the restoration to the land of promise, and, ultimately, in the Messiah within the larger frame of redemptive history.[48]

Fourth, preachers should interpret prophetic oracles from the transformation perspective, for God is at work in creating things "new"—a

---

[44]Tremper Longman III, "Lament," in *Cracking OT Codes*, 208-10.

[45]Kaiser, *Preaching and Teaching*, 138.

[46]See Ted A. Hildebrandt, "Proverb," and Andrew E. Hill, "Non-Proverbial Wisdom," in *Cracking OT Codes*, 248-49, and 273-76, respectively.

[47]Kaiser, *Preaching and Teaching*, 102, 111-12.

[48]See Greidanus, *Modern Preacher*, 256-58.

new people, a new Davidic King, a new earth. Finally, interpreters need to evaluate prophecies concerning Christ in light of His initial coming or His second coming. Such an evaluation points either to the completed work of Christ in the past or eschatological hope/warning for the future.[49]

Gospel

The Gospel genre consists of a collage of other literary features, including historical-narrative, law, wisdom, prophecy, and poetry. Thus, preachers must evaluate each context appropriately. When interpreting the Gospels, the reader must remember to keep Jesus Christ central. Even though the Gospel writers introduce a number of supporting cast members, the message is still the good news about God in Christ Jesus. Further, the entire canon serves as the broadest context for the Gospels and one must not miss Jesus' role in redemptive history.[50] Simply put, a person can only truly understand Jesus' life and ministry in light of the Old Testament.

Jesus' multi-faceted ministry of preaching, teaching and healing serves to highlight certain Christological themes: Son of Man, Son of David, Son of God, great "I am," Son of Abraham, God incarnate, Suffering Servant, etc. Although the Gospel accounts also cover related issues of theology proper, pneumatology, and hamartiology, interpreters should give special attention to the Christological and soteriological themes.

A few instructions are necessary on the theological interpretation of parables.[51] Obviously, if Jesus provides an interpretation of the parable, the reader will want to focus on the main doctrinal issue, which has to do with some aspect of the kingdom of God. Additionally, the audience hearing the parable in its original context plays a *huge* role in determining theological meaning. The audience may be disciples, religious leaders, normal crowds, a mixture of different people, or anonymous (in which case, the reader will need to consider the context in the Gospel). Also, issues which receive the most space in the parable and the ending of each parable emphasize the

---

[49]See William A. VanGemeren, "Oracles of Salvation," and Trent C. Butler, "Announcements of Judgments," in *Cracking OT Codes*, 146-52, and 166-68, respectively. For general theological implications from each of the Writing Prophets, see Gary V. Smith, *The Prophets as Preachers: An Introduction to the Hebrew Prophets* (Nashville: Broadman & Holman, 1994).

[50]Greidanus, *Modern Preacher*, 305-06.

[51]For basic guidelines for interpreting parables, see Stein, *Basic Guide to Interpreting*, 137-50; Fee and Stuart, *How to Read the Bible*, 135-48. Parables also exist throughout the OT but I cover them here because of people's familiarity with Jesus' parables.

basic point of the parable, pointing the reader to its theological focus.

Epistle

The epistles serve as the bulk of theological discourse about the gospel message. Because of its didactic nature, deriving doctrine from this genre comes quite easily in comparison to other genres. The main principle of theological interpretation is for the preacher to concentrate more on the doctrinal argument rather than the peculiarities of each letter. With regards to Paul's writings, his concern tends to be God's grace in Christ, the cross of Christ, the resurrection, faith in Christ, obedience to Christ, and Jesus' second coming. Therefore, preachers should evaluate everything Paul says with respect to his Christocentric viewpoint.[52]

Apocalyptic

Apocalyptic literature, usually a subgenre of prophecy, is by far the most mysterious and the most difficult genre to interpret. Goldsworthy humorously speaks of this mysterious genre: "What is an apocalypse? It seems that an apocalypse is what scholars and other experts decide to refer to as an apocalypse!"[53] Found in both the Old and New Testaments, apocalyptic literature is extremely popular among some Christians (Hal Lindsey, Tim LaHaye, and many dispensationalists) and almost a foreign thought among others (many amillennialists). Even though apocalyptic literature is mysterious, a few observations stand out that will aid theological interpretation. First, these

> writings proclaim a message that rests solidly upon the central confessions of Yahwistic and, especially, prophetic faith. Accordingly, the God of Israel is portrayed as a just and compassionate God who will not forsake the faithful and who will steadfastly guide history according to divine purpose. . . . Second, it is important to interpret the apocalyptic writings within the context of the Bible as a whole, so that the important lines of connection with other types of biblical literature become apparent and the specific contributions of each section of the Bible become clear.[54]

As with all the Scriptures, preachers must approach the apocalyptic writings with humility and awe before the majesty and glory of God. With this attitude toward Scripture, the reader should begin by setting the

---

[52]Greidanus, *Modern Preacher*, 332.

[53]Goldsworthy, *Preaching the Whole Bible*, 218.

[54]Paul D. Hanson, *Old Testament Apocalyptic* (Nashville: Abingdon Press, 1987), 42-43.

apocalyptic passages in their historical setting before placing them in the wider picture. Certain historical factors may clue the reader in on the prophet's intention.[55] Second, readers must avoid interpreting all of the metaphors in apocalyptic literature. Those who see great significance behind every figurative detail are in danger of missing the meaning. Third, interpreters are wise to keep several options open as to the fulfillment of prophecy within the apocalyptic genre. Date-setters and identifiers of the Antichrist often end up looking foolish while lacking integrity as *truth-tellers*. Preachers need to remember that confessing "I don't know" about the mysterious is both honest and valid.[56] Finally, readers need to clarify the main point of the apocalyptic text. Although all of the details must wait until Christ's return, faithful interpreters can glean and apply the main doctrinal message.[57] The ultimate goal in interpreting apocalyptic literature theologically is "to assure that these writings mediate God's Word and to awaken modern listeners to God's presence today as they did in biblical times."[58]

All of these general and specific observations aid the interpreter in his pursuit of theological meaning. This entire theological process results in a theological product, which is the doctrinal teaching of a particular text. This product is valuable in the homiletical process in communicating biblical doctrine via the sermon and for strengthening spiritual lives.

---

[55]Goldsworthy, *Preaching the Whole Bible*, 214.

[56]Though uttered centuries ago, Irenaeus' advice on this issue remains sound. Commenting on the number of the mark of the beast, he states that it is "more certain, and less hazardous, to await the fulfillment of the prophecy, than to be making surmises, and casting about for any names that may present themselves, inasmuch as many names can be found possessing the number mentioned; and the same question will, after all, remain unsolved" (Irenaeus, *Against Heresies*, in The Ante-Nicene Fathers: Translations of the Writings of the Fathers Down to A. D. 325, vol. 1, ed. Alexander Roberts and James Donaldson, in The Master's Christian Library [CD-ROM] [Albany, OR: Ages Software, 1997], 1121).

[57]See D. Brent Sandy and Martin G. Abegg, Jr., "Apocalyptic," in *Cracking OT Codes*, 188-90.

[58]Hanson, *OT Apocalyptic*, 61.

CHAPTER 12
HOMILETICAL METHODOLOGY FOR DOCTRINAL EXPOSITION: BUILDING MUSCLE MASS

Now that the preacher-interpreter has an approach to deriving doctrine from a passage of Scripture, he needs to transform the theological exegesis into homiletical form. This transition begins with some general principles for the sermon's focus and form. The transformation does not end there, however, for true exposition applies the genre to the sermon's shape. Further, the preacher must take the exegetical and theological idea and state it in terms of the sermon. This discipline moves beyond toning your spiritual muscles and establishing a regular routine, for it builds muscle mass to go deeper in your workout, exercising both upper and lower muscles to provide a well-rounded workout.

General Principles for Keeping the Homiletical Form Doctrinally Focused

Although discussions on sermon structure and outlines are found in many traditional textbooks on preaching,[1] a few general observations will help in

---

[1]See Bryan Chapell, *Christ-Centered Preaching: Redeeming the Expository Sermon* (Grand Rapids: Baker Books, 1994, 2005), 127-59; Haddon W. Robinson, *Biblical Preaching: The Development and Delivery of Expository Messages*, 2nd ed. (Grand Rapids: Baker Academic, 2001), 115-37; Stephen F. Olford and David L. Olford, *Anointed Expository Preaching* (Nashville: Broadman & Holman, 1998), 139-55; Jerry Vines and Jim Shaddix, *Power in the Pulpit: How to Prepare and Deliver Expository Sermons* (Chicago: Moody Press, 1999), 143-71; Hershael W. York and Bert Decker, *Preaching with Bold Assurance: A Solid and Enduring Approach to Engaging Exposition* (Nashville: Broadman & Holman, 2003), 103-46. For a number of possibilities in outlining, see Hugh

doctrinal exposition. These principles will help guide the preacher in transforming the product from theological interpretation into the sermon. First, the preacher must set the biblical text and message in the larger context of the single message of the Bible. Though this point has been repeated throughout this chapter, the reader must not forget it. A word of caution is in order here: the doctrinal expositor must be patient in leading a congregation to understand the details of Scripture in relation to the whole message. Consistency and perseverance are absolutely necessary for a preacher to declare "the whole counsel of God."

Second, the most biblical way to expound exposition of the theological product is to preach with a Christocentric undergirding. Many times, this approach results in direct Christocentric preaching, where OT and NT alike proclaim and magnify Christ. In some cases, like preaching on the Song of Solomon, there needs to be a Christ-centered basis that teaches biblical sexuality as God-glorifying and Christ-honoring.[2] All of this is to say that, no matter what the passage is, the sermon's focus should reflect the Bible's focus and point people to understand the Bible's message about God's plan in Christ. Part 3 showed that NT preaching continually emphasizes the gospel of God in Christ. Regarding this feature, Greidanus writes,

> Christocentric preaching is the preaching of God's acts from the perspective of the New Testament. In other words, Christocentric preaching requires that a passage receive a theocentric interpretation not only in its own (Old Testament) horizon but also in the broader horizon of the whole canon. In this way one can do justice to two sets of biblical testimonies: on the one hand, Christ as the eternal Logos is present and active in Old Testament times, and, on the other hand, Christ is the fulfillment of the Old

---

Litchfield, "Outlining the Sermon," in *Handbook of Contemporary Preaching: A Wealth of Counsel for Creative and Effective Proclamation*, ed. Michael Duduit (Nashville: Broadman Press, 1992), 162-74.

[2]Preaching on love and sex from the Song of Solomon still needs to declare Christ as the foundation for a man and wife in a marriage covenant. The Triune God gave sex to husband and wife for both procreation and recreation (see Gen 1:28). Moreover, God fashioned a woman for man, ordaining marriage in the process. Paul relates marital love and sexual union from Gen 2:24 ("the two shall become one flesh") to the covenantal union between Christ and the church (Eph 5:31-32). Thus, a Christocentric undergirding to the Song of Solomon is quite valid. See also Duane A. Garrett, *Proverbs, Ecclesiastes, Song of Songs*, The New American Commentary, vol. 14 (Nashville: Broadman & Holman, 1993), 380.

Testament.[3]

Similarly, Larsen asserts,

> The Christian proclaimer, whether preaching from the Old Testament or the New, must present Christ as the ultimate frame of reference. The Christian proclaimer can preach no text in the Old Testament as a rabbi would preach it because the fulfillment of the promise has come in Christ and we live under the new covenant. The Christian proclaimer has a lifelong love affair with the Old Testament, the Bible which Christ and the apostles cherished. But our preaching of any part of Scripture must stand within a clear sense of theological construct, and for the Christian proclaimer that construct is Christocentric.[4]

This Christ-centered focus helps remind the expositor that the sermon's structure should move toward the Person or work of Christ.

Third, the preacher should find both encouragement and caution in the creative use of structuring the sermon in light of doctrinal exposition. Summary statements of biblical teachings must flow from the text rather than be forced on the text. Jotting down related terms through some careful, yet creative thinking may not only benefit the process of theological investigation but may also help convey theological meaning of the text.[5]

Fourth, while relating the individual text to the whole of revelation, the expositor should consider its significance for contemporary hearers.[6] This

---

[3]Sidney Greidanus, *The Modern Preacher and the Ancient Text: Interpreting and Preaching Biblical Literature* (Grand Rapids: Wm. B. Eerdmans, 1988), 119.

[4]David L. Larsen, *The Anatomy of Preaching: Identifying the Issues in Preaching Today* (Grand Rapids: Baker Book House, 1989), 163-64. Of course, "to view a text christocentrically is not a license to preach the gospel by misinterpreting the text!" (Olford and Olford, *Anointed Expository Preaching*, 134).

[5]Graeme Goldsworthy, *Preaching the Whole Bible as Christian Scripture: The Application of Biblical Theology to Expository Preaching* (Grand Rapids: Eerdmans, 2000), 246. Goldsworthy strongly cautions against confusing any given word with a concept or theme (ibid., 247). For instance, just because the term "proclamation" occurs in Scripture does not necessarily mean it refers to preaching in the theological sense (cf. Jonah 3:7). For more on creativity in preaching, see part 5 below.

[6]Edmund P. Clowney, *Preaching and Biblical Theology* (Grand Rapids: Eerdmans, 1961), 98.

principle largely deals with the application of doctrine. Warren mentions an important point here: "While both exegesis and theology remain stable (one meaning), homiletics varies according to the differing audiences (many applications)."[7] Although a more thorough treatment of applying doctrine comes in chapter 14 below, suffice it to say here that doctrinal exposition deals with theological exegesis, explanation, and application.[8]

Finally, noting the particular genre of the passage contributes to the way the preacher preaches the text. Because the Bible as God's Word has the right to provide both substance and shape to the message, preaching on various genres of Scripture should portray differences in presentation.[9] Commenting on biblical narratives, Deuel asks, "Why change the format when preaching them? If the preacher's goal is to be expositional, what is more expositional than preaching the text in its story-line form?"[10] A few examples of this proposal follow.

---

[7]Timothy S. Warren, "A Paradigm for Preaching," *Bibliotheca Sacra* 148, no. 592 (1991): 479.

[8]As to constructing doctrinal statements from exegetical and theological interpretation, Erickson and Heflin offer a four-step process. First, one must determine the original meaning and application of the message. Second, the interpreter needs to set the teaching of the text within the whole doctrine. Third, he should isolate the timeless principles of the text. Finally, the preacher constructs these principles in relation to the contemporary audience (Millard J. Erickson and James L. Heflin, *Old Wine in New Wineskins: Doctrinal Preaching in a Changing World* [Grand Rapids: Baker Books, 1997], 102-03).

[9]Ronald J. Allen asserts, "There is no single form or structure for doctrinal or theological preaching" (*Preaching Is Believing: The Sermon as Theological Reflection* [Louisville: Westminster John Knox Press, 2002], 82). See also Thomas G. Long, "Form," in *Concise Encyclopedia of Preaching*, ed. William H. Willimon and Richard Lischer (Louisville: Westminster John Knox Press, 1995), 144-51. Cf. Walter B. Russell III, "Literary Forms in the Hands of Preachers and Teachers," in *Cracking Old Testament Codes: Interpreting the Literary Genres of the Old Testament*, ed. D. Brent Sandy and Ronald L. Giese, Jr. (Nashville: Broadman & Holman, 1995), 291-94. For various preaching forms and structures, see Bryan Chapell, "Alternative Models," in *Handbook of Contemporary Preaching*, 117-31; Kenton C. Anderson, *Choosing to Preach: A Comprehensive Introduction to Sermon Options and Structures* (Grand Rapids: Zondervan, 2006).

[10]David C. Deuel, "Suggestions for Expositional Preaching of Old Testament Narrative," *The Master's Seminary Journal* 2, no. 1 (1991): 48.

Applying Genres in Doctrinal Exposition

Specifically, the various literary genres should impact the sermon's form. That is, doctrinal exposition upholds the Word of God, allowing it to determine the sermon's substance and shape. The following treatment includes the genres of narrative, Torah, poetry, wisdom, Gospels, and epistles.

Narrative

The treatment of preaching narrative is often rough and rigid, forcing the story into a propositional mold. The use of a well-planned approach, however, can result in an engaging form of doctrinal exposition. First, when preaching on narrative, it seems best to employ something of an inductive-deductive approach.[11] While not fully advocating the narrative preaching of the New Homiletic and its inductive method, I see value in preaching narrative passages by retelling the story with some application-principles sprinkled throughout the message. Steven Mathewson describes this arrangement where "the first part of the sermon tells the story inductively, while the second part spends time developing the idea."[12]

In answering how to preach narrative, Deuel observes, "Perhaps the easiest, most effective way, the way truest to the biblical form, is just to retell the story, allowing the story itself to heighten points of application."[13]

---

[11]York and Decker acknowledge, "While our preaching might indeed have inductive *elements*, we really cannot shy away from the fact that the preaching of the prophets and apostles was almost exclusively deductive and directly applicational" (*Preaching with Bold Assurance*, 17), contra Robinson, who writes, "Narratives are most effective when the audience hears the story and arrives at the speaker's ideas without the idea being stated directly" (*Biblical Preaching*, 130). An inductive-deductive method begins with some principles, moves toward the theme (general truth), and ends with particular applications. For other ways of preaching doctrine in general, including using deductive, inductive, inductive-deductive, and narrative, see Jerry E. Oswalt, *Proclaiming the Whole Counsel of God: Suggestions for Planning and Preparing Doctrinal Sermons* (New York: University Press of America, 1993), 13-52.

[12]Steven D. Mathewson, *The Art of Preaching Old Testament Narrative* (Grand Rapids: Baker Books, 2002), 118-19. The author labels other forms of narrative preaching as inductive, the flashback approach, the semi-inductive approach, and first-person narratives (ibid., 113-20). For the last approach, see Haddon W. Robinson and Torrey W. Robinson, *It's All in How You Tell It: Preaching First-Person Expository Messages* (Grand Rapids: Baker Books, 2003).

[13]Deuel, "Suggestions for Expositional Preaching," 61. Deuel goes on to say, "When a preacher states an abstraction, he usually follows it with an

The major elements of this narrative-doctrinal exposition are conveying the text's theological meaning, showing the movement of the text through developing the storyline, and engaging the audience through relevant application.[14] Moreover, the preacher needs to focus the movement of the plot toward the theology of the text. Thus, preaching on narrative texts such as Jacob, Ruth, Jonah, and Esther will highlight the role of God and His sovereign plan.

In selecting a unit of thought in the biblical text, the expositor will usually deal with a larger chunk of narrative than he would were he preaching from the epistles. A unit of thought in a narrative text is "a whole story."[15] Preaching the storyline and hitting the high points theologically will help move the preacher through large sections of Scripture.

Torah

In reference to preaching Torah, the expositor needs to observe the three-fold use of the law: 1) it was given to restrain human wickedness, 2) it convicts of sin, and 3) it instructs God's people in righteousness.[16] This purpose can carry over to the doctrinal expository sermon by focusing on God's holiness and justice along with man's sinfulness. Furthermore, the preacher may find it necessary to structure the sermon conditionally when preaching on casuistic laws or imperatively with apodictic laws.

Poetry

When expounding a poetical text, the preacher would do well to convey the feeling of the text, whether praise with gladness or lament with sadness.[17]

---

illustration to enhance comprehension of the abstraction. Narrative preached as narrative has already incorporated the illustration" (ibid.).

[14]Modified from David L. Larsen, *Telling the Old, Old Story: The Art of Narrative Preaching* (Wheaton: Crossway Books, 1995), 66-69. For ways to preach narrative better, see Larsen, *Telling the Old, Old Story*, 56-69, 94-97; Calvin Miller, *Preaching: The Art of Narrative Exposition* (Grand Rapids: Baker Books, 2006). For particular nuances of preaching narrative, such as parables, miracle-stories, and biography, see Larsen, *Telling the Old, Old Story*, 143-237. Application, too, needs to let the genre have a voice (see Robinson, "Heresy," 26). See chapter 14 for application in doctrinal exposition.

[15]Mathewson, *Art of Preaching OT Narrative*, 32. He also suggests certain clues which mark changes in narrative (ibid., 32-33).

[16]Goldsworthy, *Preaching the Whole Bible*, 166.

[17]William D. Thompson, *Preaching Biblically: Exegesis and Interpretation*

Similarly, preaching poetry may be the best place to employ such homiletical devices as alliteration, rhythm, parallelism, and repetition. Such devices in preaching do not disregard the doctrinal substance, rather they help the preacher reach the listeners' head by going through their heart.[18]

Concerning imprecatory psalms specifically, which are almost always found in laments, doctrinal exposition must treat them openly and honestly, for example, Psalm 137:8-9: "O daughter of Babylon, who are to be destroyed, happy the one who repays you as you have served us! Happy the one who takes and dashes your little ones against the rock!" While the psalmist is not asking for bloodthirsty vengeance, he does express

> a desire for God's justice to be accomplished. He wishes for God's righteous judgment to fall upon the evil kingdom of Babylon. In his desire for divine justice he uses the imagery of his day to describe the overthrow of nations. It is interesting to note that in several ancient illustrations of a king's reign we find that the son of the king is sitting on his father's lap and the defeated and subject peoples are depicted beneath not the father's feet but the son's! Thus, the judgment of the king of Babylon must also involve the judgment of his sons. Only in this way will the evil dynasty be judged and destroyed.[19]

Such an understanding does not contradict a Christ-centered view of the Bible and Jesus' words about loving one's enemies (see Matt 5:44), for even the command to love others is subservient to the greatest command to love, serve, and obey God.[20] Thus, seeking God and His will takes priority

---

(Nashville: Abingdon Press, 1981), 108.

[18]For the relationship between the emotional center and rational side of the human brain, see York and Decker, *Preaching with Bold Assurance*, 207-13. They contend that if preachers really want to impact their listeners so that the Bible's message changes them, preaching must appeal to people's primitive, emotional side in order to reach the rational, intellectual, and decision-making part of humans.

[19]Robert H. Stein, *A Basic Guide to Interpreting the Bible: Playing by the Rules* (Grand Rapids: Baker Books, 1994), 120. For similar ways of understanding imprecatory psalms, see Gordon D. Fee and Douglas Stuart, *How to Read the Bible for All Its Worth: A Guide to Understanding the Bible*. 2nd ed. (Grand Rapids: Zondervan, 1993), 202-04; Grant R. Osbourne, *The Hermeneutical Spiral: A Comprehensive Introduction to Biblical Interpretation* (Downers Grove: InterVarsity Press, 1991), 185.

[20]Much of Jesus' teaching draws from Deuteronomy. There one finds the extreme loyalty required by those in covenant commitment with Yahweh.

in all things; this view, too, stresses the theocentric, and even Christocentric, message of the Scriptures.

Wisdom

Expositional, doctrinal preaching of wisdom literature should be done with care. Since universalizing proverbs is difficult and too simplistic, one should avoid doing so in the sermon.[21] Furthermore, an expository sermon or series through Proverbs probably falls outside the normal definition of expository preaching, for preaching straight through the wise sayings of Proverbs seems *un*wise and would most likely profit little. A topical-expositional approach to this book gathers several verses on a particular subject in Proverbs, analyzing them separately and offering a synthesis of the book's teaching. As to other non-proverbial wisdom literature such as Job and Ecclesiastes, the preacher may want to preach systematically through the book, always keeping the epilogue in view.[22] Moreover, the application of the message should focalize on Christ.

Gospel

Preaching through the Gospels presents several options on the sermon's form. Expositors may handle narratives and parables in an inductive-deductive manner, emphasizing the doctrinal content.[23] Passages dealing with Jesus' teaching and preaching should follow His own deductive approach, using propositional statements to summarize major and minor truths. A series of sermons straight through one of the Gospels should show the various Gospel genres of historical-narrative, wisdom, poetry, prophecy, apocalyptic, parable, and didactic. Such an approach is quite possibly the most expositional method. Further, it helps the audience see the bigger picture the Gospel writer seeks to convey and helps them appreciate the literary features of God's Word.

Failure to obey God results in divine curses (see Deut 28:15-68).

[21]Walter C. Kaiser, Jr. *Preaching and Teaching from the Old Testament: A Guide for the Church* (Grand Rapids: Baker Books, 2003), 86-87.

[22]See Goldsworthy, *Preaching the Whole Bible*, 194-95.

[23]For different options for preaching through Luke's Gospel, see Keith F. Nickle, *Preaching the Gospel of Luke: Proclaiming God's Royal Rule* (Louisville: Westminster John Knox Press, 2000). Greidanus observes, "The sermon form need not necessarily be the same as the form of the text but should at least respect its characteristics" (Sidney Greidanus, "Preaching in the Gospels," in *Handbook of Contemporary Preaching*, 341).

Epistle

Forming a sermon from the epistles comes easier for most expositors than preaching any other kind of genre. Many expository textbooks contain ways to outline and preach sermons in a deductive fashion. Such deductive preaching best fits the epistles, because of their own nature. Moreover, because much of the Western world thinks deductively, it is convenient to shape sermons in like manner.

The didactic nature of the epistles makes it easier for theological content to come out in preaching. Scott Hafemann reminds readers that "the goal of preaching in the Epistles is the same as the goal of preaching in any other portion of Scripture, namely, to affect the congregation with the theological truth of the text."[24] In addition to this goal, the doctrinal substance should fall in line with the main points of the epistle. Further, because of the epistles' common use of imperatives, the sermon's structure needs to aim at exhorting listeners similarly.[25]

In the end, if one struggles over how to preach a particular literary genre, it seems best to stick with a deductive approach. While this style does not fully honor the way in which the Scriptures were written in certain cases, it still proves to be a good way of conveying the meaning of the text. Furthermore, it lets people know what they are to do with what they have heard.

Homiletical Principles of the Theological Product

Just because the expositor completes the work of biblical and theological exegesis does not mean he is ready to step into the pulpit. An amateur who lifts a few weights is not ready to train others in weightlifting! Even figuring out the sermon form does not guarantee an exposition of a biblical text and its doctrine. The preacher must translate the theological product into an outline for doctrinal expository preaching. To do this, you will need to follow a few principles.

First, the preacher needs to state the theological product of the biblical text in such a way that it applies to the audience in both an interesting and relevant way. Second, preachers should employ contemporary language, striving especially for concreteness and specificity (see chapter 14 below for more on applying doctrine today). Third, this approach to preaching takes the timeless truth of Scripture and phrases it for the present audience. Fourth, the use of imperatives helps reinforce the necessity of application in

---

[24]Scott Hafemann, "Preaching in the Epistles," in *Handbook of Contemporary Preaching*, 361.

[25]Ibid., 368-77.

doctrinal exposition, letting the audience know what they are expected to do in response to God's message. This issue is of particular importance in exposition, for such preaching aims to motivate the audience into action.[26] Finally, the whole sermon structure should build toward the climax (see Table 3 in the Appendices).

These principles will help the expositor make sure he is faithful to the biblical text and relevant to the contemporary audience. Of course, one can *discuss* how something should be done, but it is often better if he *shows* how it is done—the best trainers show others how to train! Therefore, this work provides a few examples of exegetical, theological, and homiletical propositions in Table 4 (Appendices).[27]

Two Main Kinds of Doctrinal Expository Preaching

At this point in the work, one can assume that "the preacher's only real question should not be 'Shall I preach doctrine?' but 'How shall I preach doctrine?'"[28] In order to do this and declare the whole counsel of God, doctrinal exposition needs to be comprehensive. This approach suggests both broadness and balance in handling biblical doctrine. Its broadness will cover the larger subjects of the Trinity, sin, and atonement, as well as issues such as prayer, the sanctity of human life, and spiritual gifts. At the same time, a balanced approach will necessarily cover the larger and more important doctrines of the Bible without excluding the minor topics. In accomplishing this enormous task, doctrinal exposition takes two main forms—textual or consecutive.[29]

Textual Doctrinal Exposition—Exposition of a Particular Doctrine

Regardless of whether one practices expository preaching as textually or

---

[26] For this approach to preaching in an applicational, imperatival way, see York and Decker, *Preaching with Bold Assurance*, 139-47.

[27] For other examples of this kind, see Timothy S. Warren, "The Theological Process in Sermon Preparation," *Bibliotheca Sacra* 156, no. 623 (1999): 354-55.

[28] Thomas E. McCollough, "Preaching's Rediscovery of Theology," *Review and Expositor* 56, no. 1 (1959): 52. He answers this question by pointing readers to see how the theologians have done it (ibid., 53).

[29] R. B. Kuiper ("Scriptural Preaching," in *The Infallible Word*, ed. N. B. Stonehouse and Paul Woolley [Philadelphia: The Presbyterian Guardian Publishing Company, 1946], 246-50) labels these as thematic (doctrinal-topical) and homily (running commentary). For broadness and balance in doctrinal preaching, see Oswalt, *Proclaiming the Whole Counsel of God*, 1.

consecutively, the proper interpretation of a passage will bring a particular doctrine out, one which relates to the Bible's entire message.[30] Some preachers who are more doctrinally-wired may prefer to expound isolated texts on Christian doctrine. While this approach is not as favorable as consecutive exposition, it is certainly profitable and valid. In support of this view, Harold Bryson understands expository preaching as "the art of preaching a series of sermons, either consecutive or *selective*, from a Bible book" (emphasis mine).[31]

Similar to the great doctrinal preaching of the post-Reformation era, textual doctrinal preaching contains much theological substance. It begins with biblical doctrine and preaches it within a particular text. In line with the Puritans' doctrinal-thematic (or doctrinal-topical) preaching style, this view asserts the validity in preaching through doctrines systematically. On the other hand, this preaching differs from the all-too-common one or two verse text for preaching by insisting on a *passage* of Scripture. Carson observes,

> The advantage of an older style preaching in which the text served as a springboard for an entire systematic theology was that the big picture was constantly maintained—but the cost was distance from the text, and it was only rarely shown how this larger theological structure could be derived from Scripture itself.[32]

Furthermore, because of the close association with Scripture, the doctrinal elements will naturally flow from a text.[33]

The preacher will want to make sure that he sets the individual text and doctrine within the larger context of the Bible's message. This issue is where textual exposition becomes more difficult than consecutive exposition. In the latter, the preacher has the advantage of connecting the

---

[30]D. Martyn Lloyd-Jones, *Preaching & Preachers* (Grand Rapids: Zondervan, 1971), 76.

[31]Harold T. Bryson, *Expository Preaching: The Art of Preaching through a Book of the Bible* (Nashville: Broadman & Holman, 1995), 39. As the title reveals, Bryson favors the consecutive method.

[32]D. A. Carson, "The *SBJT* Forum: Profiles of Expository Preaching," *The Southern Baptist Journal of Theology* 3, no. 2 (1999): 95-96.

[33]When covering doctrinal issues, "it is not always necessary to go to the main passage on a doctrine (it may well have been covered in a recent sermon), but [one] should at least look for a passage that clearly teaches that doctrine rather than alluding to it obliquely" (Walter L. Liefeld, *New Testament Exposition: From Text to Sermon* [Grand Rapids: Zondervan, 1984], 102).

smaller themes of each passage with the main theme of the book week-in and week-out. Furthermore, the preacher can more easily interpret the smaller themes within the story of God's redemption plan. The textual approach, however, must constantly interpret each new text within its own context before tying it to the Scriptures' storyline.

As to sermon titles, one may prefer to label his messages as particular doctrines, such as Christ's atoning work, justification by faith alone, or the indwelling ministry of the Holy Spirit. While such titles may not be as catchy in this world of clichés, they will most certainly clue the audience in on the content of the message.[34] Also, a doctrinal series of expository messages on the deity of Christ, for example, might consider passages like John 1:1-18; Colossians 1:15-20; Philippians 2:5-11; and Hebrews 1:1-4.

Consecutive Doctrinal Exposition—Pure Exposition with Doctrinal Substance

Preaching doctrine through an expositional series (i.e., consecutively) is quite arguably the best way to practice doctrinal exposition. Expository preaching in this fashion, writes Adam,

> is the obvious way to preach the Bible, as it reflects the way in which God caused Scripture to be written (in books, not isolated texts or paragraphs). It enables [preachers] to imitate God in respecting the humanity of the authors and their style and historical context. It also reflects the usual way of reading books, and models a good use of Scripture to the congregation.[35]

The arrangement of some Scripture, however, such as Psalms and Proverbs, may warrant the need to preach through sections of a book rather than simply straight through a book.

Preaching doctrine through a section of a biblical book. Rather than preach through an entire book at once (especially Isaiah or the Psalms!), the preacher may decide to preach consecutively on doctrine through sections of a book. Thus, he may deal with an expository series of messages on creation (Gen 1-2), election (Rom 9-11), the resurrection (1 Cor 15), worship (select Psalms), or true wisdom (select Proverbs in topical-exposition). With respect to the Psalms, a sermon series might also

---

[34]See Clarence S. Roddy, "On the Preaching of Theology," *Christianity Today* 3, no. 23 (1959): 6.

[35]P. J. H. Adam, "Preaching and Biblical Theology," in *New Dictionary of Biblical Theology: Exploring the Unity & Diversity of Scripture*, ed. T. Desmond Alexander and others (Downers Grove: InterVarsity Press, 2000), 108.

highlight different types of Psalms—didactic, royal Messianic, creation, lamentation, salvation history, or hymns of praise.[36] Preaching through sections of the Gospels could focus on Jesus' parables in teaching about the kingdom of God. Sermons on Jesus' miracles or His "I am" statements might stress a particular characteristic of Christ. In the end, this approach to preaching sections of Scripture, while still not as favorable as preaching book-by-book, can give more possibilities for subject matter to the preacher in a given year while adding variety to sermon series.

Preaching doctrine through a biblical book. Perhaps the best expository preaching involves a book-by-book approach. One advocate for defining expository preaching along this line is F. B. Meyer, who defines one aspect of expository preaching as *"the consecutive treatment of some book or extended portion of Scripture."*[37] Only those filling the same pulpit week in and week out, however, are able to accomplish the consecutive approach. That is, chapel speakers, pulpit supplies, and guest preachers are just a few of those who do not get this advantage.

When preaching through a Bible book, the preacher will want to divide the messages around the text's doctrinal themes. Thus, preaching through Hebrews will cover a number of Christological themes (including Christ's deity, absolute superiority, high priestly role and atoning work), while also handling sanctification (living by faith, obedience and perseverance) and God's holiness and judgment. These divisions will help set the sermon's parameters while establishing doctrinal unity and focus.

This chapter has provided a proposal on how the preacher can integrate both doctrine and exposition in an effective manner. Both theological exegesis and explanation within an expository framework have been treated. The roles of both biblical and systematic theology are extremely valuable for doctrinal expository preaching. Further, considerations for biblical genre affect both theological interpretation and preaching. These theological and homiletical issues contribute to the two main ways of practicing doctrinal exposition—textually and consecutively. Hopefully, these matters will encourage preachers to integrate both doctrine and exposition in their normal approach to preaching, so that preaching builds strong bodies.

---

[36]Goldsworthy, *Preaching the Whole Bible*, 203-11.

[37]F. B. Meyer, *Expository Preaching Plans and Methods* (New York: George H. Doran Co., 1912), 29. This definition covers both "sectional" exposition and pure exposition.

Part 5: Practical Aspects for Doctrinal Exposition

CHAPTER 13
CHALLENGES OF A POSTMODERN WORLD:
COMPETING AGAINST EASY-SUCCESS MODELS

Even if the reader agrees with the need for doctrinal exposition today, the postmodern culture makes its implementation difficult, to say the least. With this implementation in mind, this section's goal is to show how doctrinal expository preaching can be done in a postmodern setting. Issues such as truth, entertainment, language, imaging, and story are all significant for contemporary preaching. As television infomercials promise easy results from costly machines, so the postmodern culture seeks to lure people away from truly building their lives in conformity to Christ. The competition is real and we must rise up to meet the challenge.

Truth in a Truth-less Society

American society consists of technological advancements like never before—automobiles, household appliances, the Internet, and cell phones, to name a few. These advances and others like them allow people to accomplish more activities within a given timeframe, providing the time to pursue matters of special interest—web browsing, reading, or watching television.[1] In a previous era, it seems that people with so much "free time" would pursue life's most ultimate questions, such as God, truth, and eternity.

In this postmodern era, however, issues pertaining to truth are virtually

---

[1]David F. Wells claims that our comfortable lifestyle is unlike any previous generation with "more money, more goods, more comforts, more protections, and more freedoms" ("Introduction: The Word in the World," in *The Compromised Church: The Present Evangelical Crisis*, ed. John H. Armstrong [Wheaton: Crossway Books, 1998], 21).

moot, since many consider it to be relative to each and every individual. Therefore, few define truth objectively but, rather, subjectively. One even says that in postmodernism, "truth is up for grabs."[2] Anyone in search of truth must look inward toward personal experience and feeling. A fairly recent study shows that fifty-four percent of Americans believe that "truth can be discovered only through logic, human reasoning, and personal experience."[3] These people resist those who are dogmatic about truth, and this resistance has had its effects on the church. People

> almost expect the minister, if he is to be politically correct, to say, 'Well maybe it is this and maybe it is that,' because [they] don't want the minister to offend anybody by a proclamation that communicates too much certainty or authority.[4]

Taking a Stand on Truth

At the same time the postmodern climate bends truth to fit its fancy, today's American culture is becoming ripe for truth and theological thinking. The events of 9-11 and the recent wars in Afghanistan and Iraq

---

[2]Graham Johnston, *Preaching to a Postmodern World: A Guide to Reaching Twenty-First Century Listeners* (Grand Rapids: Baker Books, 2001), 30. Postmodernism also defines truth by its own standards of pragmatism, inclusivism, and openness (ibid., 41, 95). Related to postmodernism's rejection of truth is its rejection of meta-narrative, "an expression of transcendent reality, objective and absolute truth. Postmodernists have rejected all such 'grand narratives' in favor of an antifoundationalism that abandons all 'large-scale theoretical interpretations purportedly of universal application'" (Timothy S. Warren, "The Theological Process in Sermon Preparation," *Bibliotheca Sacra* 156, no. 623 (1999): 339-40). Warren cites Gene Edward Veith, Jr., *Postmodern Times: A Christian Guide to Contemporary Thought and Culture* (Wheaton: Crossway, 1994), 48-49. For more on postmodernism's rejection of meta-narrative, see Gary Phillips, "Religious Pluralism in a Postmodern World," in *The Challenge of Postmodernism: An Evangelical Engagement*, 2nd ed., ed. David S. Dockery (Grand Rapids: Baker Academic, 2001), 132; R. Albert Mohler, Jr., "The Integrity of the Evangelical Tradition and the Challenge of the Postmodern Paradigm," in *The Challenge of Postmodernism*, 71; Johnston, *Preaching to a Postmodern World*, 32-33.

[3]"Doctrinal Confusion Abounds in the U. S.," *Church Planting & Evangelism Today* (Winter 2003): 11; *The Barna Update* (8 October 2002) cited in "Straying from the Truth of the Gospel," *On Mission* (Special Issue 2003): 9.

[4]R. C. Sproul, "The Teaching Preacher," in *Feed My Sheep: A Passionate Plea for Preaching*, ed. Don Kistler (Morgan, PA: Soli Deo Gloria, 2002), 138-39.

have resulted in an increase in sales among Islam literature as people, both Christian and non-Christian, are wondering what the Muslim world believes. Likewise, the postmodern culture consists of openness to spirituality, a renewed interest in some matters of faith, and a certain admiration of Jesus.[5] Thus, now that some people are once again asking life's most ultimate questions, Christians can and must champion truth, and there are no better persons than solid expositors of God's Word to accept this challenge.[6]

This stand on truth is where preaching, even doctrinal exposition, remains of utmost importance. Living in a world that despises preaching and dogmatism, preachers "must determine to let [their] convictions be shaped by the unchanging Word of God and not by the shifting currents of modern culture."[7] Moreover, when people mock expositors for their insistence on truth, preachers can take comfort in the preaching of Jesus and the Apostle Paul. Commenting on the former, Samuel Logan, Jr. writes,

> What Jesus preached was anchored in the propositional bedrock of historical accuracy, and that is why recognition and proclamation of the inerrancy of all biblical affirmations is so crucial in the church today.[8]

Furthermore, Paul remained faithful to the truth (2 Tim 4:6-8) and his

> insistence that truth is given objectively in Christ, not subjectively through private intuition as the pagans thought, would make him sound strangely out of touch. . . . [and even though] his preaching would be judged hopelessly irrelevant because its theological focus would put it out of step with modern habits.[9]

Additionally, upholding objective truth is vital now more than ever, for

---

[5]Johnston, *Preaching to a Postmodern World*, 17, 97, 120.

[6]Of course, conservative evangelicals, though a minority both in America and throughout the world, insist on absolute, objective truth. Such truth comes from God, the source of all truth. God's Word—both the written Word and the incarnate Word—clearly reveals this truth.

[7]Tom Ascol, "The Pastor's Chief Duty," *The Founders Journal*, no. 23 (1996): 2.

[8]Samuel T. Logan, Jr., "The Phenomenology of Preaching," in *The Preacher and Preaching: Reviving the Art in the Twentieth Century*, ed. Samuel T. Logan, Jr. (Phillipsburg, NJ: Presbyterian and Reformed Publishing, 1986), 143.

[9]David F. Wells, *No Place for Truth, or Whatever Happened to Evangelical Theology?* (Grand Rapids: Wm. B. Eerdmans, 1993), 290-91.

without any solid, unchanging view of truth, meaning has no value. A reason the deconstructionist movement within postmodernism will never prevail is because its main contention is that there is no such thing as original meaning, leaving everything, including the purpose of life itself, in a state of meaninglessness. Johnston notes, however, that even among postmodernists, "deep down, people want life to make sense. Absurdity is all right in small doses, but nobody wants to live in it."[10] Doctrinal exposition's high regard for truth can help these people make sense of life.

In order for truth to confront this postmodern world, preachers, more than anyone, must have a *passion* for the truth. They must live it, love it, and preach it as though it really *matters*, because it most certainly *does*! John Armstrong, in an earlier work, offers several thoughts on preaching's emphasis of the truth, four of which follow: 1) both the manner and matter of preaching should show "that God is truth;" 2) the failure to love the truth leads to "spiritual destruction," for the only way to know God is to know Him "in truth;" 3) truth is absolutely necessary for salvation; and 4) Christian living must always rest on "obedience to the truth."[11] Clearly, one could claim, "Not only does truth *matter*, but it matters for all *eternity*!"

Preaching Truth Is Not As Easy As It Used to Be

Of course, expounding truth in a truth-less society is a formidable task. With brevity and clarity, Kent Hughes describes the problem of preaching truth today:

> To be fair, preaching is far more difficult today than in past decades. There was a time across America when Sunday's sermon was the most stimulating event of the week. Then came the wireless and ABC and NBC in megadecibels. With this came the advent of the notorious "shortened attention span." Media-sotted people simply cannot listen as well or as long as their grandparents. And now we have a postliterate culture that does not read and has difficulty following reasoned discourse apart from visual

---

[10]Johnston, *Preaching to a Postmodern World*, 141. For an extremely thorough critique of the deconstructionist movement, see Kevin J. Vanhoozer, *Is There a Meaning in This Text? The Bible, the Reader, and the Morality of Literary Knowledge* (Grand Rapids: Zondervan, 1998).

[11]John Armstrong, "Preaching to the Mind," in *Feed My Sheep*, 175-83. Unfortunately, Armstrong's position has morphed in light of postmodernism in recent years. See John H. Armstrong, "How I Changed My Mind: Theological Method," *Viewpoint*, 7.4 (September-October 2003) at postbiblical.info/PDFS/How_Franke_Changed_Armstrong's_Mind.pdf; accessed 17 September 2009.

simulation.

Toss into this mix a loose set of attitudes known as postmodernity, which enthrones subjectivity and self-focus, and today becomes as challenging a time to preach the Word as has ever existed in Western culture. Nevertheless, God has chosen to speak through His written Word and its verbal proclamation.[12]

Erickson and Heflin, likewise, list twenty-seven possible factors which make preaching doctrine in today's world difficult. Such factors include naturalism, relativism, secularism, pluralism, ministerial pragmatism, anti-denominationalism, and anti-education-ism.[13] These factors, while challenging to doctrinal exposition, are not insurmountable to the one equipped with the Word of the omnipotent God.

God's Word is not the only tool the expositor needs to carry with him, however, in this postmodern world. Understanding his hearers will aid the preacher in knowing how to handle God's Word more effectively. Carson sees the need for preachers to think like missionaries by studying their culture. He writes,

The better seminaries have long included courses in the missions curriculum to help prospective missionaries "read" the culture they are about to enter. . . .

But such courses are rarely required of students in the pastoral track. The assumption is that these students are returning to their *own* culture, so they do not need such assistance. But the rising empirical pluralism and the pressures from globalization ensure that the assumption is usually misplaced. Apart from isolated pockets, Western culture is changing so quickly that the church now struggles to understand what is going on. Indeed, it is less and less easy to speak of "Western culture" in such a monolithic fashion: there is a plethora of competing cultures in most Western nations, and many pastors will minister to several of them during their ministry. Indeed, in many metropolitan areas, pastors may

---

[12]R. Kent Hughes, "Preaching: God's Word to the Church Today," in *The Coming Evangelical Crisis: Current Challenges to the Authority of Scripture and the Gospel*, ed. John H. Armstrong (Chicago: Moody Press, 1996), 92. Piper also observes, "Preaching great and glorious truth in an atmosphere that is not great and glorious is an immense difficulty" (John Piper, "Charles Spurgeon: Preaching through Adversity," *The Founders Journal*, no. 23 [1996]: 6).

[13]See Millard J. Erickson and James L. Heflin, *Old Wine in New Wineskins: Doctrinal Preaching in a Changing World* (Grand Rapids: Baker Books, 1997), 39-57.

find themselves ministering to several of them at once.[14]

Ultimately, doctrinal exposition faces the ever-changing world with the never-changing truth of God. Preachers need a sure certainty in God's Word, a solid dedication to learning this culture, and a strong resolve to engage the culture with the Word. Those most committed to bodybuilding not only watch their own diet and workout routine, but they help others get stronger. With such commitments God can use expositors to liberate those enslaved in sin with the truth of Christ.

An Entertainment-Driven Culture

Another factor in the postmodern climate is the television and entertainment industry. Few would disagree that today's American culture is largely entertainment-driven. People have a mentality that they need to feel good and enjoy whatever they do. Even some Christians are guilty of "hopping" churches in search of one which entertains them, meets their needs, and gives them a better worship experience. It seems as though the television industry has contributed much to this entertainment frenzy, for

> the visual imagery of television has aided and abetted the rise of postmodern culture, at least at the popular level of experience. While many argue over television content, the television experience is by far the most defining influence with regard to the development of popular postmodern thinking.[15]

This craving for entertainment is nothing new to the church. Sproul observes that Martin Luther had to fight this problem, for Luther believed

> that the people in the parishes came to be entertained. Even in the 16th century, the pastors, during the middle of the Reformation, were struggling with the demands of their congregations that they entertain them with their preaching. Luther claimed that it is not the task of the pastor to entertain, but to nurture, to feed, and to be

---

[14]Donald A. Carson, *The Gagging of God: Christianity Confronts Pluralism* (Grand Rapids: Zondervan, 1996), 549-50. See also Donald R. Sunukjian, *Biblical Preaching: Proclaiming Truth with Clarity and Relevance* (Grand Rapids: Kregel, 2007).

[15]William E. Brown, "Theology in a Postmodern Culture: Implications of a Video-Dependent Society," in *The Challenge of Postmodernism*, 159. Brown also states, "No feature of modern culture so dominates life and thought as does television" (ibid., 162). Veith concurs, "A major force in the shaping of the postmodern mind has been the impact of contemporary technology. The product of rationalism, the electronic media may well make rationalism impossible" (Veith, *Postmodern Times*, 121).

faithful to the Word of God.[16]

Perhaps no one from a Christian worldview has addressed the advancement of the entertainment industry and its effects on the spoken word as much as Neil Postman in his work, *Amusing Ourselves to Death*. Postman describes the history of public discourse in America, labeling 1600-1900 as the "Age of Exposition" and the twentieth century as the "Age of Show Business." These two ages represent two different cultures: a word-centered culture, where reading is for comprehension, and an image-centered culture, where reading is for leisure. Postman points to several factors which have led to the current state.[17] First, Samuel Morse's invention of the telegraph transformed the way people obtained information—by the ear rather than the eye. Second, around the 1830s, newspapers began printing irrelevant information, subjecting their readers to junk. Third, the development of photography placed information in isolation from language, no longer requiring a context for interpretation and understanding. Finally, the progress of television has moved discourse toward entertainment. Postman observes, "The problem is not that television presents us with entertaining subject matter but that all subject matter is presented as entertaining."[18]

Leith summarizes Postman's position, claiming that the entertainment industry

> has two consequences. (1) It induces people to find the meaning of life in being entertained. Entertainment (soap operas, athletic events, even anchor news which turns great events into spectacles) relieves us of uniquely human responsibilities to think for ourselves, to set goals and to accomplish them. (2) Entertainment distracts our attention from the critical issues of life, and finally our heroes become not persons of substance and achievement so much

---

[16]Sproul, "The Teaching Preacher," 143-44. A reason that some ministers give in to the entertainment crave by conjuring "up new and interesting viewpoints is because there is a lack of confidence among preachers in the effectiveness of preaching the whole counsel of God" (ibid., 157).

[17]Neil Postman, *Amusing Ourselves to Death: Public Discourse in the Age of Show Business* (New York: Penguin Books, 1986), 63-80.

[18]Ibid., 87. Postman calls television "the command center," because "through it we learn what telephone system to use, what movies to see, what books, records and magazines to buy, what radio programs to listen to. Television arranges our communications environment for us in ways that no other medium has the power to do" (ibid., 78). Of course, the Internet has quickly supplemented television's stronghold.

as celebrities who attract our attention. Form takes priority over substance. In sum, entertainment whether it is soap operas or political spectacles or athletic events, is not simply entertainment but also an escape from the hard realities of life and from the questions for which Christian faith is the answer.[19]

Therefore, "in a practical sense, the thinking involved in watching television is radically different from that which is necessary in verbal communication (reading, speaking, listening)."[20] Children and adults who spend hour after hour in front of the television end up being deficient "in the ability to read intelligently, communicate clearly, and reason morally."[21] The impact of television and the entertainment industry has led to a "dumb-ing down" effect on each new generation—kids do not really need to learn how to do basic arithmetic or spell when calculators and spell-check programs will do it for them. Moreover, these types of training models rarely force kids to think critically about important issues, allowing television programs, music lyrics, and the like to help form their views.

All of this does not mean that preaching cannot learn something from the entertainment business. As discussed below, preachers must continually assess the factor of visual communication in their sermons. In this postmodern world, a solution exists for people

> accustomed to television, movies, and entertainers. . . . The solution is not, as some have suggested, to turn worship services into entertainment—or even infotainment; the answer lies in passionate preaching of *propositional truth*.[22]

The Roles of Language, Image and Story in Doctrinal Exposition

A recent trend among preachers of the New Homiletic and some church growth specialists is explaining and applying doctrine vis-à-vis re-language and re-image.[23] The core of the biblical message, they contend, should be

---

[19]John H. Leith, *From Generation to Generation: The Renewal of the Church according to Its Own Theology and Practice* (Louisville: Westminster/John Knox Press, 1990), 94.

[20]Brown, "Theology in a Postmodern Culture," 162.

[21]Ibid., 162.

[22]Hershael W. York and Bert Decker, *Preaching with Bold Assurance: A Solid and Enduring Approach to Engaging Exposition* (Nashville: Broadman & Holman, 2003), 5.

[23]For the foundational work to the audience-response New Homiletic, see Fred Craddock, *As One without Authority: Essays on Inductive Preaching* (Enid,

told in new ways. Thus, the trend in contemporary preaching employs story in preaching so that preaching becomes less-propositional and more narrative-oriented. Language, image and story most certainly are significant for preaching today, but preachers should carefully evaluate each. Wise doctrinal expositors will adopt some elements of postmodernism, adapt other elements and oppose certain elements, as demonstrated below.[24]

The Need for New Language?

Obviously, language is a necessary element in any type of communication, especially oral communication. In preaching language must provide a link between the ancient Scriptures' theological message and contemporary anthropological reception. Tucker writes,

> The task of theology is to determine what God has said through the Word. The task of the messenger is to proclaim this discovery in *language* that today's hearer can understand. The key to this task is the congregation of believers" (emphasis mine).[25]

Problem. Robert Hughes and Robert Kysar argue that theological preaching should reformulate experience and abstraction through language, even to the point of translating tradition via re-language and re-image.[26] They go so far as to say that today's preaching on the atonement might want to underscore the correcting of "injustice through self-sacrificial love."[27] This focus, however, does not do justice to the biblical teaching of the atonement, even though their view is much more politically correct today. If only Paul had stressed this teaching in the atonement, then maybe he could have avoided some of the problems he faced!

OK: Phillips University, 1971).

[24]See especially Robertson McQuilkin, "Connecting with Postmoderns," in *The Art & Craft of Biblical Preaching: A Comprehensive Resource for Today's Communicators*, eds. Haddon Robinson and Craig Brian Larson (Grand Rapids: Zondervan, 2005), 174-76.

[25]Donald L. Tucker, "Biblical Preaching: Theology, Relevance, Empowerment," *Paraclete* 25 (Summer 1991): 26-27.

[26]Robert G. Hughes and Robert Kysar, *Preaching Doctrine: For the Twenty-First Century* (Minneapolis: Fortress Press, 1997), 27-29. Others follow the trend of Hughes and Kysar on language, image and story, but Hughes and Kysar are more unique in that they distinctly address doctrinal preaching in the twenty-first century.

[27]Ibid., 30.

At the same time, readers should use caution toward certain church growth advocates, even those who label themselves as evangelical. On the one hand, Peter Wagner gives little more than lip service to the value of solid preaching, saying that "if you can serve a diet of positive sermons focused on the real, felt needs of the people you will be preaching for growth."[28] Elsewhere, discussing whether the gift of prophecy and good preaching are synonymous, Wagner claims, "I have not yet found a correlation between one or the other and church growth."[29] While not fully denying the value of solid preaching, Wagner never explains the substance of "good preaching." With these assertions in view, doctrinal exposition, no matter how extensive, matters little in reaching people for Christ in American culture.

On the other hand, George Barna rightly recommends the contextualization principle in communicating to different audiences.[30] In the end, nevertheless, his largely secular approach to "marketing" the church offers little biblical content while, at the same time, provides a felt-needs message aimed at "satisfying the needs of the consumer" and preaching on locally "hot" issues.[31] Elsewhere, Barna asserts, "Language which is theological, judgmental, or incessantly paternalistic creates problems for many younger listeners."[32] One wonders if preaching a *gospel*

---

[28]C. Peter Wagner, *Leading Your Church to Growth* (Ventura, CA: Regal Books, 1984), 218. Only the last three pages addresses preaching within church growth, and the subject matter has little to do with biblical content (ibid., 215-18). Also, ibid., 170-71.

[29]C. Peter Wagner, *Your Spiritual Gifts Can Help Your Church Grow* (Ventura, CA: Regal Books, 1979), 229.

[30]George Barna, *Marketing the Church: What They Never Taught You about Church Growth* (Colorado Springs: NavPress, 1988), 51.

[31]Ibid., 76.

[32]George Barna, "The Pulpit-meister: Preaching to the New Majority," *Preaching* 12, no. 4 (1997): 11-12. Shortly after Barna wrote this article, Barna Research Group came out with a study as to why people choose a particular church: 58 percent (the number one reason) said that theological belief and doctrine were extremely important and 52 percent (the number three reason) listed sermon quality as extremely important ("Church Attendance," Barna Research Online; accessed 22 August 2003; available from barna.org/cgi-bin/PageCategory.asp). It seems that theology and substantial preaching still have merit after all.

about *Christ*, His *sacrifice* for *sins*, and God's *holiness* is too theological and overly expectant of such listeners.

Proposal. The more faithful approach to Scripture is to explain clearly the nature of the biblical terminology. Armstrong vehemently argues for definitional clarity in preaching. Against Barna's approach at re-language, Armstrong states,

> When the preacher must change his language or excise it of theological and biblical content, he finds himself positioned to be more of an inspirational speaker and motivator than a preacher of God's truth. . . . Barna indeed shows us the problem. But his solution is to avoid the absolutes, to go light on Scripture, not to explain the doctrines of the Word, but rather to be 'practical.'[33]

When being practical supersedes and replaces faithful explanation, then application has stepped out of place in expository preaching. The preacher must explain the content of the biblical text in order for there to be substantial application, i.e., effective and solid application always rests upon clear doctrinal exposition.[34]

John Leith says that sound

> preaching requires the acquisition of a language that is precise and clear, that has the quality of reality, and that is appropriate to communicate the Christian gospel. As long as English is spoken, this must build upon the remarkable literary and theological achievement of the Puritans. Language appropriate to the faith cannot be finally learned in academic communities but only as those learned in the tradition engage a broad range of people, learned and unlearned, in theological conversation. The scientific, technological, secular character of our culture makes the problem of language all the more important. As Calvin put the traditional theology of the church in the language of ordinary discourse, so that is our task today.[35]

Thus, preaching must retain its theological roots to be effective, and the language in preaching, while not technical, will need to be faithful to the Bible. It seems that "today the fear of 'turning people off' with having to

---

[33]John Armstrong, "Preaching to the Mind," in *Feed My Sheep*, 184-85. For Armstrong's newer position, see fn 11 in this chapter.

[34]Conversely, doctrine should be experimental, practical, and applicable for the contemporary audience (Ernest Reisinger, "The Priority of Doctrinal Preaching," *The Founders Journal*, no. 23 [1996]: 22).

[35]Leith, *From Generation to Generation*, 114.

'think' through doctrinal truths has led the pulpits overall to a shallowness that has dulled the cutting edge of soul-saving truth."[36]

Kaiser clearly argues for maintaining theological-biblical teaching in the sermon. Surely the issue of language plays an important role in his analysis:

> It is no secret that Christ's Church is not at all in good health in many places of the world. She has been languishing because she has been fed, as the current line has it, "junk food"; all kinds of artificial preservatives and all sorts of unnatural substitutes have been served up to her. As a result, theological and Biblical malnutrition has afflicted the very generation that has taken such giant steps to make sure its physical health is not damaged by using foods or products that are carcinogenic or otherwise harmful to their physical bodies. Simultaneously a worldwide spiritual famine resulting from the absence of any genuine publication of the Word of God (Amos 8:11) continues to run wild and almost unabated in most quarters of the Church.[37]

In order to speak with theological depth without going over people's heads, the preacher "must build upon values *already held* by the intended audience."[38] Without trying to belittle people's intelligence, a preacher usually

> needs to define even basic theological terms, and always in an engaging way. . . .
>
> . . . With respect to theological terms, a minister can take nothing for granted. The sermon should define even basic terms (such as Holy Spirit, sin, faith, righteousness) so that preacher and congregation communicate on the same channel.[39]

---

[36]Robert B. Selph, *Southern Baptists and the Doctrine of Election* (Harrisonburg, VA: Sprinkle Publications, 1996), 14.

[37]Walter C. Kaiser, Jr., *Toward an Exegetical Theology: Biblical Exegesis for Preaching & Teaching* (Grand Rapids: Baker Books, 1981), 7-8.

[38]Philip J. Wogaman, "Preaching the Truth in Love," *Journal of Theology* 102 (Summer 1998): 46.

[39]Ronald J. Allen, *Preaching Is Believing: The Sermon as Theological Reflection* (Louisville: Westminster John Knox Press, 2002), 85-86. Joseph Faulkener adds, "It is clearly dangerous to assume much doctrinal sophistication or even biblical literacy on the part of a congregation" (Joseph E. Faulkener, "What Are They Saying? A Content Analysis of 206 Sermons Preached in the Christian Church [Disciples of Christ] during 1988," in *A Case Study of Mainstream Protestantism: The Disciples' Relation to American*

Christians will always have a need for theology preached in their own language.[40]

At the same time, however, preachers must guard against going *too* deep in the sermon, as if they were lecturing students on theology. Employing technical language most certainly deadens interest.[41] The average church-goer does not need to hear such theological phrases as "hypostatic union," "supralapsarianism," or the "teleological argument for God's existence." Moreover, although the preacher in his study should investigate Hebrew and Greek terms, his sermon should leave them out.[42]

Finally, with regard to language, expositors need not worry so much about sermon length and boredom with doctrinal issues. Allen writes, "Theology is boring only if the preacher presents it in a boring way."[43] Moreover, studies show

> that congregations have a remarkable capacity to follow long and complex sermons when the content makes a vital connection with the experience of the congregation, when the language of the sermon is vivid, when the message moves so that the congregation can easily follow it, and when the preacher embodies the sermon in an engaging way.[44]

Culture, 1880-1989, ed. D. Newell Williams [Grand Rapids: Wm. B. Eerdmans, 1991], 438).

[40]Bernard Reymond, "Homiletics and Theology: Re-evaluating Their Relationship," *The Modern Churchman* 34, no. 5 (1993): 37.

[41]Henry Sloane Coffin, *What to Preach* (New York: Harper & Brothers, 1926), 55.

[42]Some words from theology or the biblical languages may, in rare cases, help explain or illustrate a point (such as Paul's use of γυμνασια for "exercising" is the basis for the English term "gymnasium"). Ultimately, the principle for preachers to follow on this practice is "when in doubt, leave it out."

[43]Allen, *Preaching Is Believing*, 61.

[44]Lyle Schaller, "How Long Is the Sermon?" *The Baptist Herald* 72, no. 5 (1994): 20. Similarly, John R. W. Stott observes, "Basically, it is not the length of a sermon which makes a congregation impatient for it to stop, but the tedium of a sermon in which even the preacher himself appears to be taking very little interest" (*Between Two Worlds: The Art of Preaching in the Twentieth Century* [Grand Rapids: Wm. B. Eerdmans, 1982], 292).

Of course, anyone reading through the Bible catches a glimpse of its own vivid language with its use of poetry, metaphor, stories, and such.

The Need for Imagery

When speaking of preaching in a postmodern world, many agree that "one of the ripest fields is in the postmodern appetite for image."[45] Roof adds, "Perhaps the most important impact of television was that it replaced the *word* with the *image*."[46] How a preacher should use images, however, is a matter of disagreement.

Problem. Advocates of the New Homiletic not only argue for a new language in preaching, but they are also leading the way in promoting the roles of imagery and story in doctrinal preaching. Hughes and Kysar contend that more needs to be made of images and stories in preaching. One value of these models is that they

> gain their power through ambiguity. When the image is ambiguous . . . or the story ends without a clear resolution, each takes on a new dimension. The story or image has many possible and different meanings.[47]

Although these writers have something to bring to the table in their discussion of using the imagination in conveying doctrine (discussed below), they ultimately leave the authority of textual meaning in the hands of the listeners, resulting in numerous possible meanings rather than the author's intended meaning. This leads, therefore, to more language *confusion* rather than *clarity* in understanding and applying biblical doctrine.

Additionally, any kind of enduring theological reflection in twenty-first century preaching will most certainly "take the form of imaginative discourse," contend Hughes and Kysar.[48] Further, these writers speak of "doctrinal framing" which helps hold the listeners' lives together,

> but such framing requires imagination. Humans are able to conceive their lives holistically only by imagining a holistic perspective. This means that imaginative preaching will be required,

---

[45] Michael J. Glodo, "The Bible in Stereo: New Opportunities for Biblical Interpretation in an A-Rational Age," in *The Challenge of Postmodernism*, 110.

[46] Wade Clark Roof, *A Generation of Seekers: The Spiritual Journeys of the Baby Boom Generation* (San Francisco: HarperSanFrancisco, 1993), 54.

[47] Hughes and Kysar, *Preaching Doctrine*, 57.

[48] Ibid., 13. By imagery, they "mean the mental and imaginary pictures evoked in the listener by language" (ibid., 55).

for the preacher must image anew how God language can unify the listener's experience. But, further, such preaching will invite the listeners themselves to imagine their lives within a theological image.[49]

That which Hughes and Kysar offer ends up being utterly senseless. Of course, anyone conceiving life holistically needs a holistic perspective, but how imagery and re-language seriously aids such a quest remains to be seen. It seems that they want to communicate theological language through the filter of imagination so that all that is left is little more than word-pictures which may or may not adequately convey the theological message.

Proposal. Today's expositors might as well concede that much of their expository preaching could use more imagination and creativity. Conceding such a point, however, does not mean that imagination drives the sermon or that theological communication cannot occur without it. Rather, doctrinal exposition can, and should, benefit from the use of imagery in several ways.

First, in light of the contemporary culture's proneness to learn better from visual effects, doctrinal expositors would do well to become masters of visual communication.[50] One approach to this could be through multimedia presentations in preaching. Whether the presentation reveals sermon outlines and key definitions, relevant maps, or even short video clips showing events such as Jesus' crucifixion or ascension, doctrinal exposition can benefit from modern technology's use of visual images. On the other hand, if the preacher cannot use multimedia presentations, because of location or inadequate facilities, preachers can still employ body movement and gestures for visual effectiveness.[51]

Expecting criticism to this kind of approach, Johnston hears others ask, "Must the church become pictorial in order to live?" He answers,

> I can appreciate, and even hear, the resistance some might have to such a question: "Well, the church has survived for centuries without all this nonsense—art, drama, mime, role plays,

---

[49]Ibid., 11.

[50]See York and Decker, *Preaching with Bold Assurance*, 200-13. Moreover, "it is important to recognize that, as television has taught us, congregations are not merely *listeners*, but also *viewers*" (Jay E. Adams, "Sense Appeal and Storytelling," in *The Preacher and Preaching*, 354).

[51]Many in the NT Church came to believe in Jesus Christ because they "saw" His power at work in the ministry of the Apostles (see Acts 3:9-4:4; 5:12-16; 8:6-7; 9:33-35; 13:8-12).

documentaries, dance, and a vast number of other types of audiovisual presentation."

True, the early church flourished in the absence of many things that are now used regularly: electricity, facilities, Sunday schools, biblical commentaries, seminaries, even Willow Creek formats. The use of audio-visuals is, without question, a cultural expression of our time and it too may pass.

Keep in mind, however, that how you communicate God's timeless message will constantly be changing and, yet, God's Word won't.[52]

Preachers should not view the use of modern technology for visual communication as a *substitute* for the message but as an *enhancement* of it. Rowell notes, "If I'm not passionate about God's Word, no amount of technology can correct that deficiency."[53] Many conservative evangelicals remain skeptical of certain methodologies largely because of their abuse. They often see *"the radical inconsistency that exists between the message of the bloody cross and the slick, sophisticated, Spielberg-like methods of communicating it."*[54] It does not have to be an either-or, however, for imagination does not mean imaginary or fanciful. In the end video technology can help audiences to visualize and understand the biblical message better.

Second, preachers will need to spend more time in preparation, thinking creatively and imaginatively. Warren Wiersbe asserts, "Biblical preaching means declaring God's truth *the way He declared it*, and that means *with imagination.*"[55] He defines imagination as "the image-making faculty in

---

[52]Johnston, *Preaching to a Postmodern World*, 163.

[53]Ed Rowell, "Where Preaching Is Headed: 4 Forces Shaping Tomorrow's Sermon," *Leadership* 18, no. 1 (1997): 97. The preacher's "goal is not to entertain . . . but to communicate the gospel in the most culturally relevant method possible in order to change lives" (ibid.).

[54]Arturo G. Azurdia III, "Preaching: The Decisive Function," in *The Compromised Church: The Present Evangelical Crisis*, ed. John H. Armstrong (Wheaton: Crossway Books, 1998), 190. Similarly, Brown asserts, "The visual does not supplement language, it displaces it" ("Theology in a Postmodern Culture," 162). While not wanting to take away from active reading and listening, a good "picture is [still] worth a thousand words."

[55]Warren W. Wiersbe, *Preaching & Teaching with Imagination: The Quest for Biblical Ministry* (Grand Rapids: Baker Books, 1994), 9. Henry Ward Beecher claimed, "The first element on which your preaching will largely depend for power and success, you will perhaps be surprised to learn, is *Imagination*, which I regard as the most important of all the elements that go to make the

your mind, the picture gallery in which you are constantly painting, sculpting, designing, and sometimes erasing."[56] Larsen, likewise, notes, "Imagination is an aspect of creativity. Imagination nurtures impulses, flashes of insight and excitement over ideas; creativity is the result."[57] Further, "creative delivery enables the listeners to discover the truth for themselves as opposed to having ideas dropped in their lap."[58] A creative, yet biblically-focused, imagination helps reach people in this image-saturated culture.

No matter how many preachers and theologians lament the contemporary image-culture, each must face-up to reality. To expound doctrine effectively in this postmodern world does not require "a choice of word over symbol nor of symbol over word, but rather the proper relation of the two."[59] Michael Glodo adds,

> The "word" (i.e., propositional, didactic) forms of Scripture must be enriched and vivified by the "image" forms as well as the latter being controlled and organized by the former. What makes an image-driven culture arcane or cabalistic (a la Postman) is not its image-drivenness, but the disconnection of image from word. Images become contentless or, worse, connected to propositions to which they bear no relation. An unrestrained dive into the image-character of the Bible without the proper dialogue with word could result in the same arcaneness. *But word uninformed by image will bear the*

---

preacher" (*Yale Lectures on Preaching: First, Second, and Third Series* [New York: Fords, Howard and Hubert, 1881], 109). Likewise, Arthur John Gossip writes, "To make doctrinal preaching effective for the mass of people, we must appeal to them through the imagination" ("The Whole Counsel of God: The Place of Biblical Doctrine in Preaching," *Interpretation* 1, no. 3 [1947]: 334). For suggestions on stimulating and sustaining imagination and creativity in the sermon, see David L. Larsen, *Telling the Old, Old Story: The Art of Narrative Preaching* (Wheaton: Crossway Books, 1995), 248-54.

[56]Wiersbe, *Preaching & Teaching*, 25.

[57]David L. Larsen, *The Anatomy of Preaching: Identifying the Issues in Preaching Today* (Grand Rapids: Baker Book House, 1989), 109. See also Wiersbe, *Preaching & Teaching*, 289.

[58]Johnston, *Preaching to a Postmodern World*, 75.

[59]Glodo, "The Bible in Stereo," 118. For the relationship between image and word in worship, see appendix 8.

marks of the modernist who proclaims it.[60]

One way of employing creativity and imagery in doctrinal exposition might be to dramatize the biblical text or even the preaching event. While drama should never replace the preached Word, it can most certainly enhance an audience's understanding of Scripture. Mini-dramas on Ruth, Jacob and Esau before Isaac, or Abraham and Isaac prior to preaching the sermon can enable visualization of the biblical narrative. On the other hand, a preacher portraying the Apostle Paul in dramatic monologue could recount his conversion and service to Christ, highlighting the doctrinal elements in Paul's own message.[61]

Third, preachers must work harder at translating

the abstract, Transcendent Word from scripture and doctrine into the concrete experience of human existence. Preaching is frequently too abstract, using language and images with which the listeners have no corresponding concrete identification."[62]

Referring to Jonathan Edwards's use of images in preaching, John Piper similarly writes, "Experience and Scripture teach that the heart is most powerfully touched, not when the mind is entertaining abstract ideas, but when it is filled with vivid images of amazing reality."[63] Thus, when employing images in preaching, the images will need to be explanatory

---

[60]Ibid., 120-21.

[61]The point of such dramatization is not to bring Hollywood to the church but to bridge the distance between the ancient Scriptures and the contemporary world. Commenting on dramatized exposition, Johnston says, "Sermons can become like *Rocky* pictures, if the inevitable victory becomes boring and predictable. So to best intrigue and inform, invite listeners along as you investigate the spiritual journey of Bible characters" (*Preaching to a Postmodern World*, 111). Though not speaking of formal drama, Larsen's point is still valuable: "Long ago Aristotle maintained that the soul never thinks without pictures. People today are even more taken with images than with ideas. We have too much argument—discourse stripped of its mystery—in our sermons and not enough drama" (Larsen, *Anatomy of Preaching*, 108).

[62]Kenneth L. Carder, "Doctrinal/Theological Themes for Preaching: John Wesley and the Galatian and Colossian Letters," *Quarterly Review* 12, no. 2 (1992): 105.

[63]John Piper, *The Supremacy of God in Preaching* (Grand Rapids: Baker Books, 1990), 88. Wiersbe claims that metaphorical language helps the preacher "turn people's ears into eyes and help[s] them see the truth" (Wiersbe, *Preaching & Teaching*, 43).

and/or practically applicable.[64]

The Use of Story in Doctrinal Exposition

Since mankind's beginning in the Book of Genesis, storytelling has been an important part of life as people passed on different accounts to each generation. Even today, stories make for best-sellers, whether they are biographies of famous people or novels of make-believe characters and events. The bottom line is that everyone loves a good story. Storytelling in preaching is gaining ground every day, perhaps as never before in the history of preaching. Its popularity alone demands the attention of homiletics.

Problem. In addition to re-language and re-imaging in twenty-first century preaching, proponents of the New Homiletic centralize their discussion on the use of story. In fact, they claim that "the role[s] of story and imagery. . . . are themselves the substance of the sermon and are what impacts and changes listeners' consciousness."[65] The substance they speak of is a misnomer, for they attest that images and stories may be ambiguous. In this case "each takes on a new dimension. The story or image has many possible and different meanings."[66] If image and story as the heart of preaching can have a multitude of meanings, then the substance they offer must be about as filling as cotton candy—though it can come in different flavors, it does not satisfy hunger pains.

Furthermore, the New Homiletic pushes story so far as to insist that it is fundamental, even pointing to Jesus' parabolic preaching as the model.[67] Larsen warns that "when the story is primary and the parables paradigmatic we have, in effect, a new canon."[68] Similarly, Wiersbe cautions,

---

[64]Steven D. Mathewson, *The Art of Preaching Old Testament Narrative* (Grand Rapids: Baker Academic, 2002), 142-43. See below for applying doctrine.

[65]Hughes and Kysar, *Preaching Doctrine*, 12.

[66]Ibid., 57.

[67]See David Buttrick, *Homiletic: Moves and Structures* (Philadelphia: Fortress Press, 1987); idem, *Speaking Parables: A Homiletic Guide* (Louisville: Westminster John Knox Press, 2000); Fred B. Craddock, *Preaching* (Nashville: Abingdon Press, 1985); Eugene L. Lowry, *The Homiletical Plot: The Sermon as Narrative Art Form*, rev. ed. (Louisville: Westminster John Knox Press, 2001).

[68]Larsen, *Anatomy of Preaching*, 146.

The metaphor is not the subject of the sermon. If handled properly, the metaphor expands the subject, illumines it and helps to make it vivid and personal to our listeners; but the metaphor is not the message. To turn a metaphor into an allegory is a dangerous step for the biblical preacher to take. . . .

[Furthermore], metaphor must never replace precise definition of doctrine. . . . our pictures must not be substituted for theological precepts.[69]

Story, while important, must not shape the sermon but rather supplement it.

Proposal. With all of the problems that Hughes's and Kysar's work raises, they provide some helpful advice. One of their suggestions for using story in preaching is "that story may bridge the gap between literate and post-literate mentalities."[70] Herein lies an important point: the older the group, the more likely it is to learn through *reading*; the younger the group, the more likely it is to learn through *watching*; both groups, however, are accustomed to stories. Moreover, a reason storytelling is essential today is because "the climate is right. Storytelling thrives in times and places where imagination, intuition and affect assert themselves."[71] At the same time, "The rediscovery of the story can bring us healthy variation and greater balance as well as grip our people anew with the power and appeal of the gospel."[72]

Because of the high probability of ambiguity through story, contemporary preaching must avoid strict narrative preaching. While some people may very well get the main point of a biblical text through narrative preaching, its inductive approach often leaves too many people guessing. As mentioned in chapter 12, sermons on narrative texts represent the Bible best through re-telling the story, but something of an inductive-deductive approach will make certain that the audience does not miss the point of the story.

Hughes and Kysar adamantly disagree with this approach:

---

[69]Wiersbe, *Preaching & Teaching*, 82-83.

[70]Hughes and Kysar, *Preaching Doctrine*, 66.

[71]Gabriel J. Fackre, *The Christian Story: A Narrative Interpretation of Basic Christian Doctrine*, rev. ed. (Grand Rapids: Eerdmans, 1984), 5-6. For additional help in telling stories creatively, see D. Bruce Seymour, *Creating Stories That Connect: A Pastor's Guide to Storytelling* (Grand Rapids: Kregel, 2007).

[72]Larsen, *Anatomy of Preaching*, 150.

Reflecting on a story is not the same as telling the hearers what the story *means*. To do so violates the power of the story to mean something on its own without reducing it to some moral. Reflecting on story does not close the tale. It does not limit what the hearer can find in the story for themselves.[73]

Fred Craddock defends this approach, arguing that preaching is best done as "overhearing the gospel." He favors indirect application, letting the listeners decide what to do with the message.[74] Advocates of this position often point to the preaching of Jesus, the prophets, and the apostles for their support.

Evidently, the preaching of the prophets, apostles, and Jesus were not as open-ended as New Homileticians like to think. In Nathan's story-telling, inductive approach to King David concerning his sin against Uriah and his wife Bathsheba (2 Sam 12:1-6), Nathan had to tell David the meaning—"thou art the man!"—in order for him to acknowledge his sin and repent. Simply ending the message without applied meaning would have left David angry but *unrepentant*. Moreover, Stephen's defense before the Sanhedrin seems to be a retelling of OT narrative (Acts 7:1-50). The Sanhedrin did not really understand the message until Stephen switched from an inductive analysis of the OT to a clear explanation of their own sinfulness (7:51-54). Of course, repentance did not take place in this situation, but God motivated the church to carry out her mission through this event (8:1-3).

Jesus may be the only occasional practitioner of the inductive method, but it most certainly was *occasional*. Like chapter 3 mentions, preachers should not emulate everything in Jesus' preaching. Speaking of Jesus' preaching in parables, York and Decker write,

First of all, Jesus had no single methodology of preaching parables. Sometimes they were short, other times more extended. Sometimes he clearly explained them, and other times he offered no explanation at all, simply an admonition that whoever had ears to hear, let them hear. We might wonder why Jesus did that, but the Bible provides us with the answer. After preaching the parable of the sower, Jesus concluded with, "He who has ears to hear, let him hear" (Mark 4:9). But then, afterward, his closest disciples asked

---

[73]Hughes and Kysar, *Preaching Doctrine*, 70. They conclude that "reflection on story seeks always to honor the ambiguity of a story" (ibid., 71). How the audience is supposed to learn doctrine from this kind of ambiguity still remains unanswered.

[74]See Fred B. Craddock, *Overhearing the Gospel* (Nashville: Abingdon Press, 1978).

him about the meaning of the parable. He answered them, "The secret of the kingdom of God has been given to you. But to those on the outside everything is said in parables so that, 'they may be ever seeing but never perceiving, and ever hearing but never understanding; *otherwise they might turn and be forgiven!*'" (Mark 4:11-12). It might give us pause, but the text clearly states that Jesus' sovereign purpose was to keep some of his listeners in the dark. It was all part of God's plan to culminate in Jesus' crucifixion and resurrection.[75]

These three examples indicate that, with the exception of some of Jesus' preaching, the inductive preaching in the Scriptures almost always ends deductively. Thus, doctrinal exposition of narrative texts will be most biblical when they include both inductive story and deductive doctrinal explanation. Pure inductive preaching may offer as much help as watching an exercise video without actually working out—the benefit is minimal at best.

All of this is not to say that story has little value, for preaching profits greatly from it. Story is so valuable for preaching today that a good rule of thumb would be the more theologically loaded a sermon is, the more important it is to communicate a real-life story.[76] In a discussion about preaching stories, Robinson writes,

> You can deal abstractly with a great principle—God is sovereign—in a way that gets boring. Such a sermon reminds me of a hovercraft that floats eight feet above the ground but never lands into life. Without the human element, you lose the specific, the historical narrative, the emotional interaction.[77]

Likewise, Charles Duey claims, "Theology is only stuffy when made stuffy, and only obscure when preached in erudite terms *ad nauseum*, without illustrations."[78] A sermon's use of story also helps the audience experience

---

[75]York and Decker, *Preaching with Bold Assurance*, 16.

[76]Allen claims, "Nearly every sermon that gives priority to systematic theology should contain at least one real-life story that brings theology to life" (*Preaching Is Believing*, 89). Coffin agrees, "Still another necessity is telling illustrations. Doctrinal sermons, more than any other kind of preaching, are liable to be heavy in language" (*What to Preach*, 62).

[77]Haddon W. Robinson, "The Heresy of Application," *Leadership* 18, no. 4 (1997): 27.

[78]Charles J. Duey, "Let's Preach Theology," *The Covenant Quarterly* 21, no. 2 (1963): 17. Commenting on Luther's uses of images and story, Sproul says that Luther "advises that, when preaching on abstract doctrine, the pastor find

the text, leading to a greater understanding of it.[79]

As should be evident by now, preaching must continue to use theological terms, especially those found in the Scriptures. At the same time, definitional clarity needs to be at the forefront of doctrinal exposition, so that today's listeners can better comprehend the message of the Bible. Imagery and story are significant factors in this discussion, and expositors will want to strike a proper balance between word-pictures and story on the one hand and biblical fidelity and theological substance on the other hand. Doctrinal exposition for the twenty-first century certainly must deal with the theology of each text, taking time to explain the doctrine in its passage in a way that the audience understands.[80]

---

a narrative in Scripture that communicates that truth, and to communicate the abstract through the concrete" ("The Teaching Preacher," 164).

[79]See David C. Deuel, "Suggestions for Expositional Preaching of Old Testament Narrative," *The Master's Seminary Journal* 2, no. 1 (1991): 54. For ways to tell the story more effectively, see Mathewson, *Art of Preaching OT Narrative*, 132-42; Johnston, *Preaching to a Postmodern World*, 158-62.

[80]See Walter L. Liefeld, *New Testament Exposition: From Text to Sermon* (Grand Rapids: Zondervan, 1984), 41.

CHAPTER 14
APPLICATION IN DOCTRINAL EXPOSITORY PREACHING: TRAINING OTHERS TO BECOME BODYBUILDERS

Application in expository preaching should be a given. In order for application to be as effective as possible, it needs to be both doctrinally sound and practically useful. Evangelical preachers should regret that many of the biblical doctrines of the Reformation are foreign to their contemporary listeners. Doctrines associated with such terms as justification, atonement, original sin, imputed righteousness, and even repentance need clarification so that today's church can both understand the nature of the good news and appropriate it by faith. Since this element focuses on relating doctrine to the congregation, it is helpful to think of training others to build their spiritual bodies.

Knowing the Audience
William Perkins speaks of applying doctrine as "the skill by which the doctrine which has been properly drawn from the Scriptures is handled in ways which are appropriate to the circumstances of the place and time and to the people in the congregation."[1] Touching on the congregational focus of application, Klaas Runia writes,

> A sermon is like an *ellipse with two foci*: the *text of the Bible* and the *situation of the hearers*. And preparing and delivering a sermon means that these two foci have to be interrelated in a process of continual

---

[1]William Perkins, *The Art of Prophesying; with the Calling of the Ministry* (Cambridge: J. Legatt, 1592; reprint, Carlisle, PA: The Banner of Truth Trust, 1996), 54.

reciprocity."[2]

Similarly, Johnston says that preachers have

> two burdens: Reach the listener, a fellow human being, with the
> message of Christ, and at the same time uphold the Word of God,
> faithfully and with integrity. The best biblical communicators will
> not sacrifice either burden but will allow these dual desires to fuel
> one another.[3]

These statements underscore the importance of people to preaching,
for "if the people are forgotten, then preaching is not preaching; and the
sermon is no sermon, but merely an essay which is a very different type of
thing—the consideration of some subject in the abstract."[4] Indeed, "the
pew craves clarity from the pulpit. It wants to know particulars. It wants
applications. It wants to know how a truth has impact. It wants the descent
from theory into practice, from ideas into life."[5] In order to apply doctrine
effectively, preachers must know both the text and the audience.

Showing the Relevance

Knowing the audience to whom one is preaching will aid him in focusing
the application on relevance. In this age of pragmatism, people often
wonder about the "so what?" of biblical preaching. Thus, application in
doctrinal exposition must portray both meaning and *relevance*. Lloyd-Jones
states,

> This question of relevance must never be forgotten. As I have said,
> you are not lecturing, you are not reading an essay; you are setting
> out to do something definite and particular, to influence these
> people and the whole of their lives and outlook. Obviously,
> therefore, you have got to show the relevance of all this. You are

---

[2]Klaas Runia, "What Is Preaching according to the New Testament?"
Tyndale Bulletin, no. 29 (1978): 41. Robinson, too, writes, "Let's face it. We
don't teach the Bible. We teach *people* the Bible. As vital as it is to know
content, it's not enough. We must know our audiences" (Haddon W. Robinson,
foreword to *Preaching to a Postmodern World: A Guide to Reaching Twenty-
First Century Listeners*, by Graham Johnston [Grand Rapids: Baker Books, 2001],
7).

[3]Johnston, *Preaching to a Postmodern World*, 18-19.

[4]Arthur John Gossip, "The Whole Counsel of God: The Place of Biblical
Doctrine in Preaching," *Interpretation* 1, no. 3 (1947): 332.

[5]Mark E. Yurs, "Breaking the Story: Preaching as Naming the Activity of
God Today," *Preaching* 16, no. 3 (2000): 42.

PREACHING FOR BODYBUILDING

not an antiquary lecturing on ancient history or on ancient civilisations, or something like that. The preacher is a man who is speaking to people who are alive today and confronted by the problems of life; and therefore you have to show that this is not some academic or theoretical matter which may be of interest to people who take up that particular hobby, as others take up crossword puzzles or something of that type. You are to show that this message is vitally important to them, and that they must listen with the whole of their being, because this really is going to help them to live.[6]

These aspects of meaning and relevance center on doctrine, for "to be always relevant, you have to say things which are eternal."[7]

Along with relevance comes the issue of practicality. As is often the case, "the cry has been: 'Give us practical sermons, not theology.' But nothing is so practical as doctrine of the right kind."[8] Therefore, doctrinal exposition "should be related as closely as possible to the problems of daily life in our modern world."[9] Tim Keller points readers toward the larger issue within practicality:

This is a critical and difficult balance for the Christian preacher. Every message and point must demonstrate relevance or the listener will mentally "channel surf." But once you have drawn in people with the amazing relevance and practical wisdom of the gospel, you must confront them with the most pragmatic issue of all—the claim of Christ to be absolute Lord of life.[10]

---

[6]D. Martyn Lloyd-Jones, *Preaching & Preachers* (Grand Rapids: Zondervan, 1971), 76.

[7]Os Guinness, "Sounding Out the Idols of Church Growth," in *No God but God*, ed. Os Guinness and John Seel (Chicago: Moody Press, 1992), 169. Guinness refers to Simone Weil as the origin of this quotation.

[8]Henry Sloane Coffin, *What to Preach* (New York: Harper & Brothers, 1926), 47.

[9]Donald M. Ballie, "The Preaching of Christian Doctrine," in *The Theology of the Sacraments: and Other Papers* (New York: Charles Scribner's Sons, 1957), 151. See also Hershael W. York and Scott A. Blue, "Is Application Necessary in the Expository Sermon?" *The Southern Baptist Journal of Theology* 3, no. 2 (1999): 73; Scott Avery Blue, "Application in the Expository Sermon: A Case for Its Necessary Inclusion" (Ph.D. diss., The Southern Baptist Theological Seminary, 2000).

[10]Timothy J. Keller, "Preaching Morality in an Amoral Age: How You Can

Finally, relevance in application will likely affect how the listener has experienced the doctrine. Some describe the application and experience of Christian doctrine through preaching as "experiential or experimental preaching," because

> experimental preaching seeks to explain in terms of biblical truth how matters ought to go, how they do go, and what is the goal of the Christian life. It aims to apply divine truth to the whole range of the believer's personal experience as well as in his relationships with family, the church, and the world around him.[11]

So, applied doctrine touches relevant, practical, and experiential elements of the audience.

Features of Applying Doctrine

Once the preacher accepts the necessity of application in doctrinal exposition, he can begin to appreciate some of the features of applying doctrine. First, the application of doctrine is extremely important, for one's doctrine affects his duty, even as situations change. That is, Christian living rests on Christian doctrine. Much of the Great Commission involves teaching (doctrine) to observe (duty). Thus, doctrine and application go together. Ephesians 4 is a good example of theology applied, for Paul deals with individual problems from the basis of doctrinal truth.

Furthermore, in this experience-as-truth world, one needs to teach that Christian living "involves more than experience. Biblical Christian living is grounded in sound doctrine, sound experience, and sound practice."[12] Additionally, "theology is meant to be *lived* and *prayed* and *sung*! All of the great doctrinal writings of the Bible (such as Paul's epistle to the Romans) are full of praise to God and personal application to life."[13]

Second, doctrinal exposition, while presenting the great doctrines of the faith from its numerous heroes of the past, focuses on the here-and-now. Ferguson notes,

> Those preaching helps must rather be thoroughly digested by us,

Blow the Whistle When People Don't Believe There Are Rules," *Leadership* 17, no. 1 (1996): 113.

[11]Joel R. Beeke, "The Lasting Power of Reformed Experiential Preaching," in *Feed My Sheep: A Passionate Plea for Preaching*, ed. Don Kistler (Morgan, PA: Soli Deo Gloria, 2000), 95-96.

[12]Ibid., 125.

[13]Wayne Grudem, *Systematic Theology: An Introduction to Biblical Doctrine* (Grand Rapids: Zondervan, 1994), 16-17.

made our own, and applied to people today in today's language. . . .

In this sense, biblical exposition must speak to the people sitting today in the pews, not to those who sat in them hundred [sic] of years ago![14]

Finally, expositors must apply "doctrine in a hortatory and practical way. . . . [driving] the doctrine home to the individual."[15] While discussing 2 Timothy 3:16-17, Perkins says,

Practical application has to do with life-style and behaviour and involves instruction and correction.

Instruction is the application of doctrine to enable us to live well in the context of the family, the state, and the church. It involves both encouragement and exhortation (*Rom.* 15:4).

Correction is the application of doctrine in a way that transforms lives marked by ungodliness and unrighteousness. This involves admonition.[16]

Though correction is unpopular in a "judge not lest ye be judged" mindset of many of today's people, the application of doctrine upholds the truth and encourages change in accordance with that truth. Such preaching builds up the body of Christ.

Valuable Doctrines for Evangelicalism Today

Many preachers need little persuasion when it comes to the need for doctrinal preaching today. What doctrines are important for conservative evangelicalism, however, is a matter of debate.[17] Though disagreement will

---

[14]Sinclair B. Ferguson, "Preaching to the Heart," in *Feed My Sheep*, 205.

[15]Donald Macleod, "Preaching and Systematic Theology," in *The Preacher and Preaching: Reviving the Art in the Twentieth Cenutry*, ed. Samuel T. Logan, Jr. (Phillipsburg, NJ: Presbyterian and Reformed Publishing, 1986), 265.

[16]Perkins, *The Art of Prophesying*, 65. Lloyd-Jones writes, "It is vital to the sermon that it should always end on [a] note of application or of exhortation" (*Preaching & Preachers*, 78). For ways to apply doctrine with authority, love, integrity, conviction, etc., see Macleod, "Preaching and Systematic Theology," 271; David L. Larsen, *Telling the Old, Old Story: The Art of Narrative Preaching* (Wheaton: Crossway Books, 1995), 257-69; Clarence S. Roddy, "On the Preaching of Theology," *Christianity Today* 3, no. 23 (1959): 7.

[17]I use the term "conservative evangelical" to define historical evangelicalism and its acceptance of such subjects as biblical inerrancy and divine omniscience. The more recent open theist movement evidently wants to re-define evangelicalism away from other historic definitions. For a thorough critique of open theism, showing it as outside the parameters of

most likely occur with at least some of the following issues, several valuable doctrines for evangelicalism remain.

Distinguishing between Primary and Secondary

Since some might question how one is to know what is significant enough for all evangelicals and what can be left out, they will most certainly need to begin by distinguishing between primary and secondary doctrines. Hagner writes,

> Another way of expressing the distinction is through the terms core and periphery. Some matters of scripture are obviously of central importance while others are of relatively little importance. The tabernacle furniture is clearly subordinate in importance to the Sinai covenant. Whether or not women veil their heads in public worship is obviously peripheral to their behavior as disciples of Christ.[18]

Likewise, Macleod says, "All revealed doctrines are important. But some are absolutely fundamental and primary."[19] To determine what is primary, you should employ the following four criteria:

1. Those things which "are necessary to be known, believed and observed for salvation."
2. Certain doctrines "are so clearly propounded, and opened in some place of Scripture or other, that not only the learned, but the unlearned, in a due use of the ordinary means, may attain unto a sufficient understanding of them."[20]
3. Any doctrine "on which equally devout, equally humble, equally Bible-believing and Bible-studying Christians or churches reach different conclusions must be considered secondary, not primary, peripheral not central."[21]

---

evangelicalism, see Bruce A. Ware, *God's Lesser Glory: The Diminished God of Open Theism* (Wheaton: Crossway Books, 2000). For his positive treatment of divine providence, see idem, *God's Greater Glory: The Exalted God of Scripture and the Christian Faith* (Wheaton: Crossway Books, 2004).

[18]D. A. Hagner, "Biblical Theology and Preaching," *The Expository Times* 96 (February 1985): 138.

[19]See Macleod, "Preaching and Systematic Theology," 257-58.

[20]"The Westminster Confession of Faith" 1.7, in *Creeds of the Church,* 57, in The Master Christian Library, version 5 [CD-ROM] (Albany, OR: AGES Software, 1997).

[21]John R. W. Stott, *Christ the Controversialist* (Downers Grove: Inter-

4. Most importantly, Scripture places the greatest emphasis on the most fundamental doctrines.[22]

Furthermore, Grudem discusses the difference between major and minor doctrines:

> A major doctrine is one that has a significant impact on our thinking about other doctrines, or that has a significant impact on how we live the Christian life. A minor doctrine is one that has very little impact on how we think about other doctrines, and very little impact on how we live the Christian life.[23]

Doctrines concerning biblical authority, the Trinity, Christ's deity, and justification by faith are all major doctrines within historical evangelicalism. At the same time, issues over church government, details about communion, and some last things are not as significant for evangelicalism.[24]

Preaching Primary Doctrines

A good starting place for determining primary doctrine is the doctrines of the Early Church, for people have used them throughout history to determine orthodoxy. The Apostles' Creed (ca. A.D. 150-215) and the creeds at Nicea (A.D. 325), Constantinople (A.D. 381), Ephesus (A.D. 431), and Chalcedon (A.D. 451) stress the Church's basic views concerning the Trinity and Jesus Christ. Irenaeus's "Rule of Faith" (second century) may

---

Varsity Press, 1970), 44.

[22]See, for example, Deut 6:4-5; Matt 22:37-40; John 3:1-21; 1 Cor 15:3ff; Gal 1:8-9; 1 John 4:2; etc.

[23]Grudem, *Systematic Theology*, 29. In categorizing different levels of importance among doctrine, see Al Mohler, "A Call for Theological Triage and Christian Maturity," (May 20, 2004), available at albertmohler.com/2004/05/20/a-call-for-theological-triage-and-christian-maturity-2/; accessed 16 September 2009.

[24]See Grudem, *Systematic Theology*, 29-30. Though some African-American preachers are guilty of making race a *major* doctrinal issue rather than a *minor* one, Russell D. Moore, writing about the growth of African-American churches, correctly notes that race is "a *theological* issue in the context of the Great Commission. Thus, the *Baptist Faith and Message* (2000) grounds racial justice in two gospel commitments—the *imago Dei* and the atonement of Christ" ("Resurgence vs. McWorld? American Culture and the Future of Baptist Conservatism," *The Southern Baptist Journal of Theology* 7, no. 1 [2003]: 39). See also "III. Man," in the *Baptist Faith and Message* (Nashville: LifeWay Christian Resources, 2000), 10.

very well precede even the Apostles' Creed and declares belief in the Trinity:

> . . . this faith: in one God, the Father Almighty, who made the heaven and the earth and the seas and all the things that are in them; and in one Christ Jesus, the Son of God, who was made flesh for our salvation; and in the Holy Spirit, who made known through the prophets the plan of salvation, and the coming, and the birth from a virgin, and the passion, and the resurrection from the dead, and the bodily ascension into heaven of the beloved Christ Jesus, our Lord, and his future appearing from heaven in the glory of the Father to sum up all things and to raise anew all flesh of the whole human race. . . .[25]

Moreover, the Chalcedonian Creed confesses Jesus Christ to be Lord, fully God, fully man, sinless, and eternal.[26] Therefore, evangelical doctrine must begin with orthodoxy.

Besides being orthodox, doctrinal exposition must be distinctly evangelical. Tom Nettles correctly claims, "While great openness characterizes evangelicalism, definite parameters must exist."[27] Several theological issues—both biblical and systematic—remain fundamental to evangelicalism today. As to biblical theology,

> here are some themes that may be useful: covenants, the kingdom of God, the gospel, the temple, promise and fulfillment, the people of God, the land and the inheritance, the promise of the Messiah, the promises to Abraham, atonement, resurrection, creation and new creation.[28]

---

[25]Irenaeus, "Rule of Faith," in *Creeds of the Church*, 6, in The Master Christian Library, version 5 [CD-ROM]. For other creeds of the Early Church, see *Creeds of the Church*, 8-14.

[26]See "Definition of Chalcedon," in *Creeds of the Church*, 12, in The Master Christian Library, version 5 [CD-ROM].

[27]Thomas J. Nettles, *By His Grace and for His Glory: A Historical, Theological, and Practical Study of the Doctrines of Grace in Baptist Life* (Grand Rapids: Baker Book House, 1986), 20. Nettles focuses specifically on evangelical soteriology which "asserts the uniqueness of Jesus Christ as the personal revelation of God, the completeness of his work in humiliation and exaltation for the redemption of sinners, the effectual working of the Holy Spirit through the preaching of the gospel, and the necessity of an uncoerced response of repentance and faith" (ibid., 21).

[28]Peter J. H. Adam, "Preaching and Biblical Theology," in *New Dictionary of Biblical Theology: Exploring the Unity & Diversity of Scripture*, ed. T. Desmond

Such themes will certainly provide a Christ-centered focus for both doctrine and preaching.

Concerning systematic theology, expositors must, first, teach theology proper. Such teaching should deal with God's Trinitarian nature and His various attributes, including His holiness, sovereignty, omnipotence, omniscience, justice, grace, mercy, and love. Second, biblical anthropology remains an important issue. The Bible presents man as a sinner in need of salvation by His Creator. Sin's origin is with Adam and its penalty is eternal death.

Third, doctrinal expositors must consistently declare Christology and soteriology. Both the deity and humanity of Jesus Christ are essential, as well as the exclusivity of faith in Him and His atoning work on the cross for sin. Leon Morris speaks of the latter as the "key doctrine. The atonement is the crucial doctrine of the faith. Unless we are right here it matters little, or so it seems to me, what we are like elsewhere."[29] Moreover, Christ's glorious resurrection proves He is the Messiah and is the foundation for the future resurrection of believers.[30]

Fourth, evangelical preaching must retain the Spirit's work in sanctification as well as human responsibility. Issues of personal holiness, obedience, faith, repentance, and service focus more on practical doctrine, but it is biblical doctrine nonetheless. Expositors must uphold the church as the body of Christ and speak of it in terms of its gospel mission. Finally, doctrinal exposition must not forget matters of eternity. Heaven and hell are real, Christ will soon return to judge the living and the dead, and everyone begins life on the road to hell, spared only by receiving God's glorious gospel of grace by faith.[31]

Individual preachers will most surely want to emphasize certain denominational doctrines, and they should by all means do so. Even though

Alexander and others (Downers Grove: InterVarsity Press, 2000), 109.

[29]Leon Morris, *The Cross in the New Testament* (Grand Rapids: Wm. B. Eerdmans, 1965), 5.

[30]Graeme Goldsworthy observes, "Evangelical thinking has tended to stress, rightly, the substitutionary atoning death of Jesus. Sometimes this is at the expense of the importance of the resurrection" (*Preaching the Whole Bible as Christian Scripture: The Application of Biblical Theology to Expository Preaching* [Grand Rapids: Wm. B. Eerdmans, 2000], 57).

[31]Beeke, "Power of Reformed Experiential Preaching," 125-28. Cf. Coffin (*What to Preach*, 75-80), who highlights divine providence, prayer, the cross of Christ, and redemption as necessary subjects for doctrinal preaching.

evangelicals cannot agree on every minor doctrine, doctrinal expository preaching must herald these primary doctrines, for without doing so, there will be little edification for the body of Christ.

When expositors focus on such doctrines, they will declare that

1. All are sinners—not sick and in need help [sic] but dead and in need life [sic].
2. Jesus Christ, God's Son, is the only perfect, able, and willing Savior of sinners (even the worst).
3. The Father and the Son have promised that all who know themselves to be such sinners and put their faith in Christ as Savior shall be received into favor, and none will be cast out.
4. God has made repentance and faith a duty, requiring of every man who hears the gospel a serious and full casting of the soul upon Christ as the all-sufficient Savior, ready, able, and willing to save *all* that come to God by Him.[32]

Such evangelical doctrines uphold the full authority of God's Word and stress the Bible's central message about the Person and work of Jesus Christ.

This chapter has shown how doctrinal expository preaching can be done in a postmodern setting. The postmodern culture demands that preachers deal seriously with truth, language, imaging, and story in contemporary preaching. Further, the pragmatic attitude of postmodernism makes applying doctrine crucially important. This study has noted several individual doctrines as primary within conservative evangelicalism and today's doctrinal expository preaching must retain these doctrines. May evangelical preachers engage the present postmodern culture with the sure message of truth from the One True God so that our preaching strengthens the people of God!

---

[32]Ernest Reisinger, "The Human Will and Doctrinal Decline," *The Founders Journal*, no. 26 (1996) [journal on-line]; accessed 2 April 2003; available from founders.org/FJ26/article2_fr.html.

Part 6: Beneficial Elements of Doctrinal Exposition

CHAPTER 15
THOUGH DIFFICULT, DOCTRINAL EXPOSITION IS WORTH IT: COOLING DOWN AND ASSESSING YOUR WORKOUT

I hope you have seen both the necessity and relevance of doctrinal expository preaching as a kind of preaching that builds up a body of believers. Before summarizing the main arguments of this study, several beneficial elements concerning doctrinal expository preaching should help emphasize its practicality as well as the need for its implementation. The following areas also reiterate some of the distinctive features of doctrinal exposition. Think of this section as the cooling down phase of a workout—you assess how you feel and begin to think about whether the exercise was worth the energy. Though you feel the pain more initially, the benefits become clearer the more you go through the routine.

Reasons for Doctrinal Expository Preaching
In light of the biblical foundation for doctrinal exposition, a number of reasons for this approach stand out. These reasons are both theological and practical. First, doctrinal exposition reminds preachers to allow God to set the agenda in preaching.[1] All expository preaching begins with God's Word, letting it drive the content and focus of the message. Doctrinal exposition, at the same time, permits the theology of the text to shape the sermon.

Second, doctrinal exposition treats the Scriptures the way God did, respecting the history, literary features, and styles of the human authors.[2]

---

[1]Peter Adam, *Speaking God's Words: A Practical Theology of Expository Preaching* (Downers Grove: InterVarsity Press, 1996), 128.

[2]Ibid.

Furthermore, in the book-by-book approach preachers must necessarily deal with both familiar and difficult passages. Preachers determined to preach the whole counsel of God can balance passages of God's love with texts on His holiness. In this approach expositors also treat issues they might rather avoid, such as divorce, just war, and church discipline. Additionally, since God saw fit to display an array of literary genres, preachers would do well to interpret the Bible accordingly. The fact that the Bible is a theological book also means that interpreters should observe the doctrinal content of each passage.

Third, this kind of preaching gives confidence and authority to the preacher. After careful biblical and theological exegesis, he can stand before people with an open Bible and a "thus saith the Lord" message.[3] As the expositor faithfully declares the Word, the Word itself assures him of its effectiveness in the lives of others (cf. Isa 55:11).

Fourth, doctrinal exposition provides enough time for preachers to clarify the larger contexts of the particular passage at hand week-in and week-out.[4] Moreover, preachers have little to worry about when it comes to preaching each Sunday, for the individual contexts of each book and its theological emphasis will set the boundaries of the sermon. Doctrinal expository preaching feeds people with the grand themes of the Scriptures in small morsels, providing ongoing nourishment for their lives.

Fifth, doctrinal exposition helps keep preachers humble.[5] Realizing the vast expanse of the Bible's teachings in practicing doctrinal exposition makes us as preachers remember our own insignificance. At the same time, an attitude of gratitude should mark the expositor as he thanks God for using him for such an awesome task.

Sixth, while this method of preaching humbles the preacher, it also matures him in his understanding of the Bible and its theology. Since every pastor is a theologian, he should strive to be "mighty in the Scriptures." Doctrinal exposition drives the preacher to this goal.

Seventh, many people are hungry for a holistic approach to preaching,[6] and doctrinal exposition can satisfy their hunger. Even those who are not

[3]Kent Hughes, "The Anatomy of Exposition: *Logos, Ethos,* and *Pathos," The Southern Baptist Journal of Theology* 3, no. 2 (1999): 51.

[4]Adam, *Speaking God's Words,* 128.

[5]Charles J. Duey, "Let's Preach Theology," *The Covenant Quarterly* 21, no. 2 (1963): 14-15.

[6]Ronald J. Allen, *Preaching Is Believing: The Sermon as Theological Reflection* (Louisville: Westminster John Knox Press, 2002), 25-26.

visually hungry for this method need it for their spiritual health. As Reisinger states,

> Biblical doctrine is more important than most church members realize. Doctrine not only expresses our experiences and beliefs; it also determines our direction. Doctrine shapes our lives and church programs. Doctrine to the Christian and the church is what the bones are to the body. It gives unity and stability.[7]

One way doctrinal exposition achieves this holistic approach is by employing systematic theology as the unifying factor in Scripture. At the same time, biblical theology helps keep the message focused while exposition particularizes a portion of God's entire message.

Eighth, doctrinal expository preaching helps fight against the problem of theological illiteracy in today's pews. Preaching both doctrinally and expositionally "raises doctrinal literacy which in turn encourages careful study and prayer by the preacher."[8] Even though some criticize expository preaching as mere informational preaching which does not affect one's behavior, research shows that teaching biblical doctrine affects both how one thinks and acts.[9] Furthermore, this preaching helps prevent church members from falling prey to the cults. Commenting on the growth of cults, Oswalt notes, "A weighty portion of their converts are from churches of all denominations, leaving no doubt that inadequate teaching of the central doctrines of the Bible by the churches is one primary reason why their members are vulnerable to false doctrine."[10]

Finally, doctrinal exposition done rightly is the most interesting, effective, and biblical of all preaching.[11] It teaches the truths of God

---

[7]Ernest Reisinger, "The Human Will and Doctrinal Decline," *The Founders Journal*, no. 26 (1996) [journal on-line]; accessed 2 April 2003; available from founders.org/FJ26/ article2_fr.html.

[8]Tom Ascol, "The Pastor as Theologian," *The Founders Journal*, no. 43 (2001) [journal on-line]; accessed 20 January 2003; available from founders.org/FJ43/editorial_fr.html.

[9]See Brian Richardson, "Do Bible Facts Change Attitudes?" *Bibliotheca Sacra* 140, no. 558 (1983): 163-72. For criticism of expository preaching, see Charles Bugg, "Back to the Bible: Toward a New Description of Expository Preaching," *Review and Expositor* 90, no. 3 (1993): 417.

[10]Jerry E. Oswalt, *Proclaiming the Whole Counsel of God: Suggestions for Planning and Preparing Doctrinal Sermons* (New York: University Press of America, 1993), ix.

[11]See Faris Daniel Whitesell, *The Art of Biblical Preaching* (Grand Rapids:

passionately, practically, and soundly. May God's servants of His Word find these reasons to be sufficient for practicing doctrinal expository preaching to build lives!

Goals in Doctrinal Expository Preaching

In addition to several reasons for doctrinal exposition, a number of goals or aims also exist. You might label these goals as the purposes of preaching. As such there exists a three-fold purpose to doctrinal exposition: service to God and Christ, service to God's Word, and service to God's people.[12]

First, the primary goal of such preaching is service to God and Christ, or aiming for the glory of God. The fact that Scripture clearly reveals God receiving glory from His servants makes this a worthy aim. Few have emphasized this goal as much as John Piper.[13] In order to fulfill this goal, preaching must be grounded in the cross of Christ, and the preacher must gladly submit to Christ in all things. These essentials in preaching and life form what Piper calls Christian hedonism—"God is most glorified in me when I am most satisfied in Him."[14] Following this line of thought, two of the main ways Christians glorify God the most are in the edification of the saints (Eph 4:11-16)—hence, preaching for bodybuilding—and in the evangelization of the sinners (Matt 28:19-20). The primary means by which God is glorified in these actions is through the preaching and teaching of His Word (Acts 2:42). Such preaching awakens the hearers' response to seize the promises of God (Heb 4:12). By aiming for the glory of God, doctrinal exposition unfolds both God's majesty and His mercy through His own self-disclosure (Rom 11:33-36).

Second, the explanation and commendation of the gospel of God's grace in Jesus Christ is a goal of doctrinal exposition.[15] As the central message of the Bible, the gospel entails a manifold aim in preaching's

---

Zondervan, 1950), 24-25. For the advantages of biblical preaching for both the audience and the preacher, see Whitesell, *The Art of Biblical Preaching*, 24-36.

[12]For a more complete discussion of this three-fold purpose, see Adam, *Speaking God's Words*, 126-35.

[13]See John Piper, *The Supremacy of God in Preaching* (Grand Rapids: Baker Books, 1990), 17-63.

[14]Piper explains this philosophy in his book *Desiring God: Meditations of a Christian Hedonist* (Sisters, OR: Multnomah Press, 1996).

[15]Adam, *Speaking God's Words*, 89.

relation to Scripture.[16] Primarily, expositors must teach the content of Scripture. The week-by-week content contributes to the goal of declaring the whole counsel of God (Acts 20:26-27). This preaching translates the theological words of the Bible without distorting their meaning (1 Thess 2:13). Also, preachers must show the purpose of Scripture. God has given Scripture not only for doctrine, but also "for reproof, for correction, for training in righteousness" (2 Tim 3:16). That is, Scripture both teaches and trains. Finally, preachers need to model a good use of Scripture. People ought to see preachers practice sound hermeneutics before them. In this way the authority of God can correct the misconceptions of tradition (Mark 2:22).

Lastly, doctrinal exposition aims at God's people in informing the mind, instructing the heart, and influencing behavior. In relation to informing the mind, this preaching teaches God's truth and challenges people to let their minds be renewed biblically and Christologically (Rom 12:2; Phil 2:5-11). Moreover, it encourages people to test the sermon by Scripture. Such preaching falls within the largest context of the whole canon of Scripture and preachers should encourage people to compare the sermon with the full biblical teachings. As to the instruction of the heart, doctrinal exposition arouses people to a need to worship their Creator (1 Tim 6:14-16; John 4:24). Moreover, doctrinal exposition enables hearers to experience God speaking personally (Jer 15:16). Finally, the aim at influencing behavior motivates people not only to think with a Christian worldview but also to live with one in today's postmodern world (Isa 55:10-11).

In summary, it is refreshing to hear the words of James Stewart on the goals of preaching. He claims that the

> aims and ends of all genuine preaching [are] to quicken the conscience by the holiness of God, to feed the mind with the truth of God, to purge the imagination by the beauty of God, to open the heart to the love of God, to devote the will to the purpose of God.[17]

Surely doctrinal expository preaching aims as high.

Some Values of Doctrinal Expository Preaching

The practice of doctrinal expository preaching also underscores a few

---

[16]See Walter L. Leifeld, *New Testament Exposition: From Text to Sermon* (Grand Rapids: Zondervan, 1984), 15-16; Adam, *Speaking God's Words*, 103-04.

[17]James S. Stewart, *Heralds of God* (New York: Charles Scribner's Sons, 1946), 73.

values for preaching, the preacher and the congregation.

For Preaching

First, as to preaching, doctrinal exposition glorifies God, the ultimate end of life.[18] Furthermore, it is valuable because it promotes a high view of several key doctrines in salvation—Scripture, God, Christ, the gospel, and the people of God.[19]

Second, doctrinal exposition also takes meaning seriously. Therefore, it defines theological terms openly, honestly, and faithfully to the biblical text. It conveys biblical truth in contemporary language.

Third, it serves as an important protection against the improper interpretation of Scripture. It defends the historic doctrines of Scripture against today's growing heresies, i.e., it can correct bad or false doctrine (2 Tim 4:1-5).[20] Moreover, it recognizes that certain doctrinal beliefs are absolute to salvation, such as the ability of God to save, the deity of Jesus Christ, and the repentance from sin to trust in Christ.

Fourth, this preaching allows Scripture to shape the sermon outline. By doing so, the sermon honors the substance and shape of the Bible. Biblical-theological exposition employs "the great variety of biblical revelation, exploring every genre of writing, every stage of biblical revelation, and every style of revelation."[21]

For the Preacher

Concerning the preacher, doctrinal exposition provides him with authority

---

[18]Alistair Begg, *Preaching for God's Glory* (Wheaton: Crossway Books, 1999), 33.

[19]Graeme Goldsworthy, *Preaching the Whole Bible as Christian Scripture: The Application of Biblical Theology to Expository Preaching* (Grand Rapids: Wm. B. Eerdmans, 2000), 30. A footnote refers readers to an expansion of this discussion in Goldsworthy, "The Pastor as Biblical Theologian," in *Interpreting God's Plan: Biblical Theology and the Pastor*, ed. R. J. Gibbons (Carlisle: Paternoster, 1997).

[20]Millard J. Erickson and James L. Heflin, *Old Wine in New Wineskins: Doctrinal Preaching in a Changing World* (Grand Rapids: Baker Books, 1997), 63.

[21]Peter J. H. Adam, "Preaching and Biblical Theology," in *New Dictionary of Biblical Theology: Exploring the Unity & Diversity of Scripture*, ed. T. Desmond Alexander and others (Downers Grove: InterVarsity Press, 2000), 110; cf. Liefeld, *NT Exposition*, 11.

and power, because he expounds the eternal truths of God's Word.[22] He can be confident in his preaching, because such preaching magnifies the Lord by relating any particular doctrine to God's redemptive plan in Christ.

Second, practicing doctrinal exposition makes it possible for the preacher to learn God's Word like no other kind of preaching. The grammatical-historical *and* the theological methods of interpretation strengthen the preacher's understanding of the text, which further equips him for the preaching event.

Third, whether one preaches consecutively through books of the Bible or systematically through expositions of doctrine, the preacher honors the Word of God. Moreover, this kind of preaching has an inexhaustible store of sermon material at its disposal and it aids expositors in preparing ahead, helping them avoid getting into ruts and worrying over what to preach.[23]

Fourth, exposition forces the preacher to deal with difficult texts and it demands that the preacher deal seriously and think deeply about *every* text. Even well-known passages should cause expositors to analyze the text critically and carefully while setting it within the larger theological framework. At the same time, this preaching can handle touchy subjects and doctrines within sequential preaching without seeming obtrusive.[24]

Fifth, doctrinal expository preaching is valuable because it declares the whole counsel of God. The passage-by-passage, book-by-book approach to exposition renders all the Scriptures as useful. At the same time, the doctrinal approach aims at connecting the passage to the larger theme of redemption-history.

Sixth, doctrinal exposition confines the preacher to the biblical truth of a given passage.[25] While explanation and supplementation may come from other Scripture, this kind of preaching puts a leash on the expositor, keeping him from wandering away from the text at hand.

---

[22]R. Alan Day, "Theology and Preaching," *The Theological Educator*, no. 57 (1998): 102; cf. Merrill F. Unger, *Principles of Expository Preaching* (Grand Rapids: Zondervan, 1955), 24-27; Liefeld, *NT Exposition*, 10.

[23]See F. B. Meyer, *Expository Preaching Plans and Methods* (New York: Hodder & Stoughton, 1912), 49, 119-30; Unger, *Principles of Expository Preaching*, 27-28; Derek Thomas, "Expository Preaching" in *Feed My Sheep: A Passionate Plea for Preaching*, ed. Don Kistler (Morgan, PA: Soli Deo Gloria, 2002), 91.

[24]Liefeld, *NT Exposition*, 11.

[25]Ibid., 10.

For the Congregation

Concerning the congregation, doctrinal expository preaching, first of all, meets human needs. It does this primarily through making much of God, confronting sin, presenting Christ, and challenging people to follow Him.[26]

Second, doctrinal exposition strengthens people spiritually, giving them *"a balanced diet of God's Word"*[27] and encourages them to become students of God's Word, for it "introduces the congregation to the entire Bible."[28] Through faithful hermeneutics and sound theology, people see how to understand the Bible better. Simultaneously, this kind of preaching broadens people's horizons about life. The result is that believers will have a greater desire to learn the Word and grow in Christ's likeness. Moreover, doctrinal exposition teaches a biblical worldview, helping people to "take captive every thought to make it obedient to Christ" (2 Cor 10:5).[29]

Third, doctrinal exposition may clarify a church's beliefs. It may also motivate churches "to *enlarge its theological vision or to recognize fresh possibilities* in its theology, life, and witness."[30] The audience receives a clearer picture of the Bible's message concerning redemptive-history. Rather than experience disconnection from God's purpose for His people, believers may have a greater sense for their own purpose to glorify the God of redemption.

Finally, doctrinal exposition is valuable because it applies doctrine to people's lives. In this pragmatic world, expositors can show people that truth is not only objective and absolute, but it is also practical, behooving people to live by it. On a similar note, doctrinal exposition contributes to the way people understand many contemporary issues; thus, it helps them make sense of the world.[31] Clearly, doctrinal exposition helps people construct their lives on God's Word.

---

[26]Unger, *Principles of Expository Preaching*, 28-29.

[27]Begg, *Preaching for God's Glory*, 36.

[28]Thomas, "Expository Preaching," 84. Sidney Greidanus comments that preaching Christ from the Old Testament—one aspect of doctrinal exposition— acquaints people specifically with the OT and provides them with a fuller understanding of the Person, work, and teaching of Christ (*Preaching Christ from the Old Testament: A Contemporary Hermeneutical Method* [Grand Rapids: Eerdmans, 1999], 62-67).

[29]Adam, "Preaching and Biblical Theology," 111.

[30]Allen, *Preaching Is Believing*, 74; also, ibid., 77.

[31]Erickson and Heflin, *Old Wine in New Wineskins*, 29.

Dangers to Avoid in Doctrinal Exposition

As beneficial as doctrinal expository preaching is, there are some dangers that preachers must avoid. First, the preacher should avoid substituting his own conceptual structure for the text's unifying structure.[32] Preachers usually commit this mistake in forcing a straight-forward deductive method on a narrative text. Such an approach tends to become monotonous, predictive, and uninteresting.

Second, the preacher must be careful he does not impose a doctrine into the text, being guilty of doctrinalizing.[33] Positively stated, he must let the text determine the doctrine. Failure to heed this warning has often resulted in heresies and cultic doctrines. Third, the preacher should keep from forcing divisions on the text.[34] Since the Scripture has the right to provide both substance and shape to the message, then one should strive for faithfulness in textual divisions. If only *two* divisions naturally arise, the preacher must avoid the temptation to find *three* points!

Fourth, the expositor needs to preach the whole counsel of God and, thus, avoid preaching strictly in one Testament and on favorite doctrines. Further, he must avoid the temptation to suppress doctrines in a text in his own system's interest.[35] Fifth, the preacher should focus on only the major and/or minor doctrine(s) of the text. William Perkins warns,

> We should not try to expound every doctrine on every occasion; but only those which can be applied appropriately to the present experiences and condition of the church. These must be carefully chosen, and limited to a few, lest those who hear God's Word expounded are overwhelmed by the sheer number of applications.[36]

---

[32]David C. Deuel, "Suggestions for Expositional Preaching of Old Testament Narrative," *The Master's Seminary Journal* 2, no. 1 (1991): 56-58.

[33]D. Martyn Lloyd-Jones, *Preaching & Preachers* (Grand Rapids: Zondervan, 1971), 66-67; Hughes, "Anatomy of Exposition," 45.

[34]Lloyd-Jones, *Preaching & Preachers*, 207.

[35]Donald Macleod, "Preaching and Systematic Theology," in *The Preacher and Preaching: Reviving the Art in the Twentieth Century*, ed. Samuel T. Logan, Jr. (Phillipsburg, NJ: Presbyterian and Reformed, 1986), 250-51.

[36]William Perkins, *The Art of Prophesying; With The Calling of the Ministry* (Cambridge: J. Legatt, 1592; reprint, Carlisle, PA: The Banner of Truth Trust, 1996), 68; cf. Macleod ("Preaching and Systematic Theology," 252), who suggests focusing on two or three points relevant to the doctrine of the text.

This is not to say that several doctrines cannot come out in a single sermon. A message on Ephesians 1:3-14 could touch on the doctrines of the Trinity, redemption, grace, election/predestination, eternal security, adoption, personal holiness, forgiveness, divine sovereignty, the gospel, and faith (to name only the obvious!). What is unwise, however, is incorporating a full systematic theology on all, or most, of these doctrines.

Sixth, the doctrinal expositor must be careful that he is not *too* detailed in his explanation.[37] Being overly meticulous can result in boredom and irrelevancy. Seventh, the preacher would do well to eliminate technical jargon from the message. The church pulpit is not the same as the classroom lectern. The people in the pew need doctrine taught in their own language. Adam claims, "Our task is to preach the text and to use its biblical theology to illuminate it, not overshadow it."[38]

Finally, in doing doctrinal exposition, one should never build a complete doctrine on a single text of Scripture.[39] Both biblical *and* systematic theology prove to be extremely valuable here. If no other texts cover a particular doctrine (e.g., baptism for the dead, 1 Cor 15:29), it is best to remain open and non-dogmatic.

Aids for Doctrinal Exposition Today

Talking about doctrinal expository preaching is one thing, actually doing it is quite another. Every expositor allows the Scriptures to drive the sermon and steer it theologically. In addition to the Bible, several tools help equip the preacher better for the task of doctrinal exposition in order that he lend aid to people in their spiritual workout.

First, the preacher must employ both biblical and systematic theology. Biblical theology will keep the preacher focused and textual. Systematic theology will help relate the message to the major doctrines of the Bible. Puritan publications, theological journals, and well-tested theological works can aid the expositor for the tremendous task before him.

Second, doctrinal expositors would do well to become very familiar with their own denomination's confessional history. Baptists, my own denomination, have a rich confessional heritage ranging from the First and Second London Confessions to the Philadelphia Confession to the New Hampshire Confession to the Abstract of Principles to the different revisions of the Baptist Faith and Message. Other denominations have

---

[37]Adam, "Preaching and Biblical Theology," 110.

[38]Ibid. See also Day, "Theology and Preaching," 98-99.

[39]Macleod, "Preaching and Systematic Theology," 250.

similar confessions.[40] Such confessions help preachers frame doctrinal exposition with one eye on the past and the other on the present.

Closely related to confessions, catechisms may prove to be invaluable in communicating doctrine today. Though known for their use among children in both the home and the church, many adults in contemporary churches could benefit from such a tool. An important reminder is that both confessions and catechisms "have no independent authority apart from the Bible, and they must always be tested by, and stand revisable in the light of, the Bible."[41] Moreover,

> creeds, confessions, and catechisms are not, in the Protestant understanding, in competition with Scripture. They do not violate the principle of sola Scriptura, but, rather, serve to strengthen it. After all, they are nothing more than the church's carefully thought-out interpretation of the infallible text.[42]

Since "a good catechism provides a theological framework for one's thinking,"[43] preachers would be wise to employ them in their preaching and teaching of God's Word.

Third, illustrating theological truth from great hymns of the faith may be helpful. Hymns like "Amazing Grace," "And Can It Be?" and "It Is Well with My Soul" stress themes of God's grace, love, and peace. Likewise, "Holy, Holy, Holy" and "Crown Him with Many Crowns" exalt the majesty and splendor of God and Christ.

Fourth, certain visual presentations can help communicate theological truth. Showing a new believer being baptized by immersion naturally pictures Christ's death, burial, and resurrection as well as God's work in making the old new. Breaking bread and pouring wine and even video clips of Christ's passion aid preachers in communicating how Christ laid down His life and shed His blood on behalf of sinners. Furthermore, one may see

---

[40]For a variety of different confessions among other denominations, see Allen, *Preaching Is Believing*, 66-67.

[41]Timothy George, "Doctrinal Preaching," in *Handbook of Contemporary Preaching: A Wealth of Counsel for Creative and Effective Proclamation*, ed. Michael Duduit (Nashville: Broadman Press, 1992), 97. Donald Macleod notes that preachers "should use [confessions and catechisms] as aids to exegesis" ("Preaching and Systematic Theology," 266).

[42]Michael S. Horton, "Recovering the Plumb Line," in *The Coming Evangelical Crisis: Current Challenges to the Authority of Scripture and the Gospel*, ed. John H. Armstrong (Chicago: Moody Press, 1996), 250.

[43]Ascol, "The Pastor as Theologian," Internet.

more clearly some of the key themes in biblical theology and God's redemptive-plan in a diagram outlining biblical history.[44]

Fifth, doctrinal exposition can benefit from the lives of significant biblical and historical characters by way of illustration. The expositor may use the martyrdoms of the Apostles Peter and Paul, as well as church history figures like Polycarp, Athanasius, Tyndale, and Luther to underscore such doctrines as the believer's complete obedience to Christ, the Lordship of Christ, the Trinity, and biblical fidelity. George writes,

> To show how Athanasius staked his life on the doctrine of the Trinity, or how Luther struggled against the fury of hell for the doctrine of justification by faith, is to impress on the congregation the gravity and relevance of the faith once for all delivered to the saints.[45]

Finally, keeping up with current events can aid doctrinal exposition. Even though the changes in culture should not shape one's theology, the well-equipped preacher-theologian should address current, relevant issues through his expositional approach to Scripture. Widely-read newspapers, magazines, and books, along with news programs on television and radio will point the preacher in the direction to address a contemporary audience with the unchanging truth.[46]

These tools will aid the preacher in doctrinal exposition. Without them he may as well attempt to build a house with only his bare hands. With them he can use the most proven and the best up-to-date tools for constructing and finishing the sermon.

Planning Doctrinal Expository Preaching

In addition to describing the different forms of doctrinal exposition, the wise preacher puts a plan in place for practicing this preaching. Several issues will help the preacher plan his preaching accordingly.

First, every preacher needs to evaluate his own congregation. This evaluation tries to determine where the people are biblically and theologically so that textual and doctrinal considerations may be made in light of their spiritual state. The expositor can accomplish these evaluations through the use of surveys, group feedback, and areas of question/interest, among others.[47]

---

[44]Goldsworthy, *Preaching the Whole Bible*, 69-70, 101.

[45]Timothy George, "Doctrinal Preaching," 98.

[46]Ascol, "The Pastor as Theologian," Internet.

[47]These issues and others are found in Erickson and Heflin, *Old Wine in New Wineskins*, 244-55.

Second, the preacher should be sensitive to the Holy Spirit in making the most of timely opportunities and life-situations. The man of God can handle questions from people about life after death, divorce and remarriage, and exclusivist-inclusivist-pluralist issues quickly, effectively, and biblically while curiosity is high. Moreover, settings such as weddings, baptisms, funerals, and the Lord's Supper provide preachers a renewed interest among certain people to learn about faithfulness, obedience, eternal life, the atonement, and numerous other subjects. Preachers doing consecutive exposition will need to keep a few weeks out of the year open to address such unforeseen opportunities.

Third, expositors will certainly find it valuable to keep a record of the texts and doctrines they have covered. Subjects which have received a great deal of emphasis may be placed on the back-burner while addressing other important issues. At the same time, this suggestion highlights the analogy of biblical proportion and balance—those doctrines which the Scriptures emphasize the most should be declared the most.[48]

Fourth, reviewing the calendar or using the lectionary can help in planning sermons. Although subjects for sermons at Christmas and Easter are obvious, one may find it helpful to plan a series of sermons on the life and ministry of Christ from Christmas to Easter. Or, the preacher could preach the greatest events of salvation history during the year. Also, a series on selected Old Testament prophecies concerning Christ could help Christians prepare for the Christmas season. Additionally, a series on the family might fit well between Mother's Day and Father's Day, on such texts as Ephesians 5:21-6:9; 1 Corinthians 7; or 1 Peter 3-4. The possibilities here are virtually endless and valuable.

Fifth, expositors may employ current issues of local or national interest to instruct others in biblical teaching. Preachers can find helpful texts to preach on governmental elections (Rom 13:1-7; 1 Pet 2:13-17) and moral law (Exod 20; Deut 5).

Last, as stated in chapter 12, the preacher may decide to plan his preaching through several books, sections of books, or on categories of systematic theology. While the preacher will still need to plan his preaching, the former approach is more textually-driven and the latter is doctrinally-driven. Both are beneficial for people to learn as they become stronger.

---

[48]See Macleod, "Preaching and Systematic Theology," 256-60, and chapter 5 for valuable doctrines in evangelicalism today.

CHAPTER 16
CONCLUSION:
HEALTHINESS FOR YOU AND YOUR LISTENERS

This work has proposed and analyzed the integration of expository preaching and doctrinal preaching in addressing the twenty-first century. How one is taught (expositional preaching) and what one is taught (the Bible's theology) should be every preacher's concern for his church. Thus, blending expository preaching and systematic-biblical theology provides what I label "doctrinal expository preaching," or even *Preaching for Bodybuilding*. As you build this type of discipline into your sermon preparation and delivery, you will positively affect your spiritual health and that of your listeners.

Hence, this proposal of doctrinal expository preaching for the twenty-first century shows the need for underscoring doctrinal truth within expository sermons. Because of the influence of postmodernism on today's church, preachers must declare the whole counsel of God. This kind of preaching demands both a doctrinal soundness and an expository style (book-by-book) in setting forth the truth in its proper context. Although volumes on expository preaching are abundant, doctrinal preaching receives little discussion today. More importantly, except for a chapter or section in a few isolated places, a tremendous void exists in doctrinal expository preaching. The lack of theological and biblical clarity and conviction in many modern pulpits makes this study necessary, relevant, and practical.

A solution to this biblical-theological identity crisis in the church is doctrinal exposition, where expositors preach Jesus Christ and His Lordship in the believer's life.[1] Along this line, Duey asks,

---

[1]William J. Carl III, *Preaching Christian Doctrine* (Philadelphia: Fortress Press, 1984), 12-13.

> With all the marvelous depth and width and height of God's Scriptures, and with all the subjects awaiting a Christian treatment, considering how rich is life and how hungry the average person for light on eternal matters, how can any preacher neglect this responsibility to his flock? Even worse, how can he criminally suffocate thirty minutes of God's precious time with poor preaching about things which are of questionable value?[2]

Likewise, even though McCollough wrote one-half century ago, his words still ring true:

> If the preachers of our day busy themselves with many things and fail to declare the gospel in its fullness and its immediacy they will share the guilt of a generation creating its own destruction. Theology and preaching must be the concern of the whole Christian church in our day.[3]

For preaching to return to its glory days, it must focus on the great doctrines of Scripture, for "great preaching always depends upon great themes. Great themes always produce great speaking in any realm, and this is particularly true, of course, in the realm of the Church."[4]

Furthermore, such preaching is the only kind which saves. Phillips Brooks adamantly stated the need to preach the truth about Jesus Christ for the salvation of sinners:

> But I cannot do my duty in making Christ plain unless I tell them of Him all the richness that I know. I must keep nothing back. All that has come to me about Him from His Word, all that has grown clear to me about His nature or His methods by my inward or outward experience, all that He has told me of Himself, becomes part of the message that I must tell to those men whom He has sent me to call home to Himself. I will do this in its fullness. And this is the preaching of doctrine, positive, distinct, characteristic Christian truth. . . .
>
> The truth is, no preaching ever had any strong power that was not the preaching of doctrine. The preachers that have moved and held men have always preached doctrine. No exhortation to a good life that does not put behind it some truth as deep as eternity can

---

[2]Charles J. Duey, "Let's Preach Theology," *The Covenant Quarterly* 21, no. 2 (1963): 19.

[3]Thomas E. McCollough, "Preaching's Rediscovery of Theology," *Review and Expositor* 56, no. 1 (1959): 55.

[4]D. Martyn Lloyd-Jones, *Preaching & Preachers* (Grand Rapids: Zondervan, 1971), 13.

seize and hold the conscience. Preach doctrine, preach all the doctrine that you know, and learn forever more and more; but preach it always not that men may believe it; but that men may be saved by believing it.[5]

Doctrinal exposition takes seriously the message of God's gospel of grace in Christ and the lives of sinners in need of salvation.

Christian preachers, especially those who serve as pastors, have always been called to declare the whole counsel of God (cf. Acts 20:27-28). Expositors can best accomplish this tremendous task through doctrinal expository preaching, for expository preaching goes through the biblical text systematically and doctrinal preaching declares the Bible theologically. Further, doctrinal exposition is most valuable whenever preaching is equally concerned with the Bible and the congregation. Therefore, the preacher's message will be faithful in biblical exegesis, sound in theological interpretation, and fruitful in practical application. This does not mean that preachers must rid their sermons of the Bible's language, but they must be diligent in this postmodern world to explain God's message to an audience ignorant of the theology of the Scriptures. Preaching in the twenty-first century demands that preachers be both theologically attuned and culturally aware.

Although preaching in the past has tended to favor either doctrine *or* exposition, preachers are often guilty of divorcing the two disciplines. This work argues, therefore, that an integration of theology *and* biblical exposition is a possible, and even necessary, approach to preaching. Only the faithful book-by-book, biblically-driven, and theologically-saturated preaching, i.e., doctrinal exposition, fulfills the challenge to declare the whole counsel of God.

In the face of a meltdown of truth and morality, anything less than a return to doctrinal preaching will result in a failure of evangelical Christianity to address the people of the twenty-first century. Hopefully, the pillars of biblical theology and systematic theology can team up with expositional preaching in leading today's expositors to a theological-biblical kind of preaching which is both faithful to the text and fruitful in the lives of today's people. Such preaching can provide the desperately needed stability to uncertain pulpits and unsettled pews. May God's expositors return to His firm foundation of Christ and His Word and preach expositionally and doctrinally for the building up of the body of Christ!

---

[5]Phillips Brooks, *The Joy of Preaching* (formally published as *Lectures on Preaching* [London: H. R. Allenson, 1895]; reprint, Grand Rapids: Kregel, 1989), 103.

Sample Sermon 1—Doctrinal Exposition from a Narrative Text "Reclaim the Word" (2 Kings 22:1-23:30)

Have you ever heard of valuables that were lost only to be rediscovered years later—a ring in the bottom of a dresser, a priceless book in a basement, baseball cards in an attic, money in a floorboard, an antique car in mint condition left in a barn? As valuable as all of these things are, none of them stack up to the value of the Bible. Now I know all of you would trade your Bible for any costly item, because you probably have another Bible or could go buy one for $5 or so. But imagine that you've never had a Bible or no one you know has one and you have only heard parts of it here and there, but then suddenly (picking up a dust-coated Bible) someone finds a Bible, the very Word of God! Wouldn't you read it to find out what it actually said? Wouldn't you value it unlike any other possession? I want to uphold the full authority of God's Word for our lives, but since so many people have neglected it, let's reclaim it. Let's look at 2 Kings 22-23 and "Reclaim the Word."

Have you ever heard of a country or a family that was evil? Some of you have heard of Lenin and Stalin leading the Soviets or Hitler and his Nazis or Castro in Cuba or Kim Jung-il in North Korea or Saddam Hussein in Iraq—leaders guilty of killing off millions of people simply because they didn't like them or were afraid of potential revolution. 7th century BC Judah was not all that different when it comes to evil leaders—King Manasseh, who reigned 55 years, and King Amon, who reigned but 2 years, were known for living ungodly lives, for leading their people astray to serve false gods, and for killing off the good guys, the prophets who spoke God's Word.

Let's take a closer look at this story. Josiah became king when he was 8 years old and 8 years later he began to "seek the God of his father David" (2 Chronicles 34:3). When he was around 20 he began removing the items associated with idolatry (34:3-7). By his mid-20s he realized the need to repair the Temple in order to restore the public worship of God.

A much-needed house cleaning was happening, Hilkiah the priest came upon a scroll that was the Law of Moses. He gave it to Shaphan who brought it to the king and read it to him. Upon hearing the Law, Josiah tore his clothes in remorse and brought complete reform throughout his kingdom [Note: I tear off my outer T-shirt to help the audience understand the value of remorse being greater than simple possessions]. Whereas Josiah had begun to cleanse the land a few years earlier, he probably did it out of a sense of rightness or goodness. When he heard God's Word, however, his motive transformed from goodness to *godliness*. The Word had been rediscovered and he *reclaimed* it by hearing and doing all that it said—this renewal at least matches the one initiated 3 generations earlier under King Hezekiah (doing some good things doesn't mean you are right with God. God wants godliness rather than goodness & godliness begins by turning from your sins and trusting in Christ).

Though Josiah heard the prophecy of Huldah and the certain destruction that would come upon Jerusalem while experiencing a time of peace himself, Josiah never gave up or gave in, but he acted responsibly and faithfully before God.

Josiah removed false priests, idols, and shrines throughout the land. He desecrated Topheth, where people offered their own children in fire sacrifices to the false god Molech. Josiah even had pagan altars in people's homes destroyed. These actions returned Jerusalem to her pre-idolatry days in the time of David.

Josiah doesn't merely prohibit certain practices (don't do this or that) but he also orders what to do, like keep the Passover. Yet when we read portions of the first 12 chapters of Jeremiah, we see that much of what the people did during Josiah's reign was merely external and hypocritical, and this external "holiness" was thrown aside after Josiah's death (see also 2 Kings 23:26-27), so the Lord never withheld the fierceness of His great wrath

Let me give you a couple of truths to take home (2 sides of the same coin)—they are for your everyday living. First, *reclaim the Word in your life and obtain salvatio*n (22:11, 19-20; 23:24-25; cf. Hebrews 4:12; 2 Timothy 3:14-17). Genuine salvation is not merely claiming to be saved, but living in accordance with what the Lord teaches us through His Word—Josiah did *all* God had commanded him to do.

Hebrews 4:12 teaches us that God's Word is alive—since it is alive, it can bring life & direction for us [I play a portion of Casting Crowns' "The Word Is Alive," having obtained permission from the group to do so].

It is only in obedience to the Word that you can be saved (2 Timothy 3:14-17). The Bible is not just for salvation but for direction and equipping you how to live here so you'll be ready for the hereafter. That means that you have to give up some things that lead you to sin whether it be a relationship, video games, a certain sport, putting on a filter on your Internet access, or more.

The second truth to take home from this text, the other side of the coin, if you will, is for you to *reclaim the Word in your life and avoid condemnation* (22:17; 23:26-27; cf. Deut 28:15-68). Josiah's life (and reign) was a glittering bright spot in the nation's tragic slide to destruction. Direct equivalents between Israel and America cannot be made, because we weren't a theocratic government like Israel once was. We don't have kings who completely direct our nation. Even though direct parallels cannot be made with our country, they are more appropriate with our church and with our families. Great churches of the past that once stood firmly on God's Word now sit empty as they departed from the Scriptures long ago. Families who produced great Christian leaders have also seen apostates and ungodly people scar the family name. What about you? Will you avoid the pressures to live like the vast majority of the world who serve self and false gods or will you lay claim to and reclaim the Word in your lives?

Do you have a real faith like Josiah that is transformational and life-directional or merely an external washing like the rest of the country? When I was 14 and 15 years old, I was in a youth group of about 70 that came out every Wednesday and the vast majority came on Sunday. I remember looking up to so many of what I thought were the "good" ones—guys and girls called into ministry, model students and athletes, young people who came from respected families in the church and community. I was an outsider at the time because I went to a public school in the country while everyone else was at the city school. Then, our youth pastor left and there was massive fallout and word got out about rampant sexual immorality among many of them, the use of drugs and alcohol and more, and within a year and a half we were down to six of us, but the relationship we had with the Lord was real with us and we read the Bible daily to see what God was saying to us.

I remember talking with one of those guys who had been called into ministry our freshmen year, someone I looked up to, and by his senior year he was cussing and drinking (to the point of drunkenness) and living like most everyone else and one day we were in the locker room and no one else was around and I asked him, "What happened? You used to have an intense fire for the Lord and you were going into the ministry?" He responded, "Oh, that wasn't real. That was just something I did for a short time."

Look around at each other; there are others in your group that you look up to because of their popularity or good looks or family life or walk with the Lord, but some of what you see isn't real. Now I'm no prophet so

I don't know what's going to happen with each of you in the next few months and years, but I do believe that you have a choice to make as to whether you will live a life of repentance from your way of sin and pleasing self and live a life of trusting in the Lord to rule and direct your life. God directs you through His Word, so will you reclaim the Word afresh and anew in your life? Will you trust Him to lead you every step of the way? Jesus paid for all of your sins through His death on the cross. Won't you respond by giving your life to Him by turning from your sins and trusting in Him?

Sample Sermon 2—Doctrinal Exposition from a Gospel Text "The Coming King" (Matthew 3:1-12)

What would you do if you were given the opportunity to meet the President of the United States for 5 minutes? I'm not talking about meeting with your pastor in your home for a few minutes, when many of you put on nice clothes, but some of you prefer to be in a T-shirt and shorts. I mean a meeting in the White House with the President! You would pick out your best outfit (or buy a new one!) and get your hair done and brush and floss your teeth and shower and use deodorant and cologne or perfume and have your nails and hair done and your shoes shined and think long and hard about what you would say in those few minutes, wouldn't you? With that in mind, let's look at Matthew 3 and "The Coming King."

Now many scholars agree that Matthew writes primarily to Jews to convince them that Jesus is the long-awaited Messiah due to His lineage, birth, hometown, ministry, death, and resurrection. Let's meander our way through this passage and see what God is saying to us.

Matthew says, "In those days," which is a general reference of time since nearly 30 years had passed since Jesus had been 1 or 2 years old in the previous verse. Luke records Jesus' baptism and public ministry at age 30 and provides specific rulers (Luke 3:1), so those indicators help us date this passage.

Now John the Baptist (the one who baptizes, not "John the Sprinkler" or "John the Downpour") is introduced. In baptisms of antiquity, people baptized themselves, so having an administrator is a novelty introduced by John and practiced by Jesus' followers. In the Old Testament, Jews simply had to be ceremonially washed, but Gentiles converting to Judaism had to be baptized (immersed)—the fact that John baptizes everyone tells us that all are in need of repentance.

There has been speculation that John was part of the Qumran

community, or Essenes, because they were a wilderness people not far from the Jordan—they had a simple lifestyle of clothes and diet and studied the Scriptures (preserved well through the Dead Sea Scroll discoveries in Qumran in 1947). Certainty about this matter eludes us, but we do know that John's preaching is prophetic! Such preaching was quite the shocker for many Jews who hadn't heard a prophet speak in more than 400 years. Israel's prophets had predicted a new exodus in the wilderness (Hosea 2:14-15; Isaiah 40:3)—John fulfills that prediction.

John proclaims a message of repentance. The command to repent means to change one's mind; to turn from your way of life to God—not a simple "say you're sorry" but a radical demand of a once-for-all commitment to God. Thus, John places himself in the prophetic tradition of old with this call to repentance.

The reason for repentance is that the "kingdom of heaven" (which occurs 32 times in Matthew) is at hand (3:2; 4:17). This phrase is synonymous with the "kingdom of God" elsewhere, but Matthew's Jewish audience prefers to revere God's name by avoiding it if at all possible.

Theologians refer to what John says about the kingdom of heaven being "at hand" as realized eschatology—an already-but-not-yet kingdom. That simply means that Christ actively rules in His people's lives presently but He shall one day rule the entire earth at His return (Matthew's focus is present in this passage but future in 25:31, 34; 26:29).

The Baptist's ministry is one of preparing the way of the LORD. John makes ready the road for the King is coming. This reference originates with the prophet Isaiah, who refers to Yahweh. Matthew, however, clearly connects this passage to Jesus, for Jesus is God with us (Matthew is not the only one to do this, for all of the Gospels, not to mention Paul, unmistakably claim Jesus as Yahweh, the One True & Living God).

New Testament scholar Craig Blomberg says,

> The larger context of Isaiah 40-66 discloses that the prophecy depicts part of Israel's end-time restoration. The messianic era, the millennial kingdom, and eventually the new heavens and the new earth often blend together in characteristic prophetic foreshortening.[1]

The glory of the coming of Christ hit me afresh several years ago when I was in seminary. I was traveling from Kentucky with my wife and my in-laws to my home state of Indiana. As we were crossing the bridge, the song by Bill Gaither entitled "The King Is Coming" began playing. I knew I was entering into God's country!

---

[1]Craig L. Blomberg, *Matthew* in The New American Commentary, vol. 22 (Nashville: Broadman Press, 1992), 75.

Metaphorically, John's ministry is straightening the paths to level off the road—fill in the potholes—which was done when kings came for a visit. You put your best foot forward for a king. In a literal way, the palm branches laid before Jesus' entrance into Bethany softened His ride. When the President of the United States travels somewhere in a car, he doesn't get stuck in road construction, because his way is already mapped out on well-paved roads.

What John is saying is that the coming of Christ to reign in one's life demands repentance as the straightening out of that life. John's ministry as baptism, which means dip or plunge, and the passive means "be drowned"—used of ships in the sense "sink," signifies death to a whole way of life (cf. Romans 6:3). Baptism signified that people confessed their sins and were repenting—when people really repent, they say so.

Enter the dark side of ministry [music from Star Wars is appropriate here]—the presence of the Pharisees and Sadducees represented the official leadership of Judaism in Jesus' day. Though they had different beliefs, they were united in their opposition to John and then to Jesus. It is difficult to discern whether they came to where John was baptizing (NIV) or if they came for baptism (NASB)—either way John discerned that their repentance was insincere, so he labels them a brood of vipers—offspring of venomous snakes from Arabia, which were known for murdering their mothers as they ate their way out of the womb—the utmost of human depravity is hatred and murder of one's mother.

Oozing with sarcasm, John mocks their fake repentance, "Who warned you to flee from the coming wrath?" They had no genuine repentance but a desire to escape divine retribution, God's righteous anger toward sin. Multitudes today prefer to listen to someone who puts people in comfort zones rather than call them to reckon with their sin condition. The result is that they think they can obtain fire insurance and live however they want!

John isn't interested in mere words of repentance but the fruit which is befitting repentance (the same thing Paul talks about as genuine faith). Do you want to know if you have fruit worthy of repentance? Ask someone who loves you and knows you well if they have discerned a lifestyle in you not for self but for the Lord. Look for someone who can look beyond your mere attendance at church or saying some prayers, but who can see if you have a genuine life where you don't do things your way but the Lord's way.

Genuine repentance is necessary, because John claims that ancestral heritage doesn't make one right with God, whether you are a descendant of Abraham or Billy Graham or a distant cousin to Jesus through His half-siblings. You see, God has no grandchildren, so you must have a personal relationship to Him.

Without a personal relationship, you should see God's judgment as an axe lying at the root of trees—a symbol of destruction with impending doom. This action is not merely cutting it off at the base, but at the roots! The good fruit, however, is fruit worthy of repentance—a desire to live for Christ rather than self.

I've asked a handful of people here at our church that have been here a few years if they would guess at the percentage of adults who regularly come here who are genuinely saved. Billy Graham has said that 80% of church-goers are lost. Now that accounts for all churches, even those who have failed to preach the Bible, so those who take His Word seriously should be better off than the rest. Even so, of those that I asked, they thought somewhere between 50-70% of our people are genuinely saved. If they are anywhere close to being right, then we have too many people who either don't understand the gospel or don't understand real salvation.

What's needed is a baptism for repentance, which probably means "because of" or "in reference to" repentance. Not only does the Scriptures speak against baptismal regeneration, but Josephus as a 1st century Jew and non-Christian recognized that John's baptism did not gain one forgiveness but was a consecration of the body of what had already happened in the soul.[2]

John points to Jesus as One greater than himself, pressing the seriousness of John's warning. John doesn't even deserve to be Jesus' slave. You better listen to what John says or you will pay major consequences.

To underscore Jesus' greatness, John references Jesus' baptism with the Spirit and fire. Now, some take Jesus' ministry of baptism with the Spirit and fire to refer to the indwelling and purifying work of the Spirit, because of one preposition governing two nouns (cf. Acts 2:3). Others, however, see the work of salvation and condemnation here in light of 3:10, 12. The winnowing fork in hand means the judgment is about to begin and the threshing floor will be thoroughly cleansed. Judgment will come for everyone that isn't a genuine believer. The Lord will preserve His people (the wheat) and judge the unbelievers (the chaff). Note the use of "His" in light of Jesus—"*His* winnowing fork," "*His* hand," "*His* threshing floor," and "*His* wheat" in contrast to "*the* chaff."

So what are you to do? What's the point of this passage? It is that *you must repent genuinely and live your life for Jesus, the coming King.*

Like most of us, you may never get to meet the President of the United States, but you will meet King Jesus one day and your eternal destiny will already be determined when you meet Him face-to-face. I know of a traveling evangelist who would close every revival service by going to each person individually and asking them if they were certain they would

---

[2]See Josephus, *Antiquities*, 18.5.2, in Blomberg, 79.

spend eternity in heaven because of saving faith and genuine repentance. I'll not drag out the service nor put you on the spot, but imagine for just a moment that I took the time to come to you and ask you if you were certain that you were headed to heaven, what would you say? Even Peter exhorts us to "make your calling and election sure" (2 Peter 1:10). Heed the message. Repent. Get right. The King is coming!

Sample Sermon 3—Doctrinal Exposition from a Didactic Text "Go, Show, and Tell Christianity" (Romans 10:1-17)

I want to paint you 2 scenarios. First, imagine a young boy is shipwrecked and is the only survivor and he ends up on an island all by himself, but he is just old enough to make a living for himself and he grows old and eventually dies without any outside communication. Where will he spend eternity?

The second scenario takes you back to my 9th grade show and tell speech on Roger Clemens' pitching. We've probably all done a "show-and-tell speech," so we can identify with this scenario much better than the other one.

Today, we have plenty of "show-and-tell" inside the church but not enough "Go, Show, & Tell Christianity" outside of the church (especially to the man on the island). Look with me at Romans 10.

Prior to this passage, the Apostle Paul has just shared how God unconditionally elects some by His grace and effectually calls them unto Himself as well as man's need to attain righteousness—a right standing with God—by faith. In one sense, Romans 9 deals mostly with divine sovereignty (God is in charge in salvation). Romans 10, on the other hand, centers on human responsibility (each person is responsible for obeying God).

As we zero in on this text before us, I want you to take three actions as a Christian to counter the current culture with the claims of Christ.

First, go to the non-Christian (10:14-17). The ground for Paul's argument is in verses 5-13, so I want to show you in normal logic (reversing his thoughts) how we can understand it clearly.

He presents a 5-link chain of prerequisites for salvation (10:14-15): 1) Christ sends heralds, 2) heralds go to people preaching, 3) some people hear the good news, 4) some people believe the good news, resulting in righteousness, and 5) they call on Jesus as Lord, resulting in salvation. What Paul is telling us is that before anyone can believe in Jesus and call on Him as Lord, Christians must go to them.

Such a mission shouldn't surprise Christians, because it has already been given by Jesus. We have Christ's *commission* (Matt 28:18)—"All authority has been given to Me..."; we have Christ's *command* (Matt 28:19)— "Therefore, go, make disciples..."; and we have Christ's *comfort* (Matt 28:20)—"I am with you always..."

People who carry out this task of carrying good news are labeled as "heralds." In ancient times, heralds were messengers who brought news from someone important, like the Emperor, to townspeople. Heralds who arrived with really good news were viewed as beautiful or wonderful to recipients.

One of the important issues here is that we must see that heralds are people on the go. I don't know about you, but I get impatient in traffic when a red light turns green and the person in front of me doesn't go! Let's not sit around when God has given us the green light to *go*.

In addition to going to the non-Christian, you must *show the non-Christian Christianity (10:1-4)*. In our visually-oriented society, people are watching you to see if you walk your talk—televangelists have given Christians a bad name and you and I must win the trust of non-Christians. How?

We need to *show compassion toward the unrighteous (10:1-3)*. We show compassion in a number of ways, like Paul himself, whether we grieve/sorrow over the lost (9:1-3), desire the conversion of the lost (10:1), or pray consistently for the conversion of the lost (10:1).

Several years ago, I heard a story I may never forget. One little 4-year old girl named Crystal came forward every invitation to pray for her lost parents. They didn't come to church but they allowed Crystal to be picked up and brought to church. When Crystal was 8, she trusted the Lord and when the pastor asked the parents if he could talk to Crystal about being baptized, he began sharing the gospel and asked if they would receive Jesus' offer to be their Lord and Savior. They did. The Lord had heard the prayers of little Crystal who wasn't afraid to show compassion toward her parents by praying for them at church.

Why is showing compassion so important? *Because service for God does not save (10:2)*. Having a zeal for God, a desire to serve Him, without a knowledge of the truth is futile. "Zeal" means enthusiasm, "to boil." On the other hand, Christians must be zealous (Rev 3:16-17; Rom 12:11; 1 Cor 16:22). Thus, as John Piper says, "there is a zeal that is essential and one that is suicidal, and you must flee from the one and pursue the other."[1]

---

[1] John Piper, *E. Y. Mullins Lectures on Preaching* (Louisville: The Southern

Another reason why we must show compassion is *because sincerity of self does not save (10:2-3)*. Someone's sincerity without knowledge (being ignorant) of the truth is no excuse before God. You are well aware of the fact that the world is full of sincere people who are genuinely lost (Jews, Muslims, Jehovah's Witnesses, and more). Our response to the gospel should show the world that we are not trusting self but Christ: "Nothing in my hand I bring; simply to Thy cross I cling."[2]

Not only do we show the non-Christian Christianity by showing compassion toward the unrighteous, but also by *showing conviction about God's righteousness (10:4)*. You can't be wishy-washy on the truth, the clear teachings of Scripture. We know that Jesus is the truth (John 14:6; cf. 1:1, 14, 17), God's Word is truth (John 17:17), and knowing God's truth brings spiritual freedom (John 8:31-32; cf. 4:24).

Years ago at the advent of the railroad, a watchman was given the responsibility for raising and lowering a bridge to allow boats to pass and trains to cross. If the bridge was raised, the watchman would signal to the train to stop until it was safe to cross. One early morning the watchman overslept and awoke at the sound of a distant train. Knowing the train couldn't cross, he quickly ran out to the track and waved his lantern to stop the train from going into the river. The train never stopped and everyone on board perished. Later during the trial the judge asked him "Was the train on schedule?" "Yes," the man replied. "Were you in place on time?" "Yes." "Did you wave your lantern to warn them?" "Yes, I did, your honor," was his reply. He was found not guilty. That night in his home, a friend heard him in bed crying for "those poor, poor people!" His friend awoke him and asked "Why are you crying; you were exonerated?" The bridge controller replied, "But the judge never asked me one question: 'Was my lantern lit?'"

Friends, just as this man hadn't carried out his full responsibility, if we warn non-Christians without showing them the light of Christ, then we haven't done our duty.

We must go to the non-Christian, show the non-Christian Christianity, and then we must *tell the non-Christian about Christ (10:5-13)*. We build up to Christ and the gospel by telling them things like *you cannot live by the law (10:5)*, for none is perfect but Christ. We also tell them that *you cannot change history (10:6-7)*. It is impossible for you to reach heaven or the grave to bring about the incarnation or resurrection, because they've already occurred.

Then, we are in position to *tell them you can confess Christ (10:8-13)*. The

---

Baptist Theological Seminary, 1999), videocassette.

[2]A. M. Toplady in Robert H. Mounce, *Romans*, in The New American Commentary, vol. 27 (Nashville: Broadman & Holman, 2001), 208.

reason you can confess Him is because God's saving righteousness is near, in your mouth and in your heart—the transcendent is imminent!

The hope for the nonbeliever is that believing inwardly in God's resurrection power in Christ results in a right standing with God. Confessing outwardly the Lordship of Jesus results in salvation, which speaks to the issue of Lordship salvation and the deity of Christ. The Lordship issue is clear in the text, for the confession of Jesus for salvation is confessing Him as Lord (for Christ must be both a resident and President of your life for biblical salvation). The deity of Christ is obvious because the same word for Lord in Greek (kurios) is used in reference to Jesus in 10:9 and Yahweh in 10:13 (quoting Joel 2:32). Thus, Jesus is divine.

This message of believing in Christ and confessing Him has already been announced by the Old Testament prophets Isaiah and Joel (10:11-13), whom Paul uses to offer a universal appeal of the gospel, underscored by four uses of "everyone/all" (10:11-13):

> For the Scripture says, *"Everyone* who believes in Him will not be put to shame." For there is no distinction between Jew and Greek; the same Lord is Lord of *all*, bestowing His riches on *all* who call upon Him. For *"everyone* who calls on the name of the Lord will be saved (emphasis mine).

This gospel message is important, and the burden to tell the gospel is real. Piper illustrates,

> If I knew that a plague was coming & I knew that my colleague had not received the vaccination to protect herself, would I not inquire why she refused? Would I not seek to persuade her that she should choose life? Ask yourself what you would say at the judgment day if your unbelieving friend turns to you & asks you why you didn't speak to him with more seriousness about this matter of eternal life.[3]

Now you may use something as simple as a gospel tract to help you spread the message. While waiting for a debit card or check to clear, you can say, "I do survey work as a volunteer—may I ask you a question? In your personal opinion, what do you understand it takes for a person to go to heaven?" If they answer with faith in Jesus, you can invite them to church. If they respond with anything else, you can say, "I know you're busy, but I just wanted you to know that God provided His Son Jesus Christ as the only sufficient sacrifice for sins and we must receive Him by

---

[3]John Piper, "My Heart's Desire: That They Might Be Saved," Romans 10:1 (6 January 1985), available at desiringgod.org/ResourceLibrary/Sermons/ByScripture/10/473_My_Hearts_Desire_That_They_Might_Be_Saved/; accessed 17 September 2009.

faith. I'd like for you to have this little booklet so you can read more on your own time. Thanks." While this presentation is far short of a full-fledged gospel message, it can get the person to begin thinking about the gospel claims.

Now we've come full circle back to verses 14-17. For us to be faithful, we must do more than "show-and-tell" inside the 4 walls of the church building. We must have a *"Go, Show, & Tell Christianity"* to the 4 corners of the earth. Go to the man on the island because without going, there is no knowing Jesus and an eternal hell awaits!

I've never been a Mr. Universe contestant (I know that is shocking!), but as a sophomore in high school the cheerleaders took pictures of all of us basketball players from the thighs down in a best legs contest. I'll have you know that I didn't get third, I didn't get second, I. . . didn't get first, but I got an honorable mention! Even though I got an honorable mention then, I've got beautiful feet and so do you whenever you *go, show, and tell* the good news!

APPENDICES

APPENDIX 1

Table 1. Key Old Testament Terms for Preaching[1]

Term	Meaning	Reference
פָּרַשׁ	make distinct, declare	Neh 8:8
שָׂכַל	set forth (the) understanding (i.e., the meaning)	Neh 8:8
בִּין	give understanding, make understand, teach	Neh 8:7-8
נָבִיא	spokesman, speaker, prophet	Deut 13:1; 18:20; Jer 23:21; cf. Num 11:25-29
חֹזֶה	seer (i.e., a prophet)	Amos 7:12
רֹאֶה	seer (i.e., a prophet)	1 Chr 29:29; Isa 30:10
קֹהֶלֶת	collector (of sentences), or preacher	Ecc 1:1
קָרָא	call, proclaim, read	Isa 61:1
בָּשַׂר	herald as glad tidings; the salvation of God, preach	Isa 61:1; Ps 40:9
נָטַף	drop, drip, fig. (especially of prophet) discourse	Ezek 20:46; Amos 7:16; Mic 2:6, 11
לֶקַח	learning, teaching, instruction	Deut 32:2; Job 11:4; Prov 4:2; Isa 29:24
לָמַד	teach (piel)	Deut 4:10, 12; Ezr 7:10; Ecc 12:9

---

[1]Adapted from Bryan Chapell, *Christ-Centered Preaching: Redeeming the Expository Sermon* (Grand Rapids: Baker Books, 1994), 89-90. All Hebrew definitions come from William Gesenius, *The New Brown-Driver-Briggs-Gesenius Hebrew and English Lexicon: with an Appendix Containing the Biblical Aramaic*, ed. and trans. Francis Brown, S.R. Driver, and Charles A. Briggs [BDBG] (Peabody, MA: Hendrickson Publishers, 1979)

APPENDIX 2

Table 2. Key New Testament Terms for Preaching[1]

Term	Meaning	Reference
κηρυσσω	announce, make known by a herald; proclaim aloud	Rom 10:14-15; 1 Cor 1:21-23; 2 Tim 4:2
ευαγγελιζω	bring or announce good news; proclaim, preach	Matt 11:5; Luke 4:18; Acts 8:35; 2 Pet 2:5
διδασκω	teach	Acts 5:42
διερμηνευω	explain, interpret	Luke 24:47; Acts 18:6
διανοιγω	open (figuratively, the mind); explain, interpret	Luke 24:45; Acts 17:3
διαλεγομαι	discuss, conduct a discussion; speak, preach	Acts 17:2; 18:4
παρατιθημι	put before in teaching; demonstrate, point out	Matt 13:24, 31; Acts 17:3; 28:23
λογος	speaking a word; statement	Matt 13:19-23
ρημα	that which is said, word, saying, expression	Rom 10:17; 1 Pet 1:25
καταγγελλω	proclaim	Acts 4:2; 13:5
παρρησιαζομαι	speak freely, openly, fearlessly, express oneself freely	Acts 9:27-28; 14:3; 18:26; 19:8
ελεγχω	bring to light, expose, set forth; reprove, correct	2 Tim 4:2; Tit 1:9; 2:15
παρακαλεω	appeal to, urge, exhort, encourage	2 Tim 4:2; cf. Acts 14:22
μαρτυρεω	bear witness, be a witness	Acts 20:21; 23:11; cf. 1 John 4:14
λαλεω	transitively speak and thereby assert, proclaim, say	Mark 2:2; Acts 17:19
συζητεω	dispute, debate, argue	Acts 9:29
απολογια	defense	Acts 22:1; 1 Pet 3:15

[1]Adapted from Chapell, 90-91. All Greek definitions come from Walter
Bauer, A Greek-English Lexicon of the New Testament: and Other Early Christian
, William F. Arndt, F. Wilbur Gingrich, and Frederick W.
: University of Chicago Press, 1979). A number of
ainly refer to preaching and teaching in the Scriptures.
e "Jesus spoke to the crowd" or Paul "responded to
a certain element of preaching or teaching took place.
udy omits the vast majority of such generalizations.

APPENDIX 3
THE RELATIONSHIP BETWEEN KERYGMA AND DIDACHE

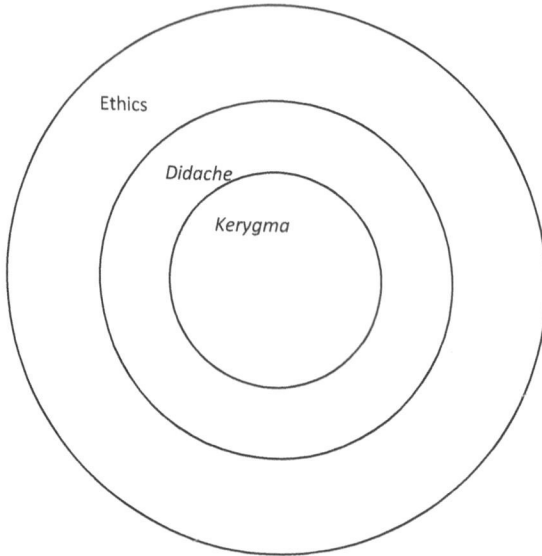

Ethics

Didache

Kerygma

Figure 1. The Relationship between *Kerygma* and *Didache*

APPENDIX 4
THE INTERPRETIVE CONTEXTS OF BIBLICAL THEOLOGY

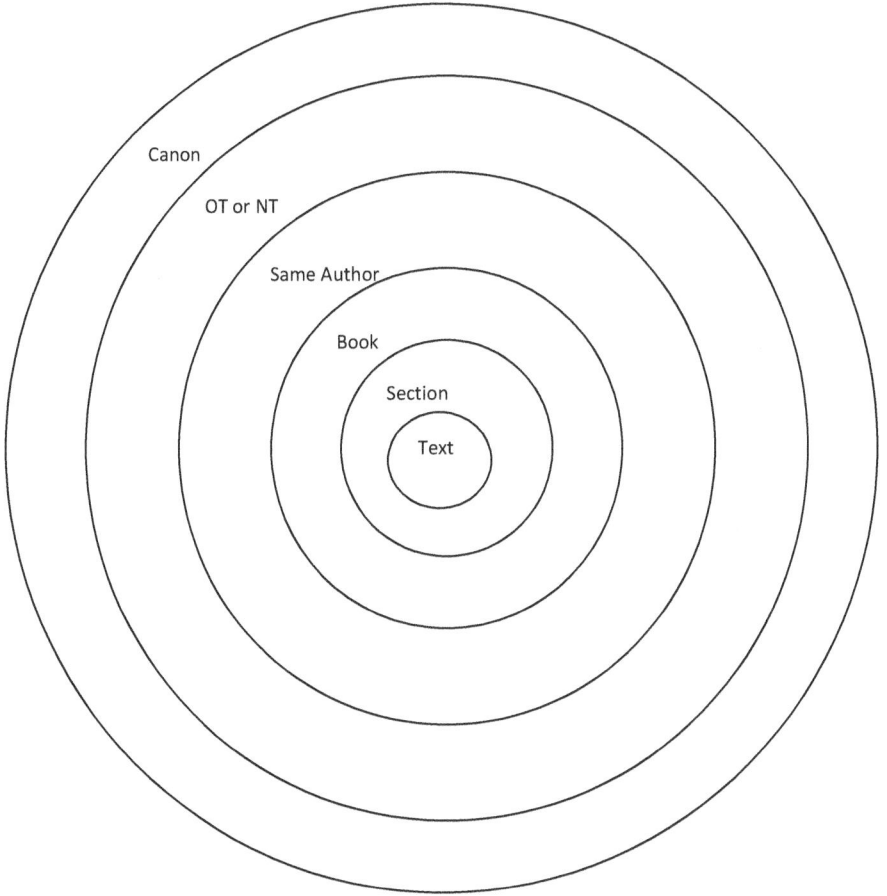

Canon

OT or NT

Same Author

Book

Section

Text

Figure 2. The Interpretive Contexts of Biblical Theology

APPENDIX 5
RELATIONSHIP OF EXEGETICAL, THEOLOGICAL
AND HOMILETICAL PROCESSES

Table 3. Distinctions between the
Exegetical, Theological and Homiletical Processes[1]

Exegetical	Theological	Homiletical
Biblical language	Timeless language	Contemporary language
Time-bound to biblical author and audience	All time with no particular audience	Time-bound to contemporary preacher and audience
Technical	Non-technical	Applicational
Explication oriented	Deep structure	Motivation oriented
Provides analytical detail	Provides integrated truth	Provides interest and relevance
Textual order of the passage	Logical order of the argument	Communicational order of the homiletical proposition
Concrete and specific	Universal and general	Concrete and specific
Indicative/Declarative	Indicative/Declarative	Imperative

[1]Timothy S. Warren, "The Theological Process in Sermon Preparation," *Bibliotheca Sacra* 156, no. 623 (1999): 354.

APPENDIX 6
EXEGETICAL, THEOLOGICAL AND HOMILETICAL PROPOSITIONS

Table 4. Exegetical, Theological and Homiletical Propositions

Text	Joshua 6-8
Exegetical	Because of the sin of Achan, God's anger burned against all Israel and victory did not come until the accursed were permanently removed through destruction.
Theological	Because of His own holiness, God judges sin and wants all of His people to live obedient, holy lives before Him, demanding that sin be removed.
Homiletical	Because God is holy, repent from your sin and live obediently to the Lord Jesus Christ.
Text	**John 8:12-20**
Exegetical	Jesus is the light of this dark world and a true witness to His message and mission from the Father.
Theological	Jesus Christ leads His people out of death's darkness and into life's light, fulfilling His mission to die for the lost.
Homiletical	Follow Jesus in order to live in His light and escape sin's judgment (or Believe Jesus' message and mission in saving sinners from death and giving them life).
Text	**1 Corinthians 15:20-28**
Exegetical	Christ has been raised from the dead and everyone in Him will be raised at His second coming, when God the Father places everything under Christ's feet.
Theological	The resurrection of Christ guarantees the future resurrection of every believer at His return to reign over all.
Homiletical	Prepare for Christ's reign as the Almighty Lord by trusting in the risen Lord.

APPENDIX 7
THE PROCESS OF DOCTRINAL EXPOSITORY
PREACHING

The process of doctrinal exposition may be likened to a funneling process. The biblical exegesis process yields an exegetical product (exegetical idea). This product passes through theological exegesis, resulting in a theological product (theological idea). The theological product then helps shape the sermon process, which in turn, yields the sermon product (homiletical idea). Figure A1 demonstrates this entire process.

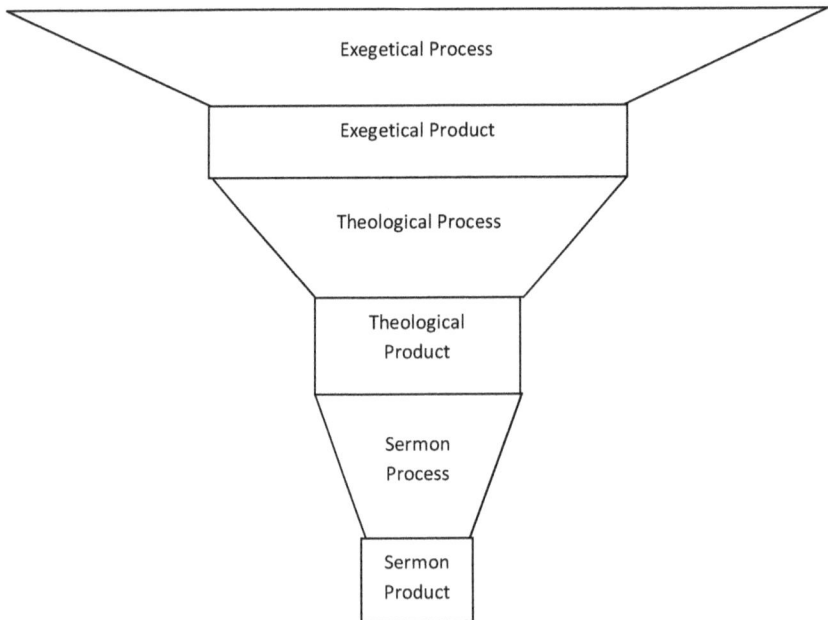

Figure A1. The Funneling Process of Doctrinal Exposition[1]

---

[1]Though portrayed quite differently, this idea came from Timothy S. Warren, "A Paradigm for Preaching," *Bibliotheca Sacra* 148, no. 592 (1991): 474.

APPENDIX 8
IMAGE AND WORD IN WORSHIP

Doctrinal expository preaching in a postmodern culture needs to employ both image and word. Figure A2 portrays how these two elements might interact in the worship setting.

Figure (word)		
Worship (image) Sacrament Singing Liturgy	**Exposition (word)** Preaching Teaching Education	
	Image Biblical imagery Motif studies Poetry Narrative	**Word** Didactic forms Prescriptive forms
Ground (image) Authentic Christian Community		

Figure A2. The Relationship of Image and Word in Doctrinal Exposition[1]

---

[1]Taken from Michael J. Glodo, "The Bible in Stereo: New Opportunities for Biblical Interpretation in an A-Rational Age," in *The Challenge of Postmodernism: An Evangelical Engagement*, 2nd ed., ed. David S. Dockery (Grand Rapids: Baker Academic, 2001), 125.

ABOUT THE AUTHOR

Joel Breidenbaugh has served churches in Kentucky and Florida as pastor since 1996. He also serves as Associate Professor of Homiletics for Liberty University's Rawlings School of Divinity. He received his PhD in preaching from The Southern Baptist Theological Seminary. His passions are preaching through books of the Bible in the local church, spreading the gospel, teaching those called to ministry, training pastors on the mission field, and, most of all, spending time with his wife and five children.

www.ingramcontent.com/pod-product-compliance
Lightning Source LLC
Chambersburg PA
CBHW021140090426
42740CB00008B/872

* 9 7 8 0 9 9 0 7 8 1 6 7 7 *